Accounting Principles for Non-Executive Directors

Good quality non-executive directors are essential to good corporate governance. They bring a wealth of experience to the boardroom, and together with their fellow board members they are responsible for the company's annual report and accounts. However, few are trained accountants.

This volume explains the key elements of a listed company's annual report and accounts. Part I explains the difference between profit and cash flows, the accounting profession, the international harmonisation of accounting rules, the origins of the rules governing the preparation of accounts, the regulation of financial reporting and the overarching principles behind accounting rules. Part II discusses issues relevant to listed companies: mergers and acquisitions; earnings per share; realised and distributable profits; financial instruments; and other key topics. An appendix sets out 50 questions, linked to the chapters, which non-executive directors might like to ask at meetings of the board and audit committee.

PETER HOLGATE is senior accounting technical partner with PricewaterhouseCoopers LLP. As such, he heads the largest accounting consulting team in the UK. A member of the ASB's Urgent Issues Task Force, he is also chairman of the Institute of Chartered Accountants in England and Wales' Centre for Business Performance management board and a member of the advisory board of the ICAEW's Financial Reporting Faculty.

ELIZABETH BUCKLEY is a consultant to PricewaterhouseCoopers LLP. She has worked in the accounting technical departments of two of the 'Big 4' accounting firms, and at the ICAEW. She is a member of the Institute of Chartered Accountants of Scotland and of the joint Institutes' working party on distributable profits.

Law Practitioner Series

The Law Practitioner Series offers practical guidance in corporate and commercial law for the practitioner. It offers high-quality comment and analysis rather than simply restating the legislation, providing a critical framework as well as exploring the fundamental concepts which shape the law. Books in the series cover carefully chosen subjects of direct relevance and use to the practitioner.

The series will appeal to experienced specialists in each field, but is also accessible to more junior practitioners looking to develop their understanding of particular fields of practice.

The Consultant Editors and Editorial Board have outstanding expertise in the UK corporate and commercial arena, ensuring academic rigour with a practical approach.

Consultant editors

Charles Allen-Jones, retired senior partner of Linklaters
Mr Justice David Richards, Judge of the High Court of Justice, Chancery Division

Editors

Chris Ashworth – Lovells LLP
Professor Eilis Ferran – University of Cambridge
Timothy Polglase – Allen & Overy
Stephen Hancock – Herbert Smith
Judith Hanratty – BP Corporate Lawyer, retired
Keith Hyman – Clifford Chance
Keith Johnston – Addleshaw Goddard
Vanessa Knapp – Freshfields Bruckhaus Deringer
Charles Mayo – Simmons & Simmons
Andrew Peck – Linklaters
Richard Snowden QC – Erskine Chambers
William Underhill – Slaughter & May
Sandra Walker – Rio Tinto

For a complete list of titles in the series see back of book

Accounting Principles for Non-Executive Directors

PETER HOLGATE AND ELIZABETH BUCKLEY

PricewaterhouseCoopers LLP

CAMBRIDGE
UNIVERSITY PRESS

CAMBRIDGE UNIVERSITY PRESS
Cambridge, New York, Melbourne, Madrid, Cape Town, Singapore, São Paulo, Delhi

Cambridge University Press
The Edinburgh Building, Cambridge CB2 8RU, UK

Published in the United States of America by Cambridge University Press, New York

www.cambridge.org
Information on this title: www.cambridge.org/9780521509787

First published 2009

Printed in the United Kingdom at the University Press, Cambridge

A catalogue record for this publication is available from the British Library

ISBN 978-0-521-50978-7 hardback

Contents

Appendices

Acknowledgements

Our thanks are due to many colleagues at PricewaterhouseCoopers LLP. To the whole Accounting Consulting Services team, for providing us with a learning environment and a stock of knowledge, much of which appears in these pages. In particular, to Barry Johnson and his team for their excellent work on the 'PwC inform' database and the two PwC Manuals of Accounting: the 'Manual of Accounting: UK GAAP' and the 'Manual of Accounting: IFRS for the UK'. Readers who need more detail than is found in this slim volume are referred to those works.

We thank Chris Nobes and Andrew Wiggins for their helpful review comments.

Finally, we thank our families, Nelda and Andrew, Chris and Jessica, for their forbearance and we dedicate this book to them.

Peter Holgate
Elizabeth Buckley

London
June 2008

Which standards and legislation has this book been based on?

This book is based on accounting standards (including interpretations) and legislation in issue at 30 June 2008. See appendices 2 and 3 for a full list of such international and UK accounting standards. Not all such standards and legislation were in force at that date, either because they were not yet mandatory or, as was the case with some international accounting standards, they were in issue but had not been adopted by the EU at that date. Where this is the case, the book nevertheless reflects such standards and legislation as they are expected to become mandatory in the UK in due course. Where a standard has been issued that will replace an existing standard, the requirements of the new standard are reflected in the book.

Glossary of terms

Introductory note on terminology

Until 2005 the terminology used in the UK was largely unchanged from that used when accounting standards were originally introduced in the early 1970s. Thus, companies referred to profit and loss accounts and balance sheets, turnover, stock and debtors, to name some of the key terms. The thinking behind what was included in the profit and loss account developed and changed over the years, but the basic statement, the profit and loss account, kept the same name and, in the main, looked much the same. In 1992 a number of changes were introduced which led to the presentation within the profit and loss account changing. At the same time the statement of total recognised gains and losses (STRGL) was introduced along with a different way of viewing performance, until then seen as stopping at the calculation of profit (after tax). This is discussed further in chapter 1 on page 9.

With the adoption of IFRSs in 2005 and the gradual aligning of UK GAAP with IFRS, much of the terminology has changed. Some of the calculations have also changed, but here we are concerned with explaining the different terminology, in particular, where it can be used interchangeably.

Income statement/Profit and loss account – this sets out how the company's profit (after tax) for the period (year, half-year or quarter) has been calculated.

Statement of comprehensive income – this statement was introduced by the 2007 version of IAS 1 and may take one of two forms: (1) where a separate income statement is presented (which is the route we expect most British companies will take) the statement of comprehensive income is an extension of the income statement, like the statement of total recognised gains and losses (STRGL) and the statement of recognised income and expense (SORIE) (see below); and (2) where a separate income statement is not presented, the statement of comprehensive income is the entire statement, the first part being the same as an income statement and the second being like the STRGL or SORIE.

Statement of recognised income and expense/Statement of total recognised gains and losses – these are both extensions of the income statement. The opening line is usually profit/loss after tax, taken from the income statement. Other gains and losses are included, such that the final total in these statements is the total change in net assets other than as a result of transactions with owners in their capacity as owners, e.g. dividends to shareholders.

Statement of financial position/Balance sheet – this is where a company's assets and liabilities are listed.

Revenue/Sales/Turnover – generally this is the first line in the income statement/profit and loss account. It represents the value of goods and services sold by the company during the period. Businesses operating in some industries may use other, more relevant, descriptions, such as rental income or finance income. Whatever the label in the income statement/profit and loss account, this is sometimes colloquially called the 'top line'.

Inventory/Stock – these are the unsold goods or (for a manufacturer) components that are held by the company at any point in time.

Receivables/Debtors – this is the amount of money due to the company from its customers or others at any point in time.

Payables/Creditors – this is the amount of money payable by the company to its suppliers or others at any point in time.

Primary statements – for IFRS, under the 2007 version of IAS 1, these are the balance sheet, income statement (although this can be subsumed within the statement of comprehensive income), statement of comprehensive income, statement of changes in equity and cash flow statement. Under the previous version of IAS 1, these are the balance sheet, income statement, either the statement of recognised income and expense or the statement of changes in equity, and cash flow statement. Under UK GAAP, these are the balance sheet, profit and loss account, statement of total recognised gains and losses and cash flow statement.

Accounts/financial statements – generally these two terms are interchangeable. IAS 1 stipulates that a complete set of financial statements comprises the primary statements together with the notes. The Companies Act does not use the term 'financial statements' and instead refers to accounts. There is a view (which stems from the terminology in the Companies Act) that accounts refers only to the primary statements and does not include the notes, and that financial statements refers to the primary statements together with the notes. However, use of these terms in practice is mixed and either term could be used when referring to the package of primary statements plus notes.

Annual report/Report and accounts – this refers to the total package, including financial statements, that is required to be produced by companies each year – see chapter 1 for a list of what is included.

Glossary of terms

AADB. Accountancy and Actuarial Discipline Board. Part of the FRC.

ACCA. The Association of Chartered Certified Accountants.

Accruals accounting. The method of accounting that underpins the income statement and balance sheet, namely recognising transactions in the period to which they relate, rather than in the period in which the cash is received or paid. Hence: (1) the charge in arriving at profit/loss for an expense is not (except by chance) the same as the amount of cash paid; and (2) the amount recognised as revenue (or turnover or sales) for the year is not (except by chance) the same as the cash received from customers.

Act (or 'the Act'). Unless specified to the contrary, 'Act' or 'the Act' refers to the Companies Act 2006.

AIM. Alternative Investment Market.

Annual report. Financial statements together with the directors' report and, for quoted companies, the directors' remuneration report, and various other information and reports to shareholders – see chapter 1.

APB. The UK Auditing Practices Board. Part of the FRC.

APM. Alternative Performance Measure. Sometimes called adjusted earnings number or non-GAAP measure.

ARC. Accounting Regulatory Committee (of the EU).

ASB. The UK Accounting Standards Board. Part of the FRC.

ASC. The UK Accounting Standards Committee, which set standards from 1970 to 1990, after which the ASB took over the activity.

Asset. In a formal sense, the IASB's Framework for the Preparation and Presentation of Financial Statements defines an asset as: 'a resource controlled by the entity as a result of past events and from which future economic benefits are expected to flow to the entity'. Less formally, an asset is something of value that a company controls; it is recognised as an asset on the balance sheet if it meets certain recognition criteria, such as whether it can be measured reliably.

Associate. An entity, including an unincorporated entity such as a partnership, over which the investor has significant influence and that is neither a subsidiary nor an interest in a joint venture (IAS 28, para. 2).

BERR. The department for Business Enterprise & Regulatory Reform. Formerly called the DTI (the Department of Trade & Industry).

Business review. Narrative reporting required to be within the directors' report. It must contain a fair review of the group's business (being, a balanced and comprehensive analysis of the development and performance of the group's business during the financial year and the position at the end of the year, consistent with the size and complexity of the business and containing, where relevant, analysis using KPIs) and a description of principal risks and uncertainties facing the group.

CA 1985. The Companies Act 1985.

CA 2006. The Companies Act 2006.

CCAB. The Consultative Committee of Accountancy Bodies in the UK and Ireland, which comprises:

- The Institute of Chartered Accountants in England and Wales (ICAEW);
- The Institute of Chartered Accountants of Scotland (ICAS);
- The Institute of Chartered Accountants in Ireland (ICAI);
- The Association of Chartered Certified Accountants (ACCA);
- The Chartered Institute of Management Accountants (CIMA); and
- The Chartered Institute of Public Finance and Accountancy (CIPFA).

CESR. The Committee of European Securities Regulators.

CIMA. The Chartered Institute of Management Accountants.

CIPFA. The Chartered Institute of Public Finance and Accountancy.

Combined Code. The UK code of corporate governance, the latest version of which (2008) is published by the Financial Reporting Council.

DB. Defined benefit (pension scheme).

DC. Defined contribution (pension scheme).

Debit/credit. These are bookkeeping terms. A debit entry represents either an expense or an asset (or a reduction of a liability). A credit entry represents either income or a liability (or a reduction of an asset). The application of accounting principles in drawing up financial statements involves determining which debits are to be treated as assets and which are to be treated as expenses; and determining which credits are to be treated as liabilities and which are to be treated as equity or income. As an example, a payment of cash of £100 to acquire inventory (stock) is represented as: Dr Inventory £100 (an increase in the asset 'inventory'); Cr Cash £100 (a decrease in the asset 'cash').

Deferred tax. A way of accounting that, generally, results in the tax consequences of a transaction or event being recognised in the same period and same place (part of profit/loss, other comprehensive income or directly in equity) as the transaction or event itself.

DTR. Disclosure and Transparency Rules issued by the FSA.

Earnings. An undefined term. Generally refers to profit after tax and minority interest. More accurately, it refers to profit after tax, minority interest and preference dividend, this being the definition of earnings used in the calculation of EPS (see below).

EBITDA. Earnings before interest, tax, depreciation and amortisation. This is a measure of earnings favoured by some analysts and companies. Depreciation and amortisation are added back because they are non-cash items. Hence

EBITDA is sometimes called 'cash earnings', although this is something of a misnomer, as it still includes many items calculated on an accruals basis.

EFRAG. The European Financial Reporting Advisory Group, part of the mechanism used by Brussels to help it to consider endorsement of International Financial Reporting Standards for use in the EU.

Entity accounts. The accounts of an entity itself – for example, the accounts of a single company – as opposed to consolidated accounts. Also sometimes called solus accounts. See chapter 8.

EPS. Earnings per share. Broadly, earnings (profit after tax, minority interest and preference dividend) divided by the number of equity shares in issue during the year. The details are set out in IAS 33.

Equity. (1) The IASB's term for share capital and reserves and what is called shareholders' funds in UK GAAP. (2) An equity share, defined in s. 548 of the Act as 'in relation to a company, its issued share capital excluding any part of that capital that, neither as respects dividends nor as respects capital, carries any right to participate beyond a specified amount in a distribution'. Note that accounting standards (international and UK) define equity shares in a different way from the Act.

Equity accounting. This is also known as 'the equity method'. It is the method of accounting adopted for associates and in certain cases for joint ventures, as explained in chapter 8.

ESOP. Employee Share Ownership Plan.

Expense. A reduction in assets, charged in arriving at profit or loss. This includes non-cash items such as depreciation of non-current assets.

FASB. The US Financial Accounting Standards Board.

Financial statements. A company's annual financial statements (or 'accounts'), which comprise the income statement, statement of comprehensive income, the balance sheet, the cash flow statement, the statement of changes in equity and various supplementary notes. They form the major part of the company's annual report; this is sent to shareholders (for quoted companies), made available on a website (for public companies), laid before the company in general meeting and (all companies) placed on the public record at Companies House. Can also refer to other contexts, such as interim financial statements.

FLA. Finance and Leasing Association.

FRC. The UK Financial Reporting Council, the body that oversees the regulation of corporate reporting and audit, including the UK ASB and the FRRP.

FRRP. The UK Financial Reporting Review Panel. Part of the FRC.

FRS. A UK Financial Reporting Standard, an accounting standard developed by the ASB. See also SSAP.

FRSSE. Financial Reporting Standard for Smaller Entities.

FSA. The UK Financial Services Authority.

GAAP. Generally accepted accounting principles, discussed in chapter 1.

Gearing. The relationship between debt and equity. Gearing can be calculated in a number of ways. See chapter 14 for details.

Gross profit. This is profit measured as revenue less cost of sales, that is, profit before deducting overhead expenses, interest and tax.

Half-yearly report. Financial information about the first half of the financial year published by listed companies as required by the FSA as Listing Authority. In the past these have frequently been referred to as the 'interims', although now there is also a requirement for interim management statements (see chapter 6), so it is preferable to use the term 'half-yearly report'.

HMRC. HM Revenue & Customs.

IAS. An international accounting standard issued by the IASC.

IASB. The International Accounting Standards Board, the global standard-setter from 2001.

IASC. The International Accounting Standards Committee, the global standard-setter until 2001.

ICAEW, ICAS, ICAI. See CCAB.

IFRIC. The International Financial Reporting Interpretations Committee, a subsidiary of the IASB.

IFRS. An international financial reporting standard issued by the IASB.

Income. An undefined term, used rather loosely. Can be used as a synonym for profit (e.g. in US parlance 'net income' means profit after tax). Sometimes also, confusingly, used to mean revenue.

Income statement. See above section 'Introductory note on terminology'.

Interest cover. The ratio of interest cost to profit before interest. So if profit before interest is one hundred and interest cost is twenty-five, interest cover is four. That is, interest is covered four times by profits.

Interims. See 'Half-yearly report' above.

Joint venture. A contractual arrangement whereby two or more parties undertake an economic activity that is subject to joint control (IAS 31, para. 3).

JV. Joint venture.

KPI. Key performance indicator.

Liability. In a formal sense, the IASB's Framework for the Preparation and Presentation of Financial Statements and IAS 37 'Provisions, Contingent Liabilities and Contingent Assets' defines a liability as 'a present obligation of the entity arising from past events, the settlement of which is expected to result in an outflow from the entity of resources embodying economic benefits'. Less formally, a liability is something that a company owes to a third party; it is recognised as a liability on the balance sheet if it meets certain recognition criteria, such as whether it can be measured reliably.

Listed company. A company whose securities are listed on the London Stock Exchange.

Listing Rules. The rules issued by the Financial Services Authority that apply to companies listed on the London Stock Exchange.

LTIP. Long-term incentive plan.

Minority interest. The interest of an outside shareholder in a partially-held subsidiary. Also called 'non-controlling interest'.

NASDAQ. National Association of Securities Dealers Automated Quotation system.

NBV. Net book value. (1) This term applies to non-current (or fixed) assets and refers to the cost or value less accumulated depreciation. (2) It also refers to the carrying value of an asset or liability as it is the amount at which it is stated, or carried, in the balance sheet.

Non-controlling interest. See minority interest.

NRV. Net realisable value.

OFR. The Operating and Financial Review. This was to have become a statutory requirement for quoted companies, but has remained a voluntary report recommended by the ASB. It is a narrative account supplementing the financial statements.

Operating profit. A measure of profit after deducting all operating expenses before deducting interest and tax and, generally, before adding share of results of associates. In UK GAAP, certain exceptional items (non-operating exceptionals or 'super-exceptionals') are also added/deducted after operating profit.

P & L. Profit and loss.

POB. The UK Professional Oversight Board. Part of the FRC.

Prelims. Preliminary announcements of results by listed companies. Previously required by the Listing Rules but now optional, although where produced must adhere to FSA requirements in the Listing Rules.

PPE. Property, plant and equipment.

Profit. A measure of the results of a business on the basis of accruals accounting (see above). (See also gross profit, operating profit, profit before tax, profit after tax.)

Profit after tax. A measure of profit after deducting all expenses, including tax.

Profit before tax. A measure of profit after deducting all expenses apart from tax.

Public company. A company that can offer shares to the public and having an allotted share capital with a nominal value of at least £50,000.

Quoted company. A company whose equity share capital is officially listed in an EEA state or is admitted to dealing on either the New York Stock Exchange or Nasdaq.

Revenue. The amount earned by an entity from selling goods and services. The terms 'sales' and 'turnover' are broadly synonymous with revenue.

Sales. See revenue.

SAS. Statement of Auditing Standards.

SEC. Securities and Exchange Commission.

Shareholders' equity. The aggregate of a company's share capital and its reserves. Called 'shareholders' funds' in UK GAAP.

SIC. Standing Interpretations Committee of the IASC.

SOCIE. See above section 'Introductory note on terminology'.

SoP. Statement of principles.

SORP. Statement of Recommended Practice.

SORIE. See above section 'Introductory note on terminology'.

Sorry. Pronunciation of SORIE (see above section 'Introductory note on terminology').

SPE. Special purpose entity.

SSAP. A UK Statement of Standard Accounting Practice, an accounting standard developed by the ASC. See also FRS.

Statement of comprehensive income. See above section 'Introductory note on terminology'.

STRGL. See above section 'Introductory note on terminology'.

Struggle. Pronunciation of STRGL. See above section 'Introductory note on terminology'.

Subsidiary/subsidiary undertaking. Under IFRS, a subsidiary is 'an entity, including an unincorporated entity such as a partnership, that is controlled by another entity (known as the parent)'. For UK GAAP and UK law purposes, there is a distinction between 'subsidiary' and 'subsidiary undertaking'. Section 1159(1) of the Act defines a 'subsidiary' for the general purposes of the Act, but not for accounting purposes. Section 1162 of the Act defines a 'subsidiary undertaking' for accounting purposes, chiefly in connection with consolidation.

Summary Financial Statements. A summarised version of the financial statements, directors' report and directors' remuneration report that can be sent to members in place of the full annual report – see chapter 6.

Turnover. See revenue.

UITF. The UK Urgent Issues Task Force. This is a subsidiary of the ASB.

XBRL. Extensible Business Reporting Language.

PART I

The accounting environment

1
Introduction

Aim of this book

Collectively, a board of directors is responsible for the company's annual report and financial statements, yet most directors are not accountants. The primary aim of this book is to explain accounting to those non-executive directors who are not accountants. The book may also be useful to executive directors who are not accountants, and even to directors who are accountants but who have not worked actively in their profession for some time. To some extent this means explaining accounting as one would to any group of intelligent non-accountants. However, we emphasise those aspects that are particularly relevant to the directors of listed companies. For example, in chapter 4 we emphasise the work of the Financial Reporting Review Panel, a body that monitors financial statements and enforces compliance with accounting standards, because while its remit remains public and large private companies, a large focus of its attention is listed companies. Similarly, the specific subjects covered in Part II reflect the likely interest of directors of listed companies: mergers and acquisitions, financial instruments, earnings per share, share-based payment and realised and distributable profits are all discussed. However, the reader will find little on inventory valuation and methods of depreciation, as these are less controversial areas. Similarly, this book does not deal with accounting for special industries and sectors such as banks, insurance companies and charities. As the group financial statements of listed companies must now be prepared using International Financial Reporting Standards (IFRS), rather than UK GAAP, the emphasis in each chapter is on IFRS. How IFRS is applied in the UK, where there are choices, is often influenced by previous UK practice and we discuss this previous UK practice where relevant. In Appendix 1, we set out 50 questions, linked to the chapters, that non-executive directors might find appropriate to ask at meetings of the board or audit committee.

What is accounting?

Accounting is a broad term. It is used to cover the initial recording of transactions in a company's accounting records, although this is better termed 'bookkeeping'. Given the almost universal use of computers for record keeping, even this term is itself only literally accurate either historically, when entries were made in books of account or (originally leather bound) ledgers, or in the smallest of businesses.

The term 'accounting' more properly refers either to the processes that accountants carry out, namely of aggregating and shaping information into reports that are useful to users of those reports; or to the outputs of those processes, namely accounting reports that can be used internally within a business ('management accounting') or externally ('financial accounting' or 'financial reporting'). External reporting can be seen in terms of compliance with legal requirements, for example the requirement under the Companies Act 2006 (CA 2006) to prepare accounts (also called 'financial statements'), circulate them to members, lay them before a general meeting of shareholders (public companies, which includes listed companies, only), and then to file them at Companies House (although small and medium-sized companies can choose to file abbreviated accounts). Other regulatory purposes arise, such as the role of the Financial Services Authority in connection with the supervision of various financial institutions.

Whilst this compliance aspect is important, accounting – both internal and external – is perhaps better seen as a process that serves the decision-making needs of business people and various classes of users of financial statements. Thus, within a company, the board and various other unit and divisional managers need accounting information to enable them to understand and control the business on a regular basis. In most medium-sized and larger businesses, budgets and, subsequently, monthly management accounts are prepared for this purpose. Managers want to know about various financial indicators, such as sales growth, margins, level of costs, amount of funds tied up in inventory (stock) and receivables (debtors) and so on. All of this has the overall objective of seeking to ensure that the company achieves its profit objectives. If the management accounting information shows that budgets are not being achieved, decisions are taken relating to matters such as pricing, level of overheads such as marketing expenditure and staff numbers, or levels of capital expenditure, to try to steer the company back on course to achieving, over the year as a whole, the sales, profit and other measures set out in the budget.

External reporting has an important decision-making focus, as well as a compliance focus. In a narrow, traditional sense, a board of directors presents to shareholders an annual report that gives an account of its stewardship of the company's assets during the year. But even implicit in that is an assumption that the shareholders will consider whether they find the performance to be acceptable. If they do not, that might lead to their refusing to reappoint some directors. So even here there is a notion of decision making.

However, in a modern context, the decision-making role is more explicit. Certainly for companies listed on a stock exchange, the board is reporting to 'the market': the analyst and fund manager community in general and not just to those who happen to be shareholders at present. The market has expectations about earnings, and if the earnings reported disappoint the market, the share price, and sometimes the directors' careers, will suffer. The fundamental decisions taking place here, of course, are concerned with whether to hold, buy or sell the company's shares.

The components of a company's annual report

An annual report, especially of a listed company, is now a very substantial document. The following are currently its main components:

- *Chairman's report.* This is voluntarily given by listed and traded companies and some other public interest entities, but not generally otherwise.
- *Operating and financial review (OFR).* This is recommended for quoted companies (officially listed in an EEA state or admitted to dealing on either the New York Stock Exchange or NASDAQ) by an Accounting Standards Board (ASB) statement of the same name. It was to have become a statutory requirement for quoted companies, but Gordon Brown, as Chancellor, stepped in at the last minute and announced the withdrawal of the requirements. The original intention was for a statutory OFR to have been required by quoted companies and a similar, but lighter-touch, business review to have been included by all other companies (other than small companies) in their directors' reports. A similar effect has still been achieved; the business review is now required to be included in the directors' report by all companies (other than small companies), but the specified content is greater for quoted companies and, for them, is similar to what would have been required in the statutory OFR.[1]
- *Directors' remuneration report.* Certain disclosures relating to directors' remuneration are required by all companies, but in the case of quoted companies these are more extensive and are presented as a separate report.[2]
- *Report on corporate governance.* This is required for listed companies and, like the OFR and remuneration report, has been a growth area in recent years.[3]
- *Auditors' report.* This is an opinion from the auditor as required by the Companies Act.[4]
- *Directors' report.* This is a legal requirement, although the contents are somewhat arbitrary and not always interesting; hence, historically, the growth of the chairman's statement and OFR as channels of communication. Since 2005, companies (other than small companies) have been required to include a business review within the directors' report. The business review is a narrative report, supplemented with analysis using key performance indicators (KPIs), and is much like an OFR. Indeed, the

1 See ch. 20.　　2 See ch. 20.　　3 See ch. 20.　　4 See ch. 4.

5

required content for quoted companies was increased with the enactment of the 2006 Act by adding in some of what would otherwise have been included in the statutory OFR had it not been withdrawn at the eleventh hour. Many companies fulfil the requirement for a business review by including an OFR (however named) in the annual report and simply including a cross-reference to it in the directors' report.

- *Performance statements.* Traditionally, the profit and loss account was the principal statement and the way in which a company or group communicated its performance in the year; the 'bottom line' being profit (or loss) for the year. The equivalent statement in IFRS is called the income statement. In the 1990s, the UK GAAP view of performance was extended to incorporate all the other gains and losses made by a company that were reported in the accounts, e.g. gains on revaluing the company's properties, although excluding items arising from transactions with shareholders in their capacity as shareholders, e.g. dividends. Hereafter performance was reported in two statements: the profit and loss account arriving at profit or loss, and the statement of total recognised gains and losses (STRGL), starting with the profit or loss and then listing the other gains and losses. A similar idea was adopted in IFRS. Until 2007, the second performance statement under IFRS could take one of two forms, the more common of which in the UK was the statement of recognised income and expense (SORIE) and this statement was broadly equivalent to the STRGL. Following the 2007 amendment of IAS 1, performance is reported in IFRS accounts either in one statement, the statement of comprehensive income (which combines the income statement and SORIE into one statement), or in two statements, the income statement and the statement of comprehensive income (which in this case would look like the SORIE). See below for a brief explanation and see chapter 9 for a detailed discussion.
- *Balance sheet or statement of financial position.* This sets out the company's assets and liabilities and its shareholders' funds. The balance sheet was traditionally seen as merely a collection of the assets and liabilities that were, so to speak, left over at the end of the year following the matching of costs and revenues in the profit and loss account. More recently, the balance sheet has come to be seen as a more important statement in its own right. For example, stricter definitions of what should be treated as assets and liabilities and the introduction of more fair valuing[5] have increased the importance of the balance sheet.
- *Cash flow statement.* This is, almost literally, a statement of the cash receipts (inflows) and payments (outflows) during the year, categorised under various headings. It may thus correspond more closely to a

5 See ch. 7.

non-accountant's view of performance than profit. See the next section for a comparison of the two.

- *Statement of accounting policies.* Even though much of accounting is specified, there is nonetheless scope in some areas for a company to select accounting policies. In this section of the annual report the company describes the significant accounting policies it has used in preparing its financial statements.
- *Notes to the financial statements.* Many pages of notes are presented in accordance with accounting standards and, for UK GAAP, company law. In general, the notes amplify what is in the income statement, statement of comprehensive income, the balance sheet and the cash flow statement. In addition, there are notes dealing with other matters such as related-party transactions, commitments entered into and key events that occurred after the end of the accounting period. For listed companies, the Listing Rules and Disclosure and Transparency Rules require some disclosures, although these can be outside the financial statements so long as they are within the annual report.

The difference between profit and cash flow

A question frequently asked by non-accountants is what exactly *profit* means and how it differs from *cash flow*. Both are measures of what has happened to a business during a year, but they shed different light on its activities. Cash flow is a natural idea, familiar to us all as individuals. By contrast, profit is an artificial construct. Profit arises from the use of *accruals accounting*, that is, recognising transactions in the period in which they occur, rather than in the period in which the cash is received or paid; it thereby measures the performance of a business. A simple example will illustrate the point.

P Limited:

- Sells goods to customers during 2007 of invoiced value £100. Of this, P receives £50 in cash during the year (the remaining £50 is received in the following year).
- Buys goods from suppliers during 2007 of invoiced value £52. P buys on extended credit and pays nothing in 2007.
- Spends £40 cash on buying office equipment.
- Pays £8 rent for premises to operate from during 2007.

P Limited's cash flow statement will show the figures indicated in Box 1.1.

The company's income statement shows an entirely different picture (see box 1.2).

The two results happen to be quite different in amount (although in other examples they might be similar) and are quite different in principle. The income statement focuses on the transactions that relate to the year in question. So, it focuses on the sales that have been made in the year (£100) and on the cost

---

Box 1.1 *P Limited*
Cash flow statement for the year ended 31 December 2007

Operating inflows	
Receipts from customers	50
Payment of rent	(8)
Net operating inflow	42
Capital expenditure	(40)
Increase in cash during the year	2

Box 1.2 *P Limited*
Income statement for the year ended 31 December 2007

Revenue (or Sales)	100
Cost of sales	(52)
Depreciation of equipment	(4)
Rental of premises	(8)
Profit before tax*	36

* Tax is ignored in this simple example

Box 1.3 *P Limited*
Balance sheet as at 31 December 2007

Non-current assets (cost £40 less depreciation £4)	36
Receivables (sales made, cash not yet collected)	50
Cash	102
Less: payables (amounts owing to suppliers)	(52)
Net assets	136

---

of those sales (£52), without reference to whether these amounts have been collected or paid for in cash. Also, the purchase of office equipment is for use in the business over an extended period; it is not held for resale. Hence it is described as capital expenditure and the cost is spread in accounting terms over its useful economic life, in this case assumed to be ten years. The rent is assumed to have been paid in full for the year.

If we assume that P Limited is a new business that started the year by issuing 100 £1 shares at par for cash, we can see that at the end of the year it will have cash of £102 (opening cash of £100 plus increase in cash during the year of £2). However, as shown in Box 1.3, its closing balance sheet will reflect all the assets and liabilities of the business.

> **Box 1.4 P Limited**
> *Shareholders' equity as at 31 December 2007*
>
> | | |
> |---|---:|
> | Opening shareholders' equity | 100 |
> | Profit for the year (retained) | 36 |
> | Closing shareholders' equity | 136 |

These net assets are equivalent to shareholders' equity, as shown in Box 1.4. This simple example illustrates a number of points. First, it shows that:

$$\text{Assets } less \text{ liabilities } = \text{shareholders' equity}$$

This simple equation demonstrates that shareholders' equity (136 in this example) is the residual interest after all liabilities (52) are deducted from all assets $(36 + 50 + 102 = 188)$.

The second point is that the income statement and the balance sheet articulate with each other. They are both prepared on an accruals basis. Third, the income statement and balance sheet show a much richer set of information than the cash flow statement. This is not to say that the cash flow statement is of little or no value. Indeed, it is important that a business generates cash, otherwise it will run into difficulty; hence cash flow information is useful in its own right. It is also useful as a cross check on the quality of profits.

The example also allows us to view profit in an economic way. Profit can be viewed as the amount that a proprietor can withdraw from a business at the end of a year, such that the business can continue in the following year. We can see from the examples in Boxes 1.2 and 1.4 that the shareholders could have withdrawn the £36 profit and the business would (leaving aside complications such as inflation) have maintained its capital and been able to continue. The £2 increase in cash in the year is not a helpful indicator in these respects.

Of course, merely to speak of 'profit' is an oversimplification. A typical company's income statement may include the figures shown in Box 1.5.

The relatively simple income statement in Box 1.5 uses four variants of the term 'profit'. Whilst they are self-explanatory, it demonstrates the need for clarity in terminology.

Performance statements

In the past, reporting of performance stopped at profit (after tax). However, the notion of performance was extended in the UK in the 1990s. It was recognised that a number of other changes are made to a company's net assets, for example, changes in the value of its assets, and that these should be reflected in the performance statements.

Let us consider further the example of P Limited above. On the first day of 2008, its second year, assume that it issued a further 100 £1 shares at par for cash, took out a bank loan of £100 and used the £200 cash to buy a property

---

Box 1.5 *Illustrative income statement*

Revenue	100
Cost of sales	(52)
Gross profit	48
Administrative expenses	(23)
Operating profit	25
Interest payable	(7)
Profit before tax	18
Tax	(5)
Profit for the year	13

Box 1.6 *P Limited*
Income statement for the year ended 31 December 2008

Revenue (or Sales)	100
Cost of sales	(52)
Depreciation of equipment	(4)
Depreciation of premises	(4)
Interest payable	(5)
Profit before tax*	35

* Tax is ignored in this simple example

---

from which to operate. Hence rent is no longer payable. If the interest for 2008 on its loan is £5 and the property is depreciated over 50 years, P's income statement, assuming that sales and cost of sales are as for 2007, will be as in Box 1.6.

Profit is lower than in the previous year. The company now owns its own premises though and on the last day of 2008 these may be valued at £203. If the gain in value of £3 is added to the profit of £35, the 'comprehensive income' made by P Limited in 2008 totals £38, higher than the £36 in the previous year.

An additional performance statement, the statement of total recognised gains and losses (STRGL), was thus introduced into UK GAAP. It started with the profit figure and then listed all other gains and losses, but only if they had been incorporated into the financial statements (rather than simply disclosed in a note). Thus, in the example of P Limited, the gain in value of the business premises would only be included in the STRGL if the property were revalued in the financial statements and the property included in the balance sheet at the end of 2008 at £203. If instead P chose not to revalue its property, the £3 gain would not be included in the STRGL. It is important to note, therefore, that not all changes in value within a business are reported in the performance statements.

When the STRGL was introduced in the UK as a second performance statement, an accompanying rule was introduced, namely that once a gain had been reported in one of the two statements, it could not be reported again (this is called 'recycling' of the gain). Thus, if P Limited sold the property for £203 on the first day of 2009, no gain or loss would be reported on the sale; the gain of £3 having already been reported (assuming that the property was included in the 2008 balance sheet at its value of £203). Although this is the same for some gains in IFRS, for example, for gains in revaluation of properties, it is not so for other gains. For example, when an overseas subsidiary is sold, the cumulative exchange differences that were reported in the second performance statement (e.g. SORIE) are reversed out of the second performance statement and included in the income statement as part of the overall gain or loss on sale of subsidiary. Accordingly, UK GAAP in this respect has been changed to align it with IFRS.

In IFRS prior to the 2007 amendment to IAS 1, the first statement was the income statement, which arrives at profit or loss, and the second statement could be either:

(1) statement of recognised income and expense (SORIE) – this is the statement that most British companies have given. It is equivalent to the STRGL and shows net profit or loss and each of the other changes in net assets (shareholders' equity) other than as a result of transactions with owners in their capacity as owners; or
(2) statement of changes in equity (SOCIE) – this is similar to the SORIE, but additionally has to show transactions with shareholders in their capacity as shareholders and the opening and closing balance of share capital and each reserve.

Why have two performance statements rather than one? Broadly, the original split between the two statements was that value changes, such as gains in property values and actuarial variances on pension liabilities, were included in the second statement, with transactions being recorded in the first statement (income statement or profit and loss account). However, a number of value changes are now included in the income statement in IFRS. These are the value changes that are seen as part of the business's operations. For example, if a business holds investment properties, these are defined as held to earn rentals or for capital appreciation or both and the relevant standard now requires not only the rental income to be included in the income statement, but also the changes in capital value of the property. Similarly, if a business holds investments for trading, the changes in value are required to be recognised in the income statement.

With the 2007 change to IAS 1, performance can now be presented in one statement, a statement of comprehensive income, which combines the income statement and SORIE. Alternatively, companies may continue to present two statements, an income statement and what is called a statement of comprehensive income. In the two-statement approach the statement of comprehensive income is like the SORIE, starting with net profit or loss and listing each item of other comprehensive income, i.e. all other changes in net assets other than as a result of transactions with shareholders in their capacity as shareholders.

We expect most British companies to go down the two-statement approach, which means continuing to present an income statement and a SORIE, albeit probably renaming the SORIE as a statement of comprehensive income.

The use of accounting terms in agreements

The earlier example of four variants of profit (Box 1.5) illustrates an important point for directors in entering into an agreement such as a contract to buy another business. A legal agreement that refers to profit should be as specific as possible as to which profit figure is envisaged. This is not just a matter of being clear as to which of the above four figures is being used. It also needs to be clear:

- which year's profits are intended;
- which GAAP is intended (UK GAAP, IFRS, etc. – see chapter 2);
- whether the profit is as per the statutory financial statements or whether it is adjusted in some way;
- according to which accounting policies the profit is calculated – for example, in an acquisition agreement is it the bidder's policies or the target's policies?

Hence a reference to 'profit calculated according to GAAP' is not helpful and can be the source of difficulty, not to say expensive and time-consuming litigation.

Similarly, other terms may be used in various legal agreements, and the same general principle applies. Further examples of imprecision are the terms 'gearing' and 'interest cover', which are often used in loan covenants. This is discussed in chapter 6.

What is GAAP?

GAAP refers to generally accepted accounting principles. There are different GAAPs in different jurisdictions, e.g. UK GAAP, US GAAP, French GAAP and so on. In addition, there are international financial reporting standards (IFRSs), also sometimes called international GAAP. These aspects are discussed in chapter 2.

Although it has no precise meaning, UK GAAP is generally taken to refer to:

- parts of company law, namely, the Companies Act 2006 and the various statutory instruments made under it, primarily SI 2008/410;

- accounting standards (Statements of Standard Accounting Practice (SSAPs) and Financial Reporting Standards (FRSs));
- abstracts from the Urgent Issues Task Force (UITF);
- for listed companies, the Listing Rules and the Disclosure and Transparency Rules; and
- reporting statements issued by the ASB.

These are the core components of GAAP.

International GAAP, or IFRS GAAP, for a British company is generally taken to refer to:

- parts of company law, namely, the Companies Act 2006 and the various statutory instruments made under it, primarily SI 2008/410;
- accounting standards (International Financial Reporting Standards (IFRSs) and International Accounting Standards (IASs) as endorsed by the EU);
- interpretations from the International Financial Reporting Interpretations Committee (IFRIC) as endorsed by the EU;
- for listed companies, the Listing Rules and the Disclosure and Transparency Rules; and
- reporting statements issued by the ASB.

Each of these components is now discussed in turn.

Company law. This is the foundation of financial statement preparation for a British company, whether under IFRS or UK GAAP. The CA 2006 sets out the basic requirement for a company to prepare accounts, circulate them to members, lay them (public companies only) before the members, file them at Companies House and make them available (quoted companies only) on a website. The Act also sets out some of the details regarding their preparation, for example, requirements as to what is a subsidiary undertaking and when consolidated accounts should be prepared. The extent of the detailed requirements applying depends upon whether the accounts are being prepared under IFRS or under UK GAAP. Chapter 3 contains a fuller discussion.

Accounting standards. The current accounting standards under international GAAP are IFRSs and these are produced by the IASB. The predecessor body until 2001 was the International Accounting Standards Committee (IASC), which produced IASs, some of which are extant. Unfortunately, it is not these standards directly that are to be applied by British companies, such as listed companies, but these standards *as adopted by* the EU; this has given rise to an additional layer of complexity, and frustration, for those companies applying international GAAP, many of which (such as the group financial statements of listed companies) are compelled to apply international GAAP. As IFRSs and IASs are intended to be applied throughout the world, they have not been developed in conjunction with any specific companies legislation. They nevertheless cover much the same topics as UK standards. A full list of extant accounting

13

standards, for international GAAP and for UK GAAP, may be found in appendices 2 and 3 respectively. Throughout the rest of this book we refer to 'IFRS' to mean international accounting standards, namely IFRSs and IASs together.

IFRIC Interpretations/UITF Abstracts. These are produced by the IFRIC and UITF respectively. Both committees have a similar role: to assist the standard-setter (IASB or ASB) in areas where an accounting standard (or, for the UITF, a Companies Act provision) exists, but where unsatisfactory or conflicting interpretations have developed or seem likely to develop and to give timely guidance on issues that have not yet been addressed by standards. Hence they deal with relatively narrow issues. Examples are IFRIC 3 'Emission rights' and IFRIC 9 'Reassessment of embedded derivatives'.

The Listing Rules and the Disclosure and Transparency Rules (DTR). These rules, insofar as they deal with accounting matters, are part of GAAP only for listed companies. In terms of regular reporting (as opposed, for example, to new listings) there are continuing obligations relating to disclosures that are additional to those in the law and accounting standards; examples are directors' interests and corporate governance issues. The Listing Rules and DTR also set out the basic requirement for interim reports. IAS 34 contains guidance on half-yearly reports for IFRS preparers. Its status is complicated, but, broadly, it now needs to be applied by UK listed companies.

Reporting Statements issued by the ASB. These are non-mandatory guidance aimed at improving best practice. Two statements have, to date, been issued in this series: the first is on the Operating and Financial Review; and the second on disclosures in respect of retirement benefit schemes (in employers', not pension schemes', accounts). Despite being issued by the ASB, both statements are intended to apply to IFRS reporters in the UK as well as to UK GAAP reporters.

In addition to the above, the term 'GAAP' in the UK for those applying IFRS encompasses the following, which are authoritative in varying degrees:

- the IASB's Framework for the preparation and presentation of financial statements ('the Framework');
- statements and recommendations from the professional bodies, such as the guidance from the Institutes of Chartered Accountants on matters such as realised profits – these are now more likely to have influence on company law issues rather than on interpretation of accounting standards;
- quite literally, principles that are generally accepted in practice, say in a particular industry;
- manuals and similar guidance from firms of accountants; and
- recent pronouncements of other standard-setting bodies that use a similar conceptual framework to develop accounting standards; this encompasses not just recent standards and guidance from the ASB and UITF, but also from other standard-setters around the world, for example, the FASB and EITF in the US.

2

Accounting in the UK and the effects of international harmonisation

The UK's Accounting Standards Board

For the first one hundred years or more of the accountancy profession in the UK, there was a basic company law framework, and a body of practice, but no codification or standardisation of accounting rules. Until the middle of the twentieth century business was relatively simple and accountants used their judgement. Increasingly, however, business became more complex and then the lack of a standardised approach led to different profit figures being reported for what were essentially the same economic events. Although the US had pioneered standard-setting from 1939, the first development in this area in the UK was soon after, in 1942, when the Institute of Chartered Accountants in England and Wales (ICAEW) developed 'Recommendations' to members as to suitable accounting principles. These had no binding force. Eventually, it became clear that these were inadequate. Hence in 1970 the Accounting Standards Committee (ASC) was formed, subsequently becoming a joint activity of the six professional accounting bodies in the UK and Ireland.

The ASC developed Statements of Standard Accounting Practice (SSAPs) in the period 1970 to 1990. Some of these are still in force today. They did not have the force of law, although the Institutes said that they expected their members to comply with them. This system worked for some years as regards the majority of standards that were uncontroversial, although its weakness started to be seen from the early 1980s in relation to the attempted imposition upon the profession and companies of various systems of adjusting financial statements for the effects of inflation, including SSAP 16 'Current cost accounting'. This standard eventually had to be withdrawn.

The inflation accounting debacle showed that a reform of standard-setting was needed. Following the report of the Dearing Committee, a new UK structure was put in place from 1990. Figure 2.1 shows this structure (see below for how it subsequently changed).

The Financial Reporting Council (FRC) oversees the structure and adds support from business, the profession, other regulators and government. The Accounting Standards Board (ASB) is the standard-setter. The Urgent Issues Task Force (UITF) is a committee of the ASB, which develops Abstracts; these are rulings that form part of UK GAAP, but which deal with narrower issues than those that are the subject of accounting standards. The Financial Reporting

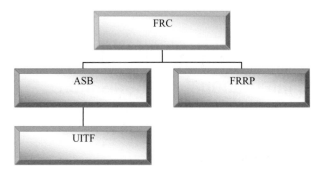

Figure 2.1 The UK accounting standard-setting structure as in 1990

Review Panel (FRRP) enforces compliance with standards and relevant parts of company law; this is discussed more fully in chapter 4. All of these bodies were newly created in 1990; the ASB took over the work of the ASC, but the other three bodies were completely new. In 2004, the FRC took over responsibility for the Auditing Practices Board and various other bodies concerned with the supervision of the accountancy profession. Subsequently, the FRC took on responsibility for actuarial regulation. The new structure that covers this wider range of activities is discussed in chapter 4.

A number of features distinguished the ASB from its predecessor, the ASC. One is more resources, including a full-time chairman and technical director, and a larger technical staff. Another was the new wider structure of which the ASB was a part, including for the first time an enforcement arm. Perhaps less obvious, but equally important, was the fact that the ASB developed an underlying framework of accounting. The ASB calls its framework a 'Statement of principles'.

The ASB established itself during the 1990s as a successful standard-setter and made many important reforms to UK accounting in that period. These included: better information about cash flows; better presentation of performance; more rigorous treatment of acquisitions and goodwill; stricter rules on provisions; reform of off-balance-sheet finance; and disclosures about financial instruments. The ASB's standards are called financial reporting standards (i.e. FRSs), to contrast them with the SSAPs developed by its predecessor. These various reforms did much to re-establish the reputation of UK GAAP during the 1990s. A full listing of UK standards may be found in appendix 3.

During the period 1990 to 2000, the ASB issued nineteen FRSs. In 2001, 2002 and 2003, no further FRSs were issued. In 2004 and 2005, ten FRSs were issued, eight of which reproduce IFRSs, or parts of them, and the other two reflect domestic issues: a change in the Companies Act; and concerns expressed in the Penrose Report on the Equitable Life inquiry. Pivotal changes in the dynamics of standard-setting occurred in 2001 and 2002 and as a result there has been a major shift in the centre of gravity to the newly formed

IASB (see under the heading 'The International Accounting Standards Board', below).

An EU Regulation was adopted in 2002 requiring EU companies whose securities are traded on a regulated market in the EU to use IFRS for their consolidated financial statements for 2005 onwards, so the previously 'flagship' UK GAAP accounts (group accounts prepared by listed companies) are now prepared directly using IFRS without reference to UK standards. UK GAAP still exists and, for most other accounts, companies can choose whether to prepare them using UK GAAP or IFRS. In practice, UK standards are still used in the preparation of the accounts of each individual company in the UK part of many groups, even where the group is listed and has to adopt IFRS in its consolidated accounts.

The ASB's role is now one of liaising with the IASB, contributing UK ideas to the debate about international harmonisation, and converging UK GAAP with IFRS. The ASB is still, nationally and internationally, an important body, but its function has changed considerably. By the end of this decade, there may be little or no difference between UK standards and IFRS.

The ASB has also been, and continues to be, involved in the development of SORPs. These do not have the same status as accounting standards, and are generally prepared by specific industry groups in conjunction with the ASB. The principal industries for which SORPs have been developed are: banking, insurance, oil and gas, investment trusts, leasing, charities, pension schemes and various other public sector bodies. The SORPs, however, have less relevance to financial statements prepared directly in accordance with IFRS.

In this section we have seen that the role of the UK's ASB has changed dramatically in the past few years. In the rest of this chapter we will explore further the reasons for this and why international harmonisation is so important.

International harmonisation

Just as accounting standards were developed in the UK and Ireland by the ASC and subsequently the ASB, committees were also set up in other countries for exactly the same purpose: to develop accounting standards for use in their home territory. Different systems of generally accepted accounting principles (GAAP) therefore developed over the years in various countries. While they were similar, in that they were based around the use of accruals accounting, the income statement and the balance sheet, they were in many respects different from each other. There were various reasons for these differences. In some countries, the stock market was relatively important as a source of finance; hence the emphasis was on performance measurement in an economic sense. In other countries, more finance came from the banking system, and so there was more emphasis on prudence. In yet other countries the influence came from the tax system.

The existence of different national GAAPs mattered relatively little until gradually business started to become more international in its nature. In the late 1960s and the early 1970s, the need for harmonisation was increasingly seen and, in 1973, the International Accounting Standards Committee (IASC) was formed. The IASC was founded and controlled by the accountancy bodies, including the same six who controlled the UK's ASC, as discussed above. It started to develop International Accounting Standards (IAS) and over the twenty-seven years of its existence it became more and more important and influential.

Initially, the IASC's role was seen in relation to developing economies; for example, the World Bank often required the use of IAS by any organisation to which it was lending. Also, it made sense for smaller, emerging economies to use IAS rather than invest in the development of their own system.

Increasingly, however, the role and use of IAS changed so that, certainly by the 1990s, the principal use of IAS was in relation to the international capital markets. That is, if a company based in, say, Switzerland or Germany wanted to raise debt or equity capital outside its own country, it would be to its advantage to use IAS rather than local GAAP, as there was more chance that investors and lenders would understand the information. As business became more global, and as the capital markets opened their doors to foreign companies, the need for international harmonisation strengthened. The fact that, say, US GAAP, UK GAAP and French GAAP reported different figures for profits and net assets became to be seen as a serious impediment to business and finance. Further, it was a source of some embarrassment to accountants that they could not agree on a global basis whether – given the same set of economic facts – a company's profits are £X or £Y, or, as sometimes happened, whether a company had made profits of £X or losses of £Y.

The International Accounting Standards Board

By the late 1990s it was becoming clear that the IASC, successful though it had been, was not up to the future task of leading the global harmonisation of accounting. A structural change was needed. A new International Accounting Standards Board (IASB) was formed and, with effect from 1 April 2001, took over the responsibility of accounting standard-setting. This is an altogether more professional organisation, with a mostly full-time board, chaired by Sir David Tweedie, who had chaired the UK ASB during the 1990s, its most dynamic period. The IASB is both a heavyweight body in its own right and is seen as a counterweight to the US Financial Accounting Standards Board (FASB). The current structure is shown in figure 2.2.

The IASB is overseen and funded by the International Accounting Standards Committee Foundation (IASCF), whose trustees appoint the board members, raise funds, set overall strategy (but do not interfere in the board's resolution of technical matters) and generally add their weight to the board's work. The

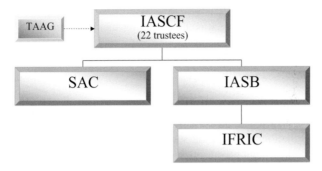

Figure 2.2 The international accounting standard-setting structure as at June 2008

trustees are assisted with appointments by the Trustee Appointments Advisory Group. There are also plans to establish a monitoring group above the trustees. The International Financial Reporting Interpretations Committee (IFRIC) is similar to the UK's UITF (see above): it deals with relatively narrow issues, developing a position where unsatisfactory or conflicting interpretations of an accounting standard have developed or seem likely to develop and on issues that have not yet been addressed by standards. There is also a Standards Advisory Council (SAC), which is drawn from a wide constituency and which advises the IASB on its agenda and gives feedback on its proposals. The IASB has sole responsibility for setting accounting standards.

On being established in 2001, the new board first adopted all the old IASs and then debated its agenda and work programme. A considerable amount of its work comprises continuing the projects of its predecessor, the IASC. This included improving many of the existing standards, for example, to eliminate options; and improving and revising the standards on financial instruments (IASs 32 and 39). However, a key change from the previous regime involves the IASB leading the development of new accounting rules, rather than seeking to harmonise the rules of the national standard-setters. Examples of this new approach are the work on share-based payments and on insurance contracts. These and other examples serve to characterise the IASB as a leader, or co-leader with the FASB, rather than a follower in the international accounting scene.

Many of the IASs remain in force despite the new regime, although over time some will be replaced, and already a number have been revised. It is noticeable that the IASB works in much more detail than the IASC. This is for a number of reasons. Partly, there is a bigger staff and a full-time board, and longer documents will automatically result. Also, the IASB needs, politically, to be seen as a valid counterweight to the FASB. This means that, whether or not the eventual standard is long, the underlying debate needs to be exhaustive.

As mentioned above, the IASC developed standards called international accounting standards (IASs) and the IASB develops standards known as international financial reporting standards (IFRSs). Although the Companies Act refers to 'international accounting standards' and 'IAS', most accountants use 'IFRS' or 'IFRSs' in referring to the total package of international standards. We use 'IFRS' in the remainder of this book to refer to international standards generally.

The EU Regulation for harmonisation within Europe

International accounting standards have no authority of their own. The IASB is a global, but private-sector, body that has no power to require its accounting standards to be followed. Nevertheless, various companies around the world decided to adopt IFRS voluntarily, and various countries decided to base their accounting on IFRS, in one of a number of ways. In some countries, such as Australia, the standard-setters have decided to base their national standards on IFRS – either literally, or with an element of local adaptation. In a few other countries, the governments have brought in, or are bringing in, legal requirements that IFRS should be used by companies, thereby giving them the status of local law. By far the most important example of this is the 2002 EU Regulation requiring EU companies whose securities are traded on a regulated market in the EU to use IFRS for their group accounts for 2005 and onwards, although, unfortunately, the Regulation requires companies to use IFRS as adopted by the EU (see below), rather than pure IFRS.

The context of this is that the EU wishes, from a political and commercial perspective, its capital markets to be a serious rival to that of the US. The US capital market is successful for a number of reasons, one of the most important being that it is subject to strong regulation by the Securities and Exchange Commission (SEC) and other bodies. In contrast, the EU capital markets are fragmented, not generally as liquid and not uniformly regulated. In order to improve their position, the EU has a Financial Services Action Plan, which seeks to harmonise and strengthen the EU capital markets in a variety of respects. One of these is the introduction of uniform financial reporting by EU listed companies. The rule may be found in Council Regulation 1606/2002/EC on the application of international accounting standards, OJ 2002 L243/1. As a Regulation, this is directly effective in Member State law, without the need for national legislation.

Needless complexity has been introduced, as the Regulation is structured so as to avoid handing over sovereignty to the IASB and thus requires EU companies to comply with IFRSs only to the extent that they have been adopted (or 'endorsed') by the EU. To assist the Commission in this regard, an Accounting Regulatory Committee (ARC) has been set up, made up of political appointees from Member States. Because of the technical nature of the work, it is assisted by the European Financial Reporting Advisory Group (EFRAG), one of whose objectives is to influence the IASB during its development of a standard, so as to ensure that the end product will be acceptable within Europe. Since early

2007, an additional layer has been introduced between EFRAG and ARC: the Standards Advice Review Group (SARG) now advises the Commission on EFRAG's review before a proposal is put to ARC. The intention of this endorsement mechanism was seen as a safeguard for the EU, but it was expected that standards developed by the IASB would be adopted. The first batch of standards was indeed adopted in 2003, but the two standards on financial instruments (IAS 32 and IAS 39) were not considered. Much of 2004 was taken up with protracted and difficult discussions among the IASB, the banks, the European Central Bank and the EU. The outcome was that the EU did finally adopt IAS 32 and a version of IAS 39 in which certain paragraphs and sentences that were problematical to some banks or regulators had been deleted. This is known as the 'carve-out' version of IAS 39.

This is a very unsatisfactory outcome, as it results in 'IFRS as adopted by the EU' being, in some respects, different from full IFRS, as set out by the IASB, and as followed elsewhere in the world. Despite the carve-out version of IAS 39, most UK listed companies have been able to follow full IFRS, whilst also being in compliance with 'IFRS as adopted by the EU', because of the limited nature of the difference between the two versions.

Even where the EU finally endorses an IFRS exactly as issued by the IASB, there is a time lag between the IASB issuing the standard and it being endorsed; generally about ten months. Thus, additional problems could be encountered when a company is preparing financial statements in this gap period.

Since the carve-out version of IAS 39, a number of new or revised standards have been adopted by the EU without incident. However, significant delay was encountered over the adoption of IFRS 8 'Operating segments' and indeed considerable uncertainty as to whether it would be adopted at all existed for a while. Objections were lodged directly with the European Parliament and the delay occurred after both EFRAG and ARC had considered the standard and proposed that it be adopted. Eventually, IFRS 8 was adopted, but only after an impact study had been carried out.

The Regulation requires all companies with securities traded on a regulated market in the EU (estimated to be about 7,000 companies, of which about 1,200 are UK companies) to prepare and publish their consolidated financial statements under IFRS (as adopted by the EU) from calendar year 2005 onwards. For other financial statements – that is, financial statements for individual entities and unlisted groups – the Regulation gives Member States a choice to allow or require adoption of IFRS. In the UK, the Department for Business Enterprise & Regulatory Reform (BERR), formerly the DTI, decided to make the move to IFRS optional for these other entities, which includes the single-entity accounts of the top-listed company in a group (see the next section). Companies traded on the Alternative Investment Market (AIM) are not required by the regulation to adopt IFRS (as adopted by the EU). However, following a rule issued by the London Stock Exchange, AIM companies have had to use IFRS in their consolidated financial statements since 2007.

The move to IFRS was a very considerable upheaval for most of the companies involved. There are some countries, such as Germany (but not the UK), where it was already permissible for companies to prepare their consolidated financial statements under IFRS, and a limited number of companies did so. However, for all other companies, a large-scale conversion exercise was required. Some of the differences between UK GAAP and IFRS are referred to in Part II of this book, but, for a comprehensive treatment of the similarities and differences, reference should be made to the detailed publications of the large accounting firms.

Examples of the kinds of difference encountered in the 2005 conversion exercises were the accounting treatment of: pensions, share-based payments (although the accounting standards are now the same), deferred tax, financial instruments, foreign currency and development costs. The conversion process, including the reconciliations from UK GAAP to IFRS required in the first year, is set out by the IASB in IFRS 1 'First time adoption of International Financial Reporting Standards'.

Convergence with US GAAP

The US standard-setter, the FASB, has been in operation since 1973 and, together with the SEC and other bodies such as the Emerging Issues Task Force, is a very active regulator of accounting in the US. The FASB has had a full-time board and large staff since its formation and has written standards on many subjects, and has written them in great detail. In many areas, US GAAP is well researched and effective. However, in recent years, events such as the collapse of Enron in 2001 have shown that US GAAP has its drawbacks, in particular in the area on consolidations. Also, the fact that US standards are written in great detail, taken together with the legalistic US business environment, has led to an unfortunate approach of some companies and their advisers seeking to get round the small print – a 'where does it say I can't do that?' attitude – rather than an acceptance that one should follow the spirit and intention of the standards. On the other hand, some accountants like US GAAP because it is comprehensive and clearly states what should be done in specific circumstances.

The US authorities, especially the FASB, were involved with the IASC for many years, but, at the same time, continued to develop US GAAP with little reference to IAS developments. Once the new IASB was formed, it became all the more important to involve the FASB in a more active way. Put simply: the US is the world's largest capital market, and if international standards are in due course accepted and used everywhere except in the US, that will be only a limited success story.

It was therefore an important event when in September 2002 the IASB and the FASB signed the 'Norwalk agreement' under which they 'each acknowledged their commitment to the development of high-quality, compatible accounting standards that could be used for both domestic and cross-border financial reporting'. Both the FASB and IASB pledged to use their best efforts to: (1) make their existing financial reporting standards fully compatible as soon as is practicable; and (2) coordinate their future work programmes to ensure that once achieved, compatibility is maintained.

At subsequent meetings the IASB and the FASB reaffirmed their commitment to the convergence of US GAAP and IFRSs and on 27 February 2006 published a 'Memorandum of Understanding'. In this, the two standard-setters set out a 'roadmap' for working between 2006 and 2008 towards convergence. The intention was not that there would be full convergence by 2008, as there was too much work to be done. Instead, the programme was divided into two: for projects in the 'short-term convergence' category, the objective was to reach a conclusion on whether major differences could be eliminated through short-term standard-setting projects and, if so, to complete or substantially complete those projects; and for the 'other joint projects', the objective was to make 'significant progress'.

In 2007, the SEC made and proposed two further important reforms. One concerns the US GAAP reconciliation. For many years, foreign companies listed in the US markets had to either prepare US GAAP accounts or (more commonly) prepare a reconciliation between their home country GAAP (now mostly IFRS) and US GAAP. However, this requirement for a reconciliation was withdrawn in late 2007, subject to certain provisos. The main condition was that the company prepared its accounts under IFRS as published by the IASB, and not a regional or other variant of IFRS such as IFRS as adopted by the EU. Although, as a transitional provision, for companies that have already adopted the EU carve-out version of IAS 39 (see above) the SEC is allowing no reconciliation to US GAAP in the first two years, but only if this is the only difference from IFRS as issued by the IASB *and* the company provides a reconciliation to IFRS as issued by the IASB.

The second of the SEC's 2007 reforms is only at the stage of a proposal, but is highly significant. The SEC has proposed that it might be possible for all SEC registrants – not just foreign companies – to use IFRS in their filings with the SEC. If the SEC does adopt this reform, and if US companies avail themselves of the facility to use IFRS rather than US GAAP, this would represent the end of US GAAP for all practical purposes, something that could scarcely have been envisaged as recently as 2006.

Implications for the UK

Growing convergence

International standards are clearly important to the UK in that, since 2005, UK listed companies have had to publish their consolidated financial statements under IFRS. However, in many respects, the importance of IFRS is greater than that. First, a number of companies have also adopted IFRS at the entity level.

23

Second, even if UK companies that are subsidiaries do not decide to opt into IFRS for their entity accounts, they will typically have to provide information (often called 'group returns' or 'consolidation packs') to their parent companies. Where these parent companies are listed in the EU, the group returns will need to be prepared under IFRS.

Third, even where companies remain under UK GAAP at the entity level, the differences between UK GAAP and IFRS are gradually dwindling, as a result of the policy of the UK ASB of converging its standards with those of the IASB.

By early 2008, the ASB had not converged all of its standards with IFRS, although it had considered a number of possible approaches. At the time of writing, a likely approach is to base UK GAAP on the work being done by the IASB in relation to a form of IFRS for small and medium-sized entities (SMEs). The IASB is developing an IFRS for SMEs in response to requests from those who regard full IFRS as too complex for smaller companies or, as others regard it, unnecessarily complex for companies that are not publicly accountable. An approach for the UK that is gaining momentum is for listed companies, and perhaps other large or important entities, to apply full IFRS; unlisted companies other than the smallest ones would apply the IFRS for SMEs; and the smallest layer would continue to apply the ASB's existing Financial Reporting Standard for Smaller Entities (FRSSE), but in time the FRSSE would be aligned with IFRS.

BERR and entity accounts

Under the Companies Act, as noted above, IFRS is optional at the entity level although, within a group, it is not possible to 'cherry-pick' – that is to have some UK subsidiaries move to IFRS and others stay with UK GAAP. Rather, a parent preparing consolidated financial statements and all its British subsidiaries have either to move to IFRS or stay with UK GAAP at the entity level (unless there are 'good reasons' for doing otherwise). It is, however, expressly permitted for a parent to move to IFRS for its entity financial statements – to be in line with its own group financial statements – yet for its UK subsidiaries to stay with UK GAAP (without the need to demonstrate 'good reasons').

Tax and distributable profits

Whilst there remains a choice between IFRS and UK GAAP at the individual entity level, there are two further important considerations for companies: tax and calculating which profits are distributable.

HM Revenue & Customs now accepts, for tax purposes, financial statements prepared under IFRS as a starting point. This is helpful: if it were not the case, companies would have to prepare UK GAAP financial statements as the starting point for tax assessment even if they adopted IFRS for Companies Act purposes.

However, there are special rules in certain areas, and it is important for each company to consider in detail the effect of IFRS on its tax position.[1]

Similarly, it is important for each company, in deciding whether to move to IFRS, to consider what effect the move may have on its distributable profits. Guidance to assist companies in this regard has been developed by the Institutes of Chartered Accountants.[2]

In a nutshell where are we now?

For listed and AIM-traded groups, consolidated financial statements must be prepared using IFRS as adopted by the EU. If the company is also listed in the US, a reconciliation to US GAAP no longer has to be presented providing there are no departures from IFRS as issued by the IASB. For such companies, the accounting policy choices must ensure compliance with both IFRS as adopted by the EU and IFRS as issued by the IASB. For those companies whose only departure from IFRS as issued by the IASB is using the carve-out of IAS 39, a reconciliation to US GAAP is not required for the first two accounting periods ending after 15 November 2007 providing a reconciliation to IFRS as issued by the IASB is provided.

At the single-entity level the financial statements of those companies can be prepared using IFRS as adopted by the EU or UK GAAP, although the financial statements of companies within a group should generally be prepared on the same basis.

For groups whose shares are neither listed nor traded on AIM, the position regarding their consolidated accounts is the same as for single-entity financial statements, namely, choose between IFRS or UK GAAP.

Current thinking is that 'UK GAAP' will become:

(a) small companies – apply the ASB's FRSSE;
(b) listed companies and other large/important/public interest entities – apply full IFRS; and
(c) all other entities – apply the IFRS for SMEs.

---

1 See ch. 12.   2 See ch. 19.

3

The legal framework for accounting

Introduction: the Companies Act 1985 and the Companies Act 2006

For more than two decades the Companies Act 1985 ('CA 1985') has been the main piece of primary legislation directly governing British companies. It has been added to and had bits removed, but the CA 1985 has remained the ruling force. All that changed on 8 November 2006, when the Companies Act 2006 ('CA 2006') received Royal Assent. Consisting of approximately 1,300 sections and 16 schedules, the CA 2006, the largest piece of legislation ever to be passed by Parliament, is a thorough modernisation and a substantial, but not complete, consolidation of the then existing company legislation, following an extensive review and consultation process.

The CA 2006 has redrafted company law to meet better the needs of small business by adopting a 'think small first' approach. The Act also extends GB company law to Northern Ireland, where previously it had required separate Northern Ireland legislation. In addition to reproducing much of the content of the CA 1985, the 2006 Act contains a number of new provisions, some of the key ones of which we highlight in appropriate chapters. Some of the content of the CA 1985 has been reproduced in statutory instruments supporting the CA 2006, rather than being included in the Act itself where it is harder to change subsequently; this is particularly important where detailed accounting provisions are prescribed.

Very little of the CA 2006 came into force immediately and, indeed, although full implementation was originally scheduled for October 2008, this has now been postponed until October 2009. Nevertheless, the CA 2006 has been gradually coming into force.

In the main, the accounting provisions both in the CA 2006 and in its supporting statutory instruments apply to accounting periods beginning on or after 6 April 2008. Accordingly, this chapter, and all the other chapters in the book, deals with the provisions of the CA 2006. Many of the accounting provisions in the CA 2006 are the same as those in the CA 1985 and appendix 4 lists the equivalent references to CA 1985.

Like the CA 1985 before it, the CA 2006 deals with a wide range of matters. The purpose of this chapter is restricted to highlighting the aspects that relate to accounting.

The Companies Act 2006: accounts and reports

Part 15 of the CA 2006 deals with 'accounts and reports' and further detail is found in various schedules to a number of statutory instruments, in particular: SI 2008/410 'The Large and Medium-sized Companies and Groups (Accounts and Reports) Regulations 2008'; and SI 2008/409 'The Small Companies and Groups (Accounts and Directors' Report) Regulations 2008'.

The SIs are part of a suite of regulations that support Part 15 of the CA 2006 and set out, with some amendments, the accounting and reporting requirements contained in Schedules 4, 4A, 5, 6, 7, 7A, 8, 8A, 9 and 9A to the CA 1985. Of most concern to us here are Schedule 1 'Companies Act Individual Accounts: Companies which are not banking or insurance companies' and Schedule 6 'Companies Act Group Accounts' to SI 2008/410.

In essence, Part 15 of the Act deals with procedural matters, e.g., requiring accounting records to be kept; accounts, which give a true and fair view, to be prepared for each financial year; and requiring the reports and accounts to be circulated to members; whereas Schedules 1 and 6 to SI 2008/410 stipulate rules on how the financial statements are prepared, e.g., requiring property, plant and equipment to be stated at cost or valuation, less depreciation. While Part 15 applies to all companies regardless of whether they use IFRS or UK GAAP to prepare their financial statements, Schedules 1 and 6 to SI 2008/410 apply only to those companies whose financial statements are prepared using UK GAAP. Although these two schedules apply only to UK GAAP financial statements, parts of the SI and some of the other schedules thereto apply to both IFRS and UK GAAP financial statements.

Box 3.1 shows the matters with which Part 15 of the Act deals.

Box 3.1 *Companies Act 2006, Part 15 – Accounts and reports*

Chapter 1 – Introduction (ss. 380–5)

Chapter 2 – Accounting records (ss. 386–9)

Chapter 3 – A company's financial year (ss. 390–2)

Chapter 4 – Annual accounts (ss. 393–414)

Chapter 5 – Directors' report (ss. 415–19)

Chapter 6 – Quoted companies: directors' remuneration report (ss. 420–2)

Chapter 7 – Publication of accounts and reports (ss. 423–36)

Chapter 8 – Public companies: laying of accounts and reports before general meeting (ss. 437–8)

Chapter 9 – Quoted companies: members' approval of directors' remuneration report (ss. 439–40)

Chapter 10 – Filing of accounts and reports (ss. 441–53)

Chapter 11 – Revision of defective accounts and reports (ss. 454–462)

Chapter 12 – Supplementary provisions (ss. 463–74)

The bulk of this chapter concentrates on a limited number of the above provisions, selected according to their importance in practice.

Application of the Companies Act to IFRS and UK GAAP companies

It is important to note that the Act applies in a different way according to whether a company has remained with UK GAAP or has moved to IFRS. Although the consolidated financial statements of listed groups must now be prepared using IFRS, many listed companies have chosen to retain UK GAAP for the preparation of their individual company financial statements (e.g. the parent entity and the UK subsidiaries), thus the Act might apply to differing extents to the different parts of a group or indeed to different parts of the same published accounts (i.e. if IFRS is applied to the group financial statements and UK GAAP to the parent company's own single entity financial statements). A company's accounting might have moved to IFRS either as a mandatory change for the consolidated financial statements of a listed company,[1] or as a voluntary move in the case of an unlisted group or an entity's own financial statements. In both of those cases, the company becomes subject to the EU Council Regulation 1606/2002/EC (OJ 2002 243/1). As a consequence, the detailed accounting rules in Schedules 1 and 6 to SI 2008/410 do not apply even though the basic requirements of the sections in Part 15 of the Act (as set out in Box 3.1) continue to apply.

Accounting provisions of the Act applying to IFRS and UK GAAP companies

The requirement for individual accounts

Sections 394 to 397 and 407 set out the fundamental requirement for directors to prepare what the Act terms 'individual accounts', that is, financial statements for a company showing the results, assets and liabilities of the company only. These are also sometimes called 'entity accounts' or 'solus accounts'. In each case the contrast is with group accounts (dealt with in ss. 398 to 406 and 408).

Section 394 requires the directors of a company to prepare individual accounts for each financial year and s. 395 requires that they are either IFRS accounts or UK GAAP accounts (the terminology in the Act is 'IAS individual accounts' and 'Companies Act individual accounts' respectively). Apart from charities, which must prepare UK GAAP accounts, directors have a free choice as to whether to prepare IFRS or UK GAAP accounts until the first time that IFRS accounts are prepared. Once IFRS accounts have been prepared, they must continue to be prepared in subsequent years unless the company meets one of the exceptions, such as it is sold outside the group to another group that uses UK GAAP. Section 407 also constrains the choice; for a listed group,

---

1 See ch. 2, p. 20.

unless there are 'good reasons' for doing something else, either the individual accounts of all British companies within the group are prepared using UK GAAP, or they are all prepared using IFRS, or the parent company (whose group accounts are prepared using IFRS) can prepare its individual accounts using IFRS whilst all its British subsidiaries prepare their individual accounts using UK GAAP.

For companies applying IFRS, s. 397 requires that the directors must state in the notes to those accounts that the accounts have been prepared in accordance with IFRS. Under the Act there are no further requirements with respect to IFRS accounts preparation; the directors apply IFRS and that is that! This is very different from the position for companies staying with UK GAAP.

Section 396 deals with the detail for those companies that are staying with UK GAAP. While it mandates adherence to Schedule 1 to SI 2008/410, where further detailed requirements are added (see below for details), it requires two primary financial statements – the balance sheet and the profit and loss account. That is, the law does not require a cash flow statement or a statement of total recognised gains and losses. These, although they are also primary statements, are required only by UK accounting standards. For IFRS accounts, the requirement for a balance sheet and statement of comprehensive income (equivalent to profit and loss account and STRGL) is found, not in the Act, but in an accounting standard (IAS 1).

The requirement for group accounts

Sections 398 to 408 set out equivalent requirements relating to group accounts. Directors shall prepare consolidated accounts (the Act uses the term 'group accounts') if, at the end of the year, the company is a parent company unless one of the Act's exemptions applies. The terms 'group accounts' and 'consolidated accounts' are sometimes used interchangeably. Strictly, 'group accounts' is a looser term, and can mean any form of aggregation of information relating to a group of companies. Consolidated accounts, which is the form required by accounting standards (IFRS and UK GAAP) and law (UK GAAP), means a specific technique of preparing a set of financial statements for the group as if it were a single entity, by aggregating all subsidiaries and, for example, eliminating intra-group transactions.[2]

Section 403 requires the consolidated accounts to be either IFRS accounts or UK GAAP accounts (the terminology in the Act is 'IAS group accounts' and 'Companies Act group accounts' respectively). As with the individual company accounts, unless there is a relevant change of circumstance, once consolidated accounts have been prepared using IFRS they must continue to be prepared using IFRS.

2 See ch. 8.

29

Section 404, which applies to group accounts prepared in accordance with UK GAAP, is equivalent to s. 396 except that the detailed requirements are found via Schedule 6 to SI 2008/410.

In relation to group accounts prepared in accordance with IFRS, s. 406 mirrors s. 397, in other words, it simply requires the directors to state in the notes to those accounts that the accounts have been prepared in accordance with IFRS.

Annual accounts and the true and fair view

For UK GAAP accounts, ss. 396 (individual company accounts), 404 (group accounts) and 393 (both individual company and group accounts) set out the requirement that they shall give 'a true and fair view'. Note that the law requires *a* true and fair view – not *the* true and fair view. This is taken to mean that there is potentially more than one way in which a true and fair view may be given. For example, a company might choose to keep its assets at cost, or to revalue them.

This true and fair view requirement is overriding – it is the key objective of annual accounts. Compliance with the detailed rules is important, and in nearly all cases it will result in a true and fair view being given. However, in that rare case, where this does not hold, the law is clear: if there is insufficient information, give more; and if despite that, the accounts do not give a true and fair view, depart from the detailed rules to the extent necessary. It is a very powerful concept. Typically, the override has been used in practice to override a part of the Act in order to allow compliance with an accounting standard.

The ASB's Foreword to accounting standards contains a similar override in the context of accounting standards; the above override being in the context of the Act's requirements. The override of accounting standards is hardly ever used in practice.

Section 393's requirement that accounts give a true and fair view applies to IFRS accounts as well as to UK GAAP accounts. IFRSs themselves use the expression 'present fairly' rather than 'true and fair'. For example, para. 15 of IAS 1(2007) states that:

> 'Financial statements shall present fairly the financial position, financial performance and cash flows of an entity. Fair presentation requires the faithful representation of the effects of transactions, other events and conditions in accordance with the definitions and recognition criteria for assets, liabilities, income and expenses set out in the *Framework*. The application of IFRSs, with additional disclosure when necessary, is presumed to result in financial statements that achieve a fair presentation.'

The two expressions, 'present fairly' and 'true and fair' have the same meaning; this is confirmed by the IASB's Framework[3] and by Martin Moore QC, in an

---

3 The 'Framework for the preparation and presentation of financial statements, para. 46.

opinion to the Financial Reporting Council. In his opinion, Mr Moore stated that the two phrases are a different articulation of the same concept. In addition, that this is paramount is evidenced by para. 19 of IAS 1(2007), which sets out an equivalent override.

Approval, distribution and filing of accounts

Financial statements, once prepared, should be approved by the Board, signed, on the balance sheet, on behalf of the Board by a director,[4] be audited and the audit report signed by the auditors.[5] The directors' report and directors' remuneration report must also be approved by the board; they have to be signed on behalf of the board by a director or the company secretary.[6]

The annual accounts and reports should then be sent to members[7] (for quoted companies), made available on a website maintained by or on behalf of the company[8] (for public companies), laid before the company in general meeting[9] and (all companies) delivered to the Registrar of Companies.[10] Further details are set out in the indicated sections of the Act, and further comments about the role of auditors may be found in chapter 4 at p. 40.

There are provisions in the Act for the revision of defective accounts and reports.[11] These provisions are discussed in chapter 4 at p. 39 under the heading, 'The Financial Reporting Review Panel'.

Exemptions and special provisions

Various exemptions are contained within the Act. These are not discussed in detail in this book. However, the principal categories of exemptions are:

- relief from sending the full Annual Accounts and Reports to shareholders, allowing instead a 'summary financial statement' to be sent;
- relief from certain disclosures for medium-sized companies, and greater relief for small companies;
- relief from the need to prepare group accounts for certain groups; and
- relief from the need for an audit for companies below a certain size.

Brief details relating to summary financial statements, which are likely to be of most interest to directors of listed companies, are discussed in chapter 6.

We may note also that, in UK GAAP, certain accounting standards give exemptions for companies below a certain size. In addition, the ASB has developed a Financial Reporting Standard for Smaller Entities (FRSSE). This is designed to provide small companies with a single reporting standard that is focused on their circumstances. That is, companies using the FRSSE need not generally comply with other accounting standards and UITF Abstracts. The FRSSE, however, contains essentially the same requirements as accounting

---

4 s. 414.   5 ss. 434, 475–84, 495–7 and 503–6.   6 ss. 419 and 422.   7 s. 423.
8 s. 430.   9 s. 437.   10 s. 441.   11 ss. 454–7.

standards as regards recognition and measurement, although they are expressed in simpler terms. As to disclosure matters, some of those set out in the other accounting standards are omitted. The IASB is developing an IFRS for small and medium-sized entities, and has issued an exposure draft, although its proposed scope is wider than that of the UK FRSSE as it may be applied to privately held companies generally, including wholly owned subsidiaries, irrespective of size. As discussed in chapter 2, current thinking in the UK is that the IFRS for small and medium-sized entities may be adopted by the ASB as a UK standard to be applied by UK companies above the FRSSE level and not meeting some other criteria (not yet determined, but may be listed/large/ public-interest/important) which would require the adoption of full IFRS if met.

Special provisions relating to banking and insurance companies and groups are contained in SI 2008/410 and apply only to UK GAAP accounts. The accounts of companies and groups in these categories are required to give a true and fair view, just as with the accounts of other companies. However, the detailed requirements are different. The detailed rules for individual accounts are set out in Schedules 2 (banking) and 3 (insurance) and for group accounts are set out in Parts 2 and 3 of Schedule 6.

Accounting provisions of SI 2008/410 applying to UK GAAP companies only

Introduction

This section covers the main schedules to SI 2008/410 that prescribe accounting requirements. For non-specialised companies, these are Schedules 1 and 6.

As mentioned above, the detailed rules for the accounts of banks and those for insurance companies are set out separately. In particular, the formats for the profit and loss account and balance sheet of banks and insurance companies are different from each other and from the formats of other companies. There are differences also in the measurement rules and the required disclosures.

The remainder of this section will look briefly at the requirements of Schedules 1 and 6.

Schedule 1

Schedule 1 contains detailed rules that must be applied in preparing a set of UK GAAP accounts. It does not apply to those that follow IFRS. The rules can be broadly summarised as follows:

- Formats and general rules – companies must choose one of two different balance sheet formats and one of four possible formats for the profit and loss account. There are also a number of rules relating to the formats, for example, assets may not be set against liabilities, but instead each should be shown separately. A relatively recent, and important, addition to the rules is the requirement that items shall be included in the profit and loss account and balance sheet in accordance with their substance; this was introduced to accommodate certain rules on financial instruments accounting in FRS 25 which are from IAS 32.[12]

- Accounting principles – five basic accounting principles are set out which must be followed, or details given of any departure, in calculating profits, assets and liabilities. An example is para. 14, which requires that all income and expenses that relate to a year shall be taken into account regardless of when the cash is received or paid; in other words, it requires the use of accruals accounting.
- Historical cost accounting rules – the rules in this section deal with the determination of the carrying value of fixed and current assets, in particular, setting out how cost is determined and how depreciation and impairment should be reflected.
- Alternative accounting rules – these rules permit companies to carry fixed assets, stocks and current asset investments at valuation, rather than historical cost, if they wish. The rules are not an 'all or nothing' and companies can choose to use the alternative accounting rules for just one asset if they wish. Accounting standards have imposed tighter restrictions, for example, requiring that if an asset is to be stated at valuation, as a minimum, the whole class of assets to which it belongs must also be carried at valuation. Where assets are revalued under the alternative accounting rules, the amount of the increase in carrying value must be included in a revaluation reserve; this has implications for distributable profits.
- Fair value accounting – the purpose of these rules is to permit companies to state certain financial instruments, investment property and living animals and plants to be included at fair value, to facilitate harmonising UK GAAP with IFRS. The amount of the increase or decrease in carrying value is recognised in the profit and loss account or fair value reserve (according to the rules), but not the revaluation reserve; this has important implications for distributable profits.
- Notes to the accounts – this part of the Schedule requires various note disclosures to be included in the accounts, for example, details about share capital and financial commitments. In many cases, accounting standards now duplicate, and generally add to, these requirements.
- Provisions applying to investment companies – this part contains rules on how investment companies should adapt the rest of the Schedule.

Importantly, companies can omit immaterial information when complying with Schedule 1 (and Schedules 2 and 3).

12 See ch. 17.

Schedule 6

For a UK GAAP company required by the Act to produce consolidated financial statements, compliance with the detailed requirements in Schedule 6 to SI 2008/410 is mandated. Part 2 deals with banking groups, Part 3 with insurance groups and Part 1 with all other groups.

Schedule 6 Part 1 is additional to Schedule 1. So, for example, the formats for the balance sheet and profit and loss account apply to consolidated accounts, just as they apply to individual accounts. However, Schedule 6 supplements them, for example, by specifying where in the formats minority interests are to be included.

Other areas dealt with by Schedule 6 Part 1 are:

- Basic rules of consolidation – the basic rule of consolidation is that the accounts should be prepared as if the group were one single entity and a number of specific rules that put this into practice are laid down, for example, requiring that any profits made when transferring goods between one group company and another are eliminated from the consolidated accounts if the goods are still held within the group.
- Which method of accounting should be used – the rules set out: what the acquisition method is; the conditions for using merger accounting; and what the merger method is.
- Joint ventures and associates – this deals with the way in which joint ventures and associates are included in consolidated financial statements.

In each of these areas, accounting standards lay down additional rules, often, reflecting the fact that thinking changes over time, taking away the choice permitted by the Schedule.

Further details of acquisition accounting and merger accounting are set out in chapter 11 at pp. 100–114 and accounting for associates is further elaborated in chapter 8 at pp. 77–79.

4

The accountancy profession and the regulatory framework for accounting and auditing

The accountancy profession

There are currently six major accountancy bodies in the UK and Ireland:

1. The Institute of Chartered Accountants in England and Wales (ICAEW);
2. The Institute of Chartered Accountants of Scotland (ICAS);
3. The Institute of Chartered Accountants in Ireland (ICAI);
4. The Association of Chartered Certified Accountants (ACCA);
5. The Chartered Institute of Management Accountants (CIMA); and
6. The Chartered Institute of Public Finance and Accountancy (CIPFA).

The vast majority of practising members of the profession are in one of the first three Institutes. The ICAEW is the largest body, although ICAS is proud to be the oldest. ACCA includes some practitioners and many members overseas. Many of the members of these four bodies, having trained in the profession, work in industry and commerce, and members of CIMA do so almost exclusively. CIPFA members work almost entirely in the public sector.

These bodies to some extent compete with each other – not least for students and, therefore, for members. They also cooperate on some matters through the Consultative Committee of Accountancy Bodies (CCAB). Setting accounting standards and auditing standards used to be in the domain of the CCAB – the Accounting Standards Committee and the Auditing Practices Committee were CCAB bodies from the 1970s for about twenty years. However, as explained in chapter 2, the accounting standards activity was moved away from the profession in 1990 when the new Accounting Standards Board (see below) was formed. Similarly, a new Auditing Practices Board was formed in April 2002, thus removing a second important role from the professional bodies.

The accountancy bodies have a number of important roles. One is education and training – training students, admitting new members and overseeing their continuing professional development. The Institutes also set professional and ethical rules. Furthermore, despite losing the important roles of setting accounting and auditing standards, the Institutes have a number of technical committees that are active in both generating and debating new ideas and in producing guidance for the profession. A recent example of guidance is TECH 01/08 'Guidance on the determination of realised profits and losses in the

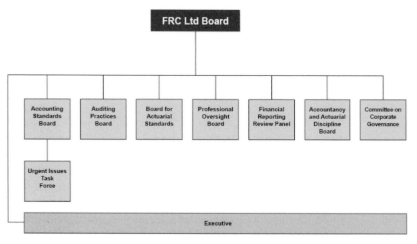

Figure 4.1 The Financial Reporting Council and its operating bodies as at June 2008

context of distributions under the Companies Act 1985', which is discussed in detail in chapter 19 at pp. 184–193.

The Financial Reporting Council

The Financial Reporting Council, which is separate from the profession, was formed in 1990, following the Dearing Report.[1] This was primarily concerned with the decreasing reputation and effectiveness of the former Accounting Standards Committee, and proposed a new structure primarily with accounting standard setting in mind. The structure initially involved a standard-setting arm – the ASB and, under it, the UITF – and alongside an enforcement arm, the FRRP. In 2004 and 2006, various additional functions were created or transferred to the FRC structure, so that it is now as shown in figure 4.1.

The Board

The Board of FRC Ltd oversees the six operating bodies (all apart from the committee on corporate governance) shown under it in the diagram in figure 4.1. It is assisted in its work monitoring the Combined Code on corporate governance by the committee on corporate governance whose members are drawn from the Board. The Board is responsible for raising finance, making appointments and setting overall strategy. It does not become involved in the detail of, for example, setting accounting standards: the ASB issues them under its own authority, having undertaken appropriate public consultation.

1 'The making of accounting standards', Report of the Review Committee (London: Institute of Chartered Accountants in England and Wales, 1988).

The Board has a wide membership and, following a restructuring in late 2007, is composed of the chair, a non-executive deputy chair, the chief executive, seven non-executive directors and the chairs of the FRC's six operating bodies.

The Accounting Standards Board

As its name might suggest, the ASB is responsible for developing and issuing accounting standards. The ASB has a full-time chairman and technical director plus, currently, another eight part-time board members. It also has a technical staff. It was very active in the 1990s in setting UK standards, but since the IASB was formed in 2001, the ASB has moved into a different phase, in which it is mostly concerned with influencing the IASB and harmonising UK practice with the international standards.

Under the ASB are a number of committees of which the best known is the UITF, described below. Of the others, CASE, the Committee on Accounting for Smaller Entities, which, as its name suggests, is concerned with the application of accounting standards to smaller entities, is perhaps the most well known.

The Urgent Issues Task Force

The UITF is a committee of the ASB, formed of seventeen members from industry and professional accounting firms. The UITF's role is 'to assist the ASB with important or significant accounting issues where there exists an accounting standard or a provision of companies legislation (including the requirement to give a true and fair view) and where unsatisfactory or conflicting interpretations have developed or seem likely to develop'.[2] In practice, this means that it is concerned with producing 'Abstracts', as its output is known, in a shorter timescale than a full accounting standard, on narrower issues than would be dealt with in an accounting standard.

The Abstracts are developed entirely by the UITF, but are approved, and formally issued, by the ASB. They are part of GAAP, in the same way as accounting standards themselves, and, like accounting standards, are subject to enforcement by the FRRP.

As with UK accounting standards, the Abstracts are increasingly becoming the adoption into UK GAAP of the equivalent international rule; in the case of the UITF the adoption of IFRIC interpretations.

The Financial Reporting Review Panel

See below.

---

2 Foreword to UITF Abstracts, para. 2.

Professional Oversight Board

Formed in 2003, the Professional Oversight Board (POB) has three main roles, all of which are audit related. One of the three roles is to establish and oversee an independent Audit Inspection Unit to monitor the audits of major listed companies and other public-interest entities, including both the audit process and the decisions taken by auditors. The other two roles involve regulating the professional accountancy bodies.

The Audit Inspection Unit took over a monitoring role previously carried out by the Joint Monitoring Unit, which was part of the Institutes. The 2004 restructuring took away from the Institutes the role insofar as it relates to listed companies and other public interest entities. However, the role in relation to other companies remains with the Institutes.

The Auditing Practices Board

The Auditing Practices Board (APB) was moved to be part of the FRC structure in 2004. Prior to this, it came under the Accountancy Foundation and, prior to that, it was part of the profession through the CCAB. The APB issues auditing standards and guidelines for the profession. Its responsibilities have recently been extended to the development of ethical standards relating to the independence, objectivity and integrity of auditors. Many of the standards and guidelines are concerned with methodology and are not discussed here. However, later in this chapter there is a section dealing with the law, auditing standards and practice in the area of standard, modified and qualified audit reports.

Board for Actuarial Standards

The Board for Actuarial Standards (BAS) is a new body, having only been established in April 2006. HM Treasury, following the publication of the Morris Review of the actuarial profession, asked the Financial Reporting Council to take on responsibility for the oversight of the UK actuarial profession and the independent setting of actuarial technical standards. BAS is to be responsible for the setting of actuarial standards.

Accountancy and Actuarial Discipline Board

Originally, the role of this board was in relation to accountants only; the role being to investigate public-interest cases involving accountants and to discipline as appropriate. While this role in relation to accountants continues, a similar role in relation to actuaries was added to the board's remit in summer 2007.

The Financial Reporting Review Panel

The Panel aims to ensure that annual financial statements of public companies and large private companies comply with the requirements of applicable accounting standards and of the Companies Act 2006. The Panel's work includes IFRS accounts as well as UK GAAP accounts. In practice, nearly all of the Panel's investigations have been concerned with listed companies.

While the accounting standards produced by the ASB during the 1990s did much to improve accounting in that period, the formation and operation of the FRRP was an important second leg. Prior to 1990, there had been no effective enforcement of accounting standards (or indeed of the accounting requirements of the Companies Act 1985), and the appearance of the Panel did much to change attitudes towards compliance.

Until 2004, the Panel was reactive. That is, it would enter a dialogue with a company where there was adverse press comment, or an allegation from, say, a shareholder or other interested party, that the financial statements did not comply with the Act or accounting standards. The Panel would then discuss the matter with the company, through correspondence and/or formal meetings. In some cases, the directors persuaded the Panel that the treatment adopted was in fact appropriate; the case was then dropped. In other cases, the Panel was not so persuaded. In these circumstances, the Panel does not have the power to force the company to change its financial statements. However, it does have the power to refer the matter to the court. In the eighteen years since the Panel was formed, no cases have gone to court. In all of these cases, the directors of the companies in question have seen the merit of acceding to the Panel's view and changing their financial statements 'voluntarily'.

From 2004, as part of a wider picture of post-Enron reforms, the Panel has moved on to being proactive in its work. That is, it continues to respond to complaints, but it also reviews financial statements as a matter of routine. The Panel initially focused its attention on larger listed companies (the top 350), but from 2008 it is focusing more on smaller listed companies, those traded on AIM and larger private companies. It will nevertheless continue to select financial statements from the full range of companies within its remit.

Recently, the Panel has been announcing in advance the sectors on which it will focus its monitoring activity. For the year to 31 March 2009, it has announced that it is to focus its activities on:

- banking;
- retail;
- travel and leisure;
- commercial property; and
- housebuilders.

The Panel's focus on banking, commercial property and housebuilders reflects its interest in those companies likely to be affected by the 2007/08 'credit crunch'. The Panel has added that it will pay particular attention to disclosures relating to financing arrangements and risks and uncertainties in the light of credit market conditions at the time of approval of financial statements.

To help it select other financial statements to review (i.e., other than from the sectors announced), the Panel is developing a risk model to identify where it considers accounting problems may be more likely. It cites poor corporate governance as an example. Topical accounting issues also help it to identify companies to review.

In the first year of targeting particular sectors, the year to 31 March 2006, the Panel looked at 66 sets of accounts from the five sectors and, as a consequence, ten companies agreed to make changes going forward. By contrast, in the year to 31 March 2007, the Panel reviewed 311 sets of accounts and 94 companies undertook to reflect the Panel's comments in future accounts. The higher proportion of amendments to future financial statements, in part, reflects the fact that this period of review activity included financial statements that were prepared for the first time under EU-adopted IFRS.

The move to proactive enforcement is part of a wider European initiative. The Committee of European Securities Regulators (CESR) is encouraging an enforcement mechanism to be put in place in all EU countries.

From 2005, the Panel's scope was extended to include, inter alia, interim reports of listed companies and the accounts of overseas companies with a primary listing in the UK. For financial years beginning on or after 1 April 2006, the Panel's scope was further extended to encompass directors' reports, including business reviews.

Audit reporting

Perhaps the most visible part of auditors' work is the audit report that is published as part of a company's annual report. The Act sets out the basic requirements. With respect to the annual accounts, the auditors are required to state whether, in their opinion, the annual accounts: give a true and fair view of the state of affairs at the end of the financial year and of the profit or loss for the financial year; have been properly prepared in accordance with the relevant financial reporting framework (IFRS or UK GAAP); and have been prepared in accordance with the Act and, where applicable, Article 4 of the IAS Regulation. Quoted companies must prepare a directors' remuneration report[3] and the auditors are required to audit part of that report, stating in the audit report whether, in their opinion, that part of the directors' remuneration report has been properly prepared in accordance with the Act. Certain more limited responsibilities of the auditors exist in relation to the directors' report and other information presented with the audited financial statements, although

3 See ch. 20.

Box 4.1 *Qualified audit opinions*

Qualified opinion ('except for')	Disagreement with management or limitation of scope of audit is not so material or pervasive as to require an adverse opinion or disclaimer of opinion
Disclaimer of opinion	Possible effect of limitation of scope is so material and pervasive that the auditors are unable to express an opinion.
Adverse opinion	Effect of disagreement is so material and pervasive that the auditors conclude that a qualification is not adequate to disclose the misleading or incomplete nature of the financial statements.

---

the auditors are required to report whether, in their opinion, the information given in the directors' report is consistent with the accounts.

International Standard on Auditing (UK and Ireland) (ISA (UK and Ireland)) 700 deals with audit report requirements and APB Bulletins provide example wording. There is a reasonably standardised wording for audit reports, although given the choice of accounting framework (IFRS or UK GAAP) for single-entity financial statements, there are a number of alternatives even for a listed group. It should be noted that the requirement of the Act and auditing standards is for the auditors to express an opinion. The auditors do not prepare the accounts and do not give a certificate. References are sometimes made to 'audit certificates', but these represent an incorrect understanding of the role of the auditors.

Where auditors are satisfied that the accounts give a true and fair view and have been properly prepared, the form of audit report wording is known as an unqualified audit report (sometimes informally called a 'clean opinion'). Where auditors are not so satisfied, they should modify their report and give a qualified opinion. There are a number of possible ways in which this can be done, as shown in Box 4.1.

There are other types of non-standard wording that do not count as 'qualified' opinions, but are still called 'modified' audit reports. The most common situation where these are used is in circumstances where the going concern status of the company is in doubt. They equally apply to any other situation where there is a significant uncertainty the resolution of which is dependent upon future events and which may affect the financial statements, for example, litigation. In these circumstances, the directors need to give disclosures about the uncertainty. If the auditors regard the uncertainty as significant, even though they believe the directors' disclosures are adequate they should include an 'emphasis of matter' paragraph in their report, with an appropriate heading, drawing attention to the significant uncertainty. Uncertainties are regarded as significant when they involve a significant level of concern about the validity of the going-concern basis or other matters whose potential effect on the financial statements is unusually great.

In the 'emphasis of matter' paragraph the auditors explain that in forming their opinion they have considered the adequacy of the disclosures in the financial statements concerning the possible outcome of the uncertainty, and they describe the uncertainty, the possible outcome and its effect, including quantification. In addition to the comments about the significant uncertainty, the auditors may explicitly clarify that their opinion is not qualified in this respect.

For audit reports in respect of financial statements for accounting periods beginning on or after 6 April 2008 (which for a calendar-year-end company will be the 2009 financial statements), the name of the audit partner who signed the audit report on behalf of the audit firm, as well as the name of the audit firm, will have to be shown on the audit report.

Limitation of liability for auditors

From 6 April 2008, the Act removes the UK's eighty-year prohibition on auditors and their clients reaching contractual limitations for the auditor's liability. However, when companies and their auditors reach such an agreement, the board will still need to secure shareholder approval at the next AGM for the agreement to take effect. The court can override agreements that it considers to be unfair or unreasonable and can substitute its own limit with the limitation of liability agreement still being valid. Where a company enters into a limited liability agreement with its auditors in respect of a financial year, disclosure is required in the notes to the accounts.

The role of accountants in capital markets transactions

Although this book is concerned with accounting rather than with the full range of what accountants do, the role of accountants in transactions still merits brief mention.

The word 'transaction' is often used rather loosely to mean a capital markets transaction such as:

- the raising of share capital, which could be a new listing of shares (an Initial Public Offering – IPO) or a further issue of shares by a company that is already listed;
- a secondary listing of shares, for example when a company already listed in London seeks a listing on another exchange;

- the raising of capital in the form of a debt issue; and
- a merger or acquisition involving a listed company.

Accountants carry out much behind-the-scenes advisory work in relation to transactions such as these. For example, they carry out investigations of varying degrees of depth in connection with potential acquisitions; these are often called due-diligence exercises.

5

Substance over form

Form v. substance

When business life was somewhat simpler than it is today, accounting for a transaction in accordance with its legal form generally gave an appropriate result. However, over the last twenty years or so, as business transactions have become more complex, there have been increasing numbers of transactions in which the legal form and economic substance have diverged from each other; gradually it became clear, in UK GAAP at least, that following the legal form did not properly reflect the commercial transaction.

To accountants, the basic legal requirement that accounts must give a 'true and fair view'[1] means that they must reflect the economic substance of a transaction and not just its legal form.

In this chapter we will discuss the UK GAAP experience regarding substance over form before concluding with a look at the position under IFRS because the UK perspective on this topic is relevant to applying IFRS in the UK.

Early examples

For some years, there were examples of substance over form being applied to common transactions, almost as second nature, rather than by applying a specific rule or even consciously applying the substance over form principle. One example is accounting for an asset being 'bought' under hire purchase. The legal analysis is that the asset is being hired (or leased) for the term of the agreement. There is then an option for the lessee to purchase the asset, generally for a nominal sum such as £1. In almost all circumstances, the option to purchase is exercised, and the commercial effect of the transaction is that, from the start, the asset is being purchased on deferred payment terms. Hire purchase transactions were accounted for in this way, that is, the asset being hired/bought was treated as capital expenditure at the outset and the obligation to pay instalments was shown on the balance sheet as a liability. No accounting standard was needed in order to require this treatment; it was done as a matter of professional practice.

---

1 Discussed in ch. 3 at pp. 30–31.

Subsequently, the principle of substance over form and the practice established for hire purchase were extended to accounting for leases[2] in both UK GAAP and IFRS.

Another early example of substance over form is goods sold subject to reservation of title. In these transactions, goods are sold, but title stays with the vendor until the purchaser settles the amount due. The substance of these transactions is that a sale is being made on credit. The reservation of legal title is merely a technique to give the vendor more security so as to reduce any losses that might occur as a result of insolvency of the customer. Following the Romalpa case in 1976, the Institute of Chartered Accountants in England and Wales published guidance which advised members on the accounting treatment to be adopted in the specific case of goods sold subject to reservation of title: 'the commercial substance of the transaction should take precedence over its legal form where they conflict'.

Emergence of the off-balance-sheet industry in the UK

Throughout the 1980s, more and more transactions were developed in which the legal form and the economic, or commercial, substance conflicted. Among these were so-called 'non-subsidiary subsidiaries'. These were companies, or other forms of entity, that were in substance subsidiaries of a parent, in that they were for all practical purposes controlled by the parent, and brought benefits to the parent. However, they did not meet the legal definition of subsidiary company; if structured as a company, this was usually done through establishing some unusual or artificial feature such as weighted voting rights for certain classes of shares. Alternatively, a number were not legally companies and so outside the then definition of a subsidiary. Accountants faced some difficulty here, as they were unsure whether it was appropriate to consolidate entities that were not, in a legal sense, part of the group. Hence, the off-balance-sheet industry was born. Various other structures were developed with a common aim of keeping entities, or assets (and, more importantly, the liabilities that financed them) off balance sheet. The Institute responded with guidance, but it had no force, and the practice of off-balance-sheet finance flourished throughout the 1980s and was a major contributor to the worsening reputation of financial statements and accountants in that period.

FRS 5 'Reporting the substance of transactions'

The situation was largely rescued by two events. One was the Companies Act 1989, which introduced new rules relating to consolidated financial statements and, in particular, new, wider definitions of the parent/subsidiary relationship. Thus, certain entities that had previously escaped consolidation were now

2 See ch. 15.

defined as subsidiary undertakings and had to be consolidated. These definitions (as enhanced in 2004 – see below) have been carried forward into the Companies Act 2006.

The second was the establishing in 1990 of the new Accounting Standards Board (ASB) to replace the old Accounting Standards Committee. The ASB acknowledged that it needed to develop an effective standard dealing with the off-balance-sheet problem. The result of the ASB's work on off-balance-sheet finance was FRS 5 'Reporting the substance of transactions'. This was first issued in April 1994. It is hard to underestimate the importance of this standard. FRS 5 is a complex standard in some respects, but at its heart it is very simple. The main principles can be summarised as follows:

- financial statements should report the substance of transactions;
- to determine substance, consider the effect of a transaction on assets and liabilities; and
- all aspects and implications should be identified and greater weight should be given to those more likely to have a commercial effect in practice.

There is, of course, much more to it than that, but accountants frequently come back to these basic principles when considering the appropriate accounting treatment of complex transactions.

Quasi-subsidiaries

A key part of FRS 5 has been its provisions relating to 'quasi-subsidiaries'. These are defined in FRS 5 as: 'a company, trust, partnership or other vehicle that, though not fulfilling the definition of a subsidiary, is directly or indirectly controlled by the reporting entity and gives rise to benefits for that entity that are in substance no different from those that would arise were the vehicle a subsidiary'.

This definition of quasi-subsidiary has often been used to pick up, for inclusion in the consolidation, trusts and companies owned by trusts, some of which carry the label 'special purpose vehicles' (or 'special purpose companies' or 'special purpose entities'), a term which, since the collapse of Enron, attracts less admiration than previously.

The importance of the FRS 5 rules on quasi-subsidiaries is now reduced, following a change in 2004 widening even further the Act's definition of subsidiary undertaking. Hence some of what were identified for consolidation only by virtue of being quasi-subsidiaries are now being included as Companies Act subsidiary undertakings.

Specific applications

FRS 5 includes guidance on a number of specific applications, in the form of 'Application notes'. The current notes are:

A Consignment stock;
B Sale and repurchase agreements;
C Factoring of debts;
D Securitised assets;
E Loan transfers;
F Private finance initiative and similar contracts; and
G Revenue recognition.

Application notes A to F are merely specific examples of the general principles outlined above. For example, if amounts receivable by a manufacturer from customers are sold to a financial institution (a factoring company), and cash is received by the manufacturer equal to 85 per cent of the face value of the receivables, what is the appropriate accounting treatment? The factoring company may administer the manufacturer's sales ledger and handle all aspects of the collection of the money from customers for a fee of, say, 2 per cent of the face value of the receivables. If the factoring company charged interest on the monies it paid to the manufacturer on transfer of the receivables (the 85 per cent of the face value of the receivables), stopped charging interest when cash was received from the manufacturer's customer in settlement of the invoice, and at the end of three months transferred back to the manufacturer any debts that the customers had not settled, the risks and rewards of the receivables would remain with the manufacturer. Although legally structured as an assignment (sale) of receivables, the commercial substance would be that of a loan. Thus, the receivables would continue to be recognised on the manufacturer's balance sheet, with the amount received from the factoring company being shown as a liability.

Application Note G is different in nature to the others. The ASB wanted in 2003 to put in place some interim rules on revenue recognition, pending the outcome of a longer-term IASB/FASB project. Consequently, the ASB did not want to present it as a full accounting standard in its own right. Because the recognition of revenue is driven, to some degree, from changes in assets and liabilities, an Application Note to FRS 5 was a convenient, alternative method of promulgating the rules.

Examples of FRS 5 in practice in the UK

Presented here are examples in which accountants use the FRS 5 principle of substance over form to determine the appropriate accounting treatment.

Failed sale of an asset

In the example in figure 5.1, we are concerned with the financial statements of the B group, which includes its subsidiary C. C has a property that it wishes to sell. A represents an investor, or a group of investors, who own B. A third-party purchaser (TP) for the property is in prospect, but no sale has been agreed, and

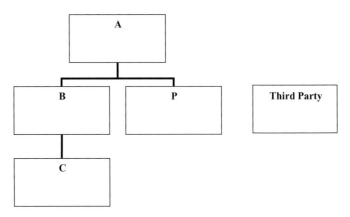

Figure 5.1 Example: failed sale of an asset

any sale to TP is unlikely to be completed until year 2. B wants to reflect the sale of the property in year 1.

There already exists, or A sets up for this purpose, P, a property company. P has no significant assets. It is arranged, just before the end of year 1, that C sells its property to P. The terms are that the sale price is expressed as £6 million, but this amount is provisional, in that if the sale to TP realises less than this, say £5 million, the price in the sale contract between C and P will be adjusted accordingly; similarly, if the price paid in due course by TP exceeds £6 million, the excess is passed on to C again by means of a price adjustment in the contract between C and P. Further, the consideration of £6 million is not paid in cash, but is left outstanding on inter-company account.

The accounting analysis of this transaction is that the B group has not effected a sale of the property (neither has C in its entity accounts). The primary reason is that the B group has not passed on to P the risks and rewards relating to the asset. B group still has the upside potential, that is, it will gain if on a sale to TP the property is found to be more valuable. Similarly, B group will lose if the property is sold to TP for less than £6 million. The conclusion is strengthened by the fact that P does not settle the price, but leaves the amount outstanding on inter-company account. However, this feature is not necessary: the same view would most likely be taken even if the consideration were paid in cash, because the key feature – that the risks and rewards have not been transferred to another party – remains present. In effect, what is happening here is a parking or warehousing of an asset, ostensibly outside the reporting entity (the B group), but no transaction of substance has taken place. The B group would report a sale when P sells the property to a third party in a way that transfers the risks and rewards of ownership to that third party.

It is important to stress that the fact that P is owned by the same investor, or group of investors, as B is not an obstacle to recognising a sale by B. It is the structuring of the sale terms and the lack of transfer of risks and rewards that is

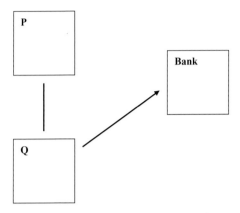

Figure 5.2 Example: warehousing of stock

the key feature. Hence if the B group were to make a clean sale of the property to P for a fixed price of £6 million, and the price were to be settled in cash, or left outstanding, but to be settled in the short term, the B group would validly report a sale of the property in its financial statements. It is true that, if A was a company, there would be no sale in any consolidated accounts prepared for the A group as a whole: in that context there has just been a sale from one subsidiary to another. However, if our context is the consolidated accounts of the B group, the B group has made a sale.

Warehousing of stock

A similar example is that a company may operate in an industry where the inventory holding period is long, and hence have a significant holding of inventory. It may wish to get the inventory and related finance off its balance sheet. A variety of techniques were developed to achieve this, mostly pre-FRS 5, although sometimes they recur. See, for example, figure 5.2.

Q is the operating subsidiary of the P group. The P group wishes to raise finance. Rather than borrow secured on the inventory, P group arranges that:

- Q will sell the inventory to the bank;
- the inventory will remain in Q's warehouse, or at a third-party location controlled and paid for by Q;
- the bank will sell the inventory back to Q whenever Q so requests;
- if Q has not called for the inventory within one year, the bank will be entitled to sell the inventory back to Q;
- the bank is not entitled to sell the inventory to a third party, except under Q's specific instruction; and
- the price at which the inventory is sold back to Q is the price of the original sale plus an interest rate applied for the period in which the bank

has held the inventory. For example, if the annually agreed interest rate is 8 per cent, and the inventory remained with the bank for six months, the repurchase price would be 104 per cent of the original sale price.

The substance of the transaction is that, despite the transfer of legal title in the inventory to the bank, the inventory remains under the control of Q, Q retains the risks and rewards relating to the inventory, and is in substance borrowing from the bank. The bank's role is that it is lending money to Q, earning a lender's rate of return and not taking possession of, or risk in relation to, the inventory. Hence Q's accounting, and therefore the accounting in the P group, is that the inventory remains an asset, the amount received from the bank is shown as a liability, and an interest cost is included in arriving at profit or loss.

Trusts and SPVs

A variety of structures is found in which either trusts alone, or trusts that own companies, are set up, often in tax havens. These structures are sometimes used in connection with securitisations or other transactions in the financial services industries, but can also be found, for example, in the area of film finance. It is often argued that the trustees of the trust perform a significant role and act independently of other parties. However, often the trustees in these circumstances are acting in a predetermined manner and do not have any significant decision-making power or, if they do have such power, they do not exercise it in practice. Accountants therefore often seek to identify another party that controls any assets that are held in such trusts, or in companies held by such trusts. Often, in accounting analysis, such trusts are regarded as quasi-subsidiaries, and probably now as subsidiary undertakings (see above), of one of the major players in a transaction and hence do not escape inclusion in group accounts.

The future of FRS 5 in UK GAAP

Despite the importance of FRS 5 to UK accounting, we are likely eventually to lose the specific standard as UK standards are aligned with those in IFRS. The sentiments of FRS 5 will, hopefully, remain though. See the next section in this chapter ('Does substance over form have a place in IFRS?').

Does substance over form have a place in IFRS?

Substance over form is a notion that underlies the concept of reliability, one of the qualitative characteristics that are detailed in the IASB's Framework. There is, however, no standard in IFRS, equivalent to the UK standard FRS 5, dealing specifically with reporting the substance of transactions. SIC 12 'Consolidation – special purpose entities' is broadly equivalent to the UK rules within FRS 5 on quasi-subsidiaries; IAS 32 requires capital instruments to be classified as debt or equity, whichever represents the substance (although application of the detailed rules sometimes undermines that objective); IAS 17 on leases takes the same approach as the UK's SSAP 21 (which is generally seen as adopting a substance approach); and IAS 8 'Accounting policies, changes in accounting estimates and errors' refers, in its discussion of selection of appropriate accounting policies, to the financial statements reflecting 'the economic substance of transactions, other events and conditions, and not merely the legal form'. Given this and the fact that substance is a concept underlying the IASB's conceptual framework, it is not unreasonable that certain aspects of FRS 5 continue to be a reference point for identifying the appropriate accounting for transactions that are not dealt with by international standards and interpretations. It is difficult, for example, to contemplate the accounting in the examples outlined above being different under IFRS than under FRS 5. Having said that, the concept of substance over form is, in practice, somewhat weaker in IFRS and there are other examples in which the accounting would be based more on legal form than in UK GAAP.

6

Communicating accounting information

Background

The Companies Act 2006 requires that UK companies should prepare a report and annual accounts and send them to shareholders. Most companies are then required to file the report and accounts on the public record at Companies House; certain small and medium-sized companies may instead file abbreviated information at Companies House. Quoted companies are required to make a copy of their report and accounts available on a website. Of particular interest to many listed companies is the provision permitting companies (previously limited to listed companies, but now available to all companies) to send a summary financial statement to shareholders in place of the full report and annual accounts (see below).

In addition to the Companies Act, listed companies have to comply with the Listing Rules and the Disclosure and Transparency Rules, both of which are issued by the Financial Services Authority. With respect to periodic financial reporting, the requirements include:

- Selected additional disclosures in the annual report and accounts – for example, relating to corporate governance matters.
- Release of half-yearly financial report for the first six months of the year. In the past these have frequently been referred to as the 'interims', although now[1] that there is also a requirement for interim management statements (see below) it is preferable to use the term 'half-yearly report'. IAS 34 must be followed[2] in the preparation of the half-yearly reports (unless the listed entity is not a group and is still applying UK GAAP, in which case an ASB statement becomes mandatory).
- Where an entity does not publish quarterly results, it must publish an 'interim management statement' during the first and second six months of a financial year. The period to be dealt with by the interim management statement is that starting on the first day of the accounting year (or first day of the second half of the year) and ending with the date of publication of the statement, which can be within a window of approximately ten weeks. The content is considerably less than for the half-yearly report,

1 For accounting periods beginning on or after 20 January 2007.
2 For accounting periods beginning on or after 20 January 2007.

and indeed can all be in narrative form, without even a summarised income statement or balance sheet.

• Preliminary announcements are no longer mandatory, although entities must comply with specific Listing Rules requirements if they do prepare one.

AIM-traded companies do not have to comply with the above rules on periodic financial reporting set out in the Listing Rules and in the Disclosure and Transparency Rules. Instead, the AIM Rules for Companies, issued by the London Stock Exchange, require half-yearly reports (with a minimum content specified) for the first six months of a year and require annual financial statements, specifying the GAAP to be used (which must be IFRS as adopted by the EU for a parent company incorporated in an EEA country) and calling for disclosure of certain related-party transactions.

Summary financial statements

As mentioned above, the Companies Act permits companies to send to shareholders a summary financial statement in place of the full annual report and accounts. The original provisions applied only to listed companies and were introduced in the light of the privatisations of the 1980s when companies were formed with a shareholder base of far greater numbers than had previously been seen; the original benefit was to reduce printing and postage costs. Now that the Act allows electronic communication with shareholders, some of this benefit falls away. Nevertheless, the summary financial statement provisions continue to be popular with listed companies (and by a wider group of companies than simply those that were subject to privatisation). With the increasing complexity of annual accounts, they provide directors with an opportunity to communicate with shareholders in a simpler way.

Safeguards have been introduced into the legislation, for example, a company cannot send summary financial statements to a member in place of its full report and accounts unless it has ascertained that the member does not wish to receive the full report and accounts. When summary financial statements were first allowed, a company could only send them to a shareholder that had positively elected to receive them. Now companies are permitted to notify shareholders that they will receive a summary financial statement unless they elect to receive the full report and accounts. The full report and accounts must still be produced, filed at Companies House, made available (quoted companies only) on a website, and sent to any shareholder requesting it. A minimum content that must be included in the summary financial statement is specified in the Act and related statutory instrument (SI 2008/374); all that is required for a quoted company preparing IFRS consolidated financial statements is an income statement and balance sheet (as in the full financial statements, although headings and sub-totals can be combined where they are of a similar nature),

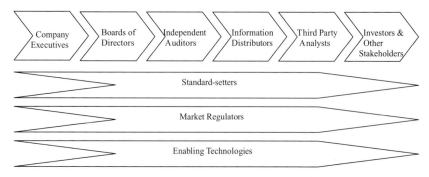

Figure 6.1 The corporate reporting supply chain

summarised directors' remuneration report, dividend information, a statement by the company's auditors and certain disclosures from the directors' report (although the disclosures from the directors' report can be circulated with the summary financial statement rather than being a part of it), along with a number of legal statements (such as a statement that the summary financial statement is only a summary of information in the company's annual financial statements and directors' remuneration report).

The corporate reporting supply chain

In practice, many groups of people are involved in the reporting process for listed companies – or the 'corporate reporting supply chain', as it has been called by Di Piazza and Eccles.[3] This may be shown as indicated in figure 6.1.

Figure 6.1 illustrates the roles and relationships among the various groups and individuals involved in the production, preparation, communication and use of corporate reporting information. Company executives and boards of directors prepare or approve the information that companies report. In a UK context, a company's audit committee, which is a committee of the board, has an important part to play. This is described in the Combined Code. Audit committees of listed companies comprise independent non-executive directors who should work with the external auditors and challenge management with regard to the draft annual report as a whole, including the statutory accounts and the accounting policies adopted therein. An audit committee also typically reviews half-yearly results, quarterly reports or interim management statements and, where produced, preliminary announcements. Recent years have seen audit committees perform a stronger and more independent role in this area, although practice in this respect is still mixed.

3 *Building public trust: the future of corporate reporting* (New York: John Wiley & Sons Inc., 2002).

Other terms used to describe participants in the corporate reporting supply chain deserve clarification:

- *Independent auditors* are firms of auditors in their capacity as auditors. Companies may also use their audit firm, or indeed other accounting firms, for other work, for example, tax.
- *Information distributors* are data vendors that consolidate reported information and provide it for others to use. This group also includes news media, websites and other communications media that provide commentary on company information.
- *Third-party analysts* are those who use the information reported by companies, usually in combination with other information and research, to evaluate a company's prospects and performance.
- *Investors and other stakeholders* are the ultimate consumers of corporate reporting information. Investors include company shareholders, but may also refer to potential shareholders. Other stakeholders include employees, business partners, customers and suppliers, community members, social and environmental groups and non-governmental organisations.
- *Standard-setters* most obviously include bodies such as the ASB and IASB. Professional accounting bodies also have a role here.
- *Market regulators* include national government agencies and regional equivalents (e.g. the EU). It includes both those that regulate companies and those that regulate stock markets.
- *Enabling technologies* are primarily internet technologies and Extensible Business Reporting Language (XBRL), a language that enables electronic standardisation of information from all companies so as to ease search and analysis.

The reality of the 'earnings game'

While figure 6.1 shows the major players in the corporate reporting supply chain, there is a different, more pragmatic, description that can be given.

Much of recent accounting reform has been directed at making it difficult for management to present smoothed results. Definitions of assets and liabilities have shifted the emphasis away from smoothed income numbers to the balance sheet, as explained in chapter 7 at p. 65.

A related reform has been to try to reduce the focus on 'the bottom line' – an undefined term, generally taken to mean the bottom line in the income statement (or in the income statement part of the statement of comprehensive income), that is, profit attributable to shareholders, namely, the profit after tax, and, in a UK GAAP context, after minorities, but in an IFRS context, before minorities. Earnings, another figure of considerable focus by the market, is similar to the bottom line as defined above after minorities, but also after deducting dividends on preference shares classified as equity. Earnings per share (EPS) is earnings expressed on a per share basis.

In the UK as far back as 1992, the ASB tried, in FRS 3, to introduce the idea that the whole of the performance of a company in a year cannot realistically be condensed into a single number. Rather, the ASB argued, there should be presented a series of measures, such as operating profit, profit before and after tax, and total recognised gains and losses (which includes, for example, revaluations of assets, and in IFRS terminology is called 'other comprehensive income'). Despite the ASB's argument, there still continues to be considerable focus on a single bottom-line earnings number. In 2007, the IASB issued a revised version of IAS 1, reiterating the ASB's stance, for example, stating that 'the financial performance of an entity can be assessed only after all aspects of the financial statements are taken into account and understood in their entirety' and that 'the Board acknowledged that the items included in profit or loss do not possess any unique characteristics that allow them to be distinguished from items that are included in other comprehensive income'.

Prior to these changes, and to some extent still, it has been the desire of some managements to present a smooth time series of numbers, characterised at the extreme by 'the chairman is pleased to report the 27th year of uninterrupted earnings growth'. Whilst this type of reporting did lack a certain credibility, analysts and other commentators find it both comforting to receive results announcements of that type and easy to deal with them. In contrast, earnings numbers that jump around from year to year in a seemingly random pattern make it very difficult to understand, and, therefore, value, the company concerned.

Against this background, there has developed in recent years the so-called 'earnings game', in which management:

- seek to deliver a track record of consistent earnings growth;
- manage earnings expectations carefully;
- aim to slightly beat market expectations; and
- make business decisions to meet or beat expectations.

Analysts, for their part:

- hammer stocks that fail to meet expectations;
- listen carefully for the 'whisper number' (that is, an unofficial management forecast of earnings); and
- hammer stocks that fail to meet the whisper number.

Whilst this description is perhaps an oversimplification, there is some truth in it; many a results announcement reporting increased profits has been met with a fall in the company's share price because, as good as the results are, they fall below analysts' expectations. There are also a number of disadvantages arising from it. The desire to meet earnings expectations can lead to suboptimal business decisions. For example, a potential acquisition or new product development may be clearly worthwhile in the medium or longer term, but reduce EPS in the short term. If it is not done because of short-term earnings considerations, that is a poor business decision. The desire to meet earnings expectations can also lead to pressure on the financial reporting process. Many conversations between company management and auditors are based around the desire to (for example) carry forward an item of cost, or recognise some revenue early, in order to meet a target profit number and thereby not to disappoint the market.

Nonetheless, the combined effect of accounting standards that focus on assets and liabilities in the balance sheet, better governance within companies (e.g. better audit committees) and better auditing have resulted in more volatile – that is, more realistic – profit numbers being reported. This has opened up another development: that of reporting alternative performance measures, or, as they are also called, adjusted, or non-GAAP, or pro-forma, earnings numbers.

Alternative performance measures

Partly in response to the pressures outlined above, some companies have developed the practice in recent years of publishing alternative performance measures (APMs), sometimes called adjusted earnings numbers, 'non-GAAP' or 'pro-forma' numbers. Whether or not this practice is valid depends on how it is done.

Companies' objectives in this area are more often based on a desire to stabilise reported earnings, rather than merely to increase them. Sometimes the objective is to focus on earnings numbers that are close to operating cash flow. Hence one tends to see, as well as the required GAAP numbers, APMs such as:

- earnings before exceptional items (exceptional items are, or are supposed to be, material one-off items that potentially distort the underlying trend);
- EBITDA (earnings before interest, tax, depreciation and amortisation) – this is regarded by some companies as being a stabilised version of operating cash flow; and
- earnings at constant exchange rates (that is, showing what the earnings would have been if last year's exchange rates had been applied to this year's earnings of overseas subsidiaries).

Prior to 2005, companies also often disclosed earnings before goodwill amortisation (adding goodwill back because it is a non-cash item and also because it was rather nebulous in nature) or earnings before goodwill amortisation and exceptional items. Goodwill is not amortised under IFRS,[4] so these figures have dropped in their frequency, although adjustment is sometimes made to eliminate a charge for the impairment of goodwill.

These adjusted numbers are sometimes presented in additional columns (for example, columns showing pre-exceptional, exceptional, total), additional

4 See ch. 11.

rows that show subtotals such as operating profit before a particular expense, or shaded boxes that have similar objectives. Two example presentations are illustrated in chapter 9.

While each of these has its own logic, the danger with them is that different companies adjust their earnings numbers in different ways; as a result there is little comparability among the adjusted results. Moreover, especially in preliminary announcements, half-yearly results and the 'front half' of annual reports (that is, in highlights statements, chairman's statements, and operating and financial reviews) sometimes more prominence is given to these adjusted earnings numbers than to the required GAAP numbers. This is a practice that concerns auditors. Reflecting this, the APB issued guidance to auditors, which was updated in 2008, pointing out, among other things: that inappropriate prominence should not be given to APMs relative to the GAAP numbers; and that any APMs should be accurately described and reconciled to the GAAP numbers. Equivalent guidance for companies is in the form of a summary, published by the Financial Services Authority, of CESR recommendations. The guidance includes the following:

- APMs should not be presented with greater prominence than defined GAAP measures;
- where APMs resemble defined performance measures in audited financial statements, but do not have the characteristics of the defined measures, the defined measures should have greater prominence than the APMs; and
- comparatives should be provided for any APM presented.

Some improvement in practice is likely to emerge as the jurisdiction of the FRRP has been extended for periods beginning on or after 1 April 2006 to include directors' reports, encompassing the business review, as well as the statutory accounts. In its report setting out its preliminary findings in respect of IFRS implementation by UK listed companies in their annual accounts, the FRRP addressed this issue, stating that:

> 'Within the narrative review sections of their reports, some companies referred to measures of profit which were not consistent with the presentation adopted for the Income Statement. Non-GAAP performance measures should be defined and reconciled to GAAP measures. Similarly, alternative measures for Earnings per Share (EPS) should be identified and reconciled to EPS figures derived from IAS 33, "Earnings per share". Undue prominence should not be given to any non-GAAP measures.'

Users and analysis of accounting information

Users of financial statements look to them for a variety of purposes. Nevertheless, it is generally accepted that the prime users are investors, or shareholders, including potential shareholders. The requirements of accounting standards are based on this assumption. A key underpinning of accounting standards is that investors want information that will allow them to forecast cash flows. This is key to valuation of companies and therefore of shares. However, suppliers, bankers and employees are also very interested in information from which they can forecast cash flows, as they wish to predict whether the company will be able to pay them, repay loans and pay salaries respectively.

Having said that, there are specific uses of financial statements and specific pieces of analysis that need to be carried out. For example, a loan agreement may include clauses (covenants) under which the company has to keep certain ratios within defined bounds. For instance, gearing (see below) should be not more than X per cent, or interest cover (see glossary) should not drop below Y times. In the event that these ratios are not satisfied, the loan becomes immediately repayable. While the terms 'gearing' and 'interest cover' are generally understood, there is no standardised definition. Gearing, for example, means broadly the relationship of debt to equity (shareholders' funds) on the balance sheet, but it can be defined in a number of ways, including:

1. long-term debt compared to equity;
2. long-term debt compared to equity plus long-term debt;
3. long-term and short-term debt compared to equity; and
4. long-term and short-term debt net of cash balances compared to equity.

Hence there has to be clarity as to exactly how the numbers that contribute to those ratios are defined.

In an agreement for the sale or purchase of a subsidiary, the price to be paid may include an initial amount plus a further amount of contingent consideration that may be payable depending on the level of profits in the period (typically one to three years) after the sale. This is sometimes called an 'earn-out' clause. This often arises because there is genuine uncertainty about the fair value of the operation being sold, and the level of profits achieved after the sale provides further evidence of the fair value.

In these circumstances, the sale and purchase agreement will include a term specifying the additional amounts that will be payable and the basis of their calculation. Again, it is important to be clear exactly how various terms are defined, for example, whose accounting policies will be used to calculate the profits, the acquirer's or acquiree's; and whether the policies will remain on a frozen GAAP basis or will they change as GAAP changes.

Protracted discussions between the parties, often with each party employing an expert, and even costly court cases, have arisen numerous times in the past due to imprecise wording of agreements. Companies carrying out transactions should be as precise as possible in using accounting terminology to avoid such expense.

7
Current trends in accounting

Why all the change?

The financial reporting environment and the financial reporting rules that have to be applied are in a constant state of flux. The annual report of a UK listed company now looks very different from its equivalent of twenty years ago. The same is true to a lesser extent for an unlisted company. The main factors that underlie the changes are:

- developments in business;
- activities of standard-setters;
- legislation and EU regulation; and
- responses to scandals.

Developments in business

Business transactions continue to be innovative and become more complex. The leasing industry, for example, has changed from being clearly in two halves – lessors who rent out equipment for the short term, and subsidiaries of banks who provide finance through finance leases – to an industry where a variety of players offer leases with varying degrees of risk for different parties, thus blurring the traditional clear divide. This has led to pressure to update the lease accounting rules to reflect contemporary business. A more obvious example is the whole area of financial instruments, including derivatives, which has witnessed an explosion in volume and sophistication in the last twenty years or so.

New industries also emerge and bring new accounting challenges. Revenue recognition – primarily the question of when (i.e. in which accounting period) revenue should be recognised – was not a problem when factories made goods, put them on a lorry and delivered them the same day. The day the goods left the factory gate coincided with the date of invoicing and that was the date the revenue was recognised. However, in the software industry, a supplier may develop software at its own expense, and then secure a customer who buys: (1) a piece of software; (2) an agreement to upgrade it for up to two years; (3) a helpline and maintenance support service running for five years. If this compound sale is made for a single price (say £1 million), the software house has to consider whether and how to disaggregate the revenue into parts and when to recognise them. If there are market values for the separate supply of each of the three components, that task is made somewhat easier, but this is not always the case.

Companies and analysts sometimes complain that accounting rules and financial statements are becoming too complex and seek to lay the blame at the door of the standard-setters or the profession. However, to a large extent the increasing complexity of accounting merely reflects business developments.

Activities of standard-setters

In the UK, the first accounting standards were developed in the early 1970s. By 1980, the annual compendium of UK accounting standards was 320 pages long. The equivalent 2007/08 edition is 3,508 pages long, of which 113 pages comprise a discussion paper on the reform of lease accounting to reflect the developments described above. A further 445 of its pages consist of rules on accounting for financial instruments. The equivalent edition of IFRS standards for 2008 is 2,719 pages long.

Accounting standard-setters are now an established part of the institutional framework. There is no sense in which they are soon likely to have finished their work, having written all the accounting rules that are necessary to deal with varied and uncertain practices that need to be standardised. New issues continually emerge and, such is the depth of the subject, there is no shortage of issues to which an active standard-setter can usefully turn its attention.

The strong focus on global convergence of accounting rules strengthens this: even where an IFRS and the equivalent US standard on a particular topic take a similar overall approach, there can be differences of application. On other topics the accounting can simply be very different. Hence the standard-setters see this as a harmonisation challenge.

Legislation and EU Regulation

A number of changes have been brought about following the introduction of legislation and EU Regulation. Some changes to the British legislation have been following domestic issues, such as the requirement for quoted companies to publish a directors' remuneration report disclosing the remuneration of individual directors by name – see chapter 20. Other changes to British legislation have been to ensure that we implement an EU Directive. Detailed rules on the presentation of balance sheets and profit and loss accounts ('formats') for UK GAAP financial statements were introduced by the Companies Act 1981 following the 4th EU Directive.

EU Regulations apply directly in each Member State without the need for national legislation. Article 4 of EU Regulation 1606/2002 had a profound effect on British companies' consolidated financial statements from 2005, requiring them to be prepared using IFRSs as adopted by the EU if the company has securities traded on a regulated market in the EU.

Response to scandals

Many pieces of legislation or other rules stem from scandals. Indeed, in the UK, the accounting standards programme was originally started partly in response to differences in accounting treatment that emerged in the GEC/AEI take-over in the late 1960s. More recently, calls for strengthened accounting standards on financial instruments followed reports of certain banks and corporates incurring large-scale losses from derivative operations, at a time when the transactions were not (by current standards) being accounted for properly, and were not even being disclosed. The international standard (IFRS 2) on share-based payment was developed partly because it was an area where accounting was simply not giving realistic answers. However, it was given a considerable fillip by the scandals about the size of executive remuneration packages in which share options played a large part and yet were not reflected in arriving at profit or loss.

The new millennium has of course been characterised by numerous corporate scandals, starting perhaps with Enron and WorldCom in the US. Parmalat in Italy in early 2004 showed that the capacity for things to go seriously awry in the corporate world was not restricted to the Americas. The reaction to these scandals has followed the traditional pattern in which governments and other regulators demand action and new, tougher rules in order that 'the same should not be allowed to happen again'. This is naive: many years ago, laws were established forbidding activities such as robbery and murder, yet we may note that they continue. This is not to say that it is pointless to react to such scandals. Indeed, it is good to take the opportunity to improve specific rules that were found to be weak. The risk is that people will mistakenly expect that there will be no further difficulties. The risk also is that new rules place a further burden of cost and process that hits the 99 per cent of companies that are good citizens. This is the case with much of the US reaction to Enron: the rules coming into force under the Sarbanes-Oxley Act ('Sarbox') and from the Public Companies Accounting Oversight Board, which Sarbox established, in the area of internal control procedures and reporting are a good example. On the other hand, one of the very good effects of Enron was that it crystallised an improvement in the US accounting requirements for disclosures about and consolidation of special purpose entities (SPEs). Prior to this, the FASB had had a project on reforming the rules for consolidations that had set something of a record by being active, if that is the right word, for eighteen years without resolution.

Current trends in thinking

Greater disclosure

Throughout society, and in particular throughout the business environment, there is a trend towards greater disclosure and transparency. Many of the current and recent changes in corporate reporting can be seen as examples of that. From an accounting point of view, this is often described as allowing shareholders and other users of accounts to see the business through the eyes of management. A good example is segment reporting. Under IFRS 8 companies are required to give analyses of revenue, profit, assets and various other measures according to a line of business or geographical segmentation. The specific segments about which information is disclosed are those segments for which information is reported internally to management (to 'the chief operating decision-maker'). The information to be disclosed in the financial statements is that disclosed to the chief operating decision-maker. Thus, whichever profit figure is reported internally as part of managing the business is the figure reported in the segmental analysis note in the financial statements.

As well as accounting changes in a narrow sense, there are many other examples: greater disclosure of corporate governance arrangements; greater disclosure of directors' remuneration packages; earlier disclosure of price-sensitive information and so on.

Principles v. rules

One of the recent and continuing issues in standard-setting has been the so-called 'principles v. rules' debate. Those on the principles side say that: as professionals they understand accounting principles, and are taught to analyse and apply judgement; to have rules imposed upon them is unnecessary both because principles work well enough and because not all circumstances are the same and hence the application of judgement gives better results than a straitjacket of rules; and, inevitably, transactions will arise that are outside the detailed rules but would be within the principles. Those on the rules side say that: principles are too vague to result in consistent application; judgement too often means flexibility and acceding to management's wishes; comparability of reporting is very important and that can only be achieved by standardisation.

This debate is likely to continue. The IASB and the UK ASB argue, with some justification, that their standards set out principles in contrast to the US approach, which is more detailed and prescriptive. This is certainly true in relative terms; but, meanwhile, more and more detailed rules continue to be written by all standard-setters.

Use of fair value

An important current trend is towards the increased use of fair values in accounting. Historical cost accounting was the original basis of accounting; the balance sheet reflected the price paid for assets and the cost was expensed in arriving at profit/loss as the asset was used up. This was subsequently adapted in the UK to allow companies, if they wished, to state certain assets at current cost, market value or fair value (these terms are broadly synonymous); this allowed companies to reflect the higher worth of assets in their balance sheets, although this is not the same as reflecting the market value of the business itself on balance sheet as many items making up the value of a business as a whole do not appear on the balance sheet at all. Current thinking is that, for an increasing number of assets and liabilities, fair value provides more relevant information than historical cost to users of the financial statements. This is even though it may be less reliable than the equivalent historical cost information. The relevance/reliability trade-off depends on the asset or liability in question. For example, shares in companies listed and actively traded on the London Stock Exchange have an easily determinable fair value. An investment in an unlisted start-up company is altogether more difficult to value.

As the following examples illustrate, international accounting and UK GAAP both currently use a 'mixed model', that is, some assets and liabilities are stated at cost, but others are stated (or may be stated) at fair value.

- Property, plant and equipment (called 'tangible fixed assets' in UK GAAP) may be stated at valuation. In practice, it is properties that are sometimes revalued; other categories, such as plant, are valued only occasionally.
- Investment properties, under IFRS (IAS 40), can either be carried at valuation or cost (but fair value must be disclosed in the notes if cost is used in the balance sheet), whereas they are required to be stated at current valuation in UK GAAP (SSAP 19). It is widely accepted that, for properties held for rental income and capital growth, value is much more relevant than cost and a well-developed valuation profession in the UK helps this to work. Not having mandatory valuation under IFRS reflects a number of factors. First, the valuation profession was not so well developed in some other countries. Second, it was to give preparers and users time to gain experience with using a fair value model.
- Financial instruments, as explained in chapter 17 at pp. 161–166, is a complex area where part of the debate is the question of how far fair value should be applied. The international standard, IAS 39, which has become part of UK GAAP through FRS 26, is a pragmatic, and somewhat unsatisfactory, example of the mixed model, with some assets fair valued and others carried at cost. There is also an option to fair value certain instruments.
- Perhaps a less obvious example is agriculture, but the international standard applies fair value accounting to this area too, based on the greater relevance of the information. It requires fair value accounting for biological assets and agricultural produce harvested from an entity's biological assets.

As may be noted, some of these examples require the use of fair value accounting, while others permit it. Moreover, in some cases, the gains and losses arising from fair valuing are recognised in arriving at profit/loss, while others are reported as other comprehensive income in IFRS (or as 'other recognised gains and losses' in the STRGL under UK GAAP). It is a very mixed picture, but the direction of change – towards increased use of fair value information – is clear.

Smoothing v. volatility

An important trend in accounting over the last few years is that it is becoming increasingly difficult for companies to report a smooth time series of results. The trend is towards greater volatility.

As noted in chapter 6, it has long been an objective of some managements to report a smooth profits trend. In the 1970s and 1980s, this was generally not too difficult to achieve. However, in the 1990s, the UK ASB brought in a number of accounting standards – many of which have international counterparts and thus continue to affect UK companies following the move to IFRS – that challenged this approach to reporting. The standard-setters made the point that businesses go through economic cycles, rates of interest vary, foreign exchange rates fluctuate and it is artificial to somehow report results as if the company were in a very stable situation. The change of approach was achieved by altering the focus of accounting from the calculation of profit/loss to the balance sheet. It put the main focus on properly identifying the assets and liabilities at the start and end of the year, and measuring them appropriately. For example, IAS 37 and FRS 12 (which were developed in conjunction with one another) on provisions made it no longer possible for a company to provide for a cost that is likely to be incurred in the following year, unless it can be shown that it is an actual liability at the year end. Previously, especially where a company had unusually good results for the year, it would sometimes provide for certain future costs, even though it was not committed to incur them at the year end. The effect would be to reduce profits of the earlier year and thereby protect the profits of the later year.

A second example is IAS 36 and FRS 11 on impairment of assets (generally non-current assets and goodwill). The objective of these standards is to ensure that such assets are not carried at above their recoverable amount, and that any impairments are identified and reported in the correct period. Impairments, of tangible and intangible assets, can be large expenses that can dominate results announcements; one recent announcement was of a goodwill impairment charge of £23.5 billion.

These two standards to some extent remove managements' discretion as to when expenses should be recognised, and hence the results become more volatile.

A similar effect arises from the trend, described above, towards more use of fair values. This is especially the case where the changes in the fair values are recognised in arriving at profit/loss. The leading example of this is accounting for financial instruments, where financial assets and liabilities that are derivatives or that are held for trading – and some others according to choice – are treated in this way. Reported profits can thus be affected by swings in interest

65

rates and foreign exchange rates as well as by changes in the underlying value of investments, e.g. arising from an equity investment becoming more valuable.

There is a very practical effect arising from the inclusion of fair value changes in profit measurement, namely that it will not be possible until the year end to know what the profit is likely to be. It has been a source of some comfort for boards, and for analysts, to have, say, a month before the year end, a good idea of the likely results for the year. This is now much more difficult to achieve.

Part II

Some specifics

8

Individual entity and consolidated financial statements

The distinction between individual entity financial statements and consolidated financial statements

General distinction

There is an important distinction between the financial statements of an individual entity, such as a company, and the consolidated financial statements of a group. An entity for this purpose could take a number of forms; the most common example is a single company, but an entity for accounting purposes could be a partnership or an unincorporated association – that is, it does not need to have separate legal personality. A group typically comprises a parent company and a number of subsidiary undertakings, but again the parent and the subsidiary undertakings need not be companies.

Individual entity financial statements, sometimes called 'single entity', or 'solus', financial statements, are the financial statements of the entity itself. Thus, where a company transacts its business through subsidiaries rather than directly itself, its individual entity financial statements will record an investment in one or more subsidiaries in its balance sheet and will record dividend income in arriving at profit/loss. The trading transactions will be included in the individual entity financial statements of the subsidiaries themselves and are not reflected in the parent's individual entity financial statements.

It is generally accepted, therefore, that the individual financial statements of a parent entity, while they have some uses, do not properly reflect the parent's results, assets and liabilities. Hence, for many years, it has been the practice to prepare 'group financial statements' for groups of companies, albeit with exceptions as discussed below. Group financial statements now almost exclusively take the form of consolidated financial statements. In practice, the terms 'group financial statements' and 'consolidated financial statements' are used interchangeably.

Consolidated financial statements aim to present a picture of the group as a whole as if the group were a single entity. Hence the revenue, expenses, profit, assets and liabilities of the group are shown in aggregate, irrespective of whether they sit in the parent entity or in a subsidiary, and reflect the transactions of the group with parties outside the group. Transactions between entities within the group, e.g. a sale from one subsidiary to another, would be

Box 8.1 *Balance sheets*

	Parent entity	Consolidation
Share capital	100	100
Retained earnings	50	(20)
Shareholders' equity	150	80
Net assets	150	80

eliminated. Subsidiaries are consolidated based on a control criterion, whether they are wholly owned, partly owned or, occasionally, not legally owned, and whether they are domestic or foreign. There are a number of qualifications and exceptions to these general statements, as discussed below.

Distributable profits

One of the most important applications of the distinction between individual entity financial statements and consolidated financial statements lies in the field of company distributions. Simply put: it is individual companies (not groups) to which the legal rules on distributions apply and that make distributions. The details about realised and distributable profits are discussed in chapter 19, but for simplicity let us assume in the following illustration that a company's accumulated distributable profits equate to the balance on its retained earnings. Suppose that the balance sheet of a parent entity and the consolidated balance sheet of the group that it heads are as shown in Box 8.1.

One might expect that the consolidated balance sheet would be stronger than that of the parent alone, and indeed this is often the case. However, a situation such as the above is by no means rare. One common underlying reason is that the parent may have made an acquisition, of which a large element was goodwill, and, in the consolidated financial statements, the goodwill was written off to reserves, as was permissible in the UK prior to 1998 and which can remain written off to reserves under the rules for conversion to IFRS (IFRS 1), thus superficially weakening the consolidated balance sheet. Alternatively, the subsidiaries might have made losses. The key point is that when the parent considers whether it can make a distribution, it refers to its single entity financial statements. These show that it has profits available for distribution of 50. The fact that there is a deficit in the group generally does not affect the parent's ability to make a distribution.

Conversely, the parent's entity financial statements might show a much smaller balance of retained earnings (say 10) than is shown in its consolidated financial statements (say 150) – for example, because the subsidiaries have not passed their profits up to the parent by way of dividend. If the parent wishes to pay a large dividend to its shareholders, it must first receive a dividend from its subsidiaries.

Entity focus for tax purposes

Another key application of entity financial statements is for tax purposes. HM Revenue & Customs assesses tax on the taxable income of entities, not on a group basis (though this is subject to various exceptions). So, for example, if a parent sells goods to a subsidiary during the year for 100, including a profit of 40, and those goods remain unsold by the subsidiary at the year end, the 40 is taxed in the parent entity, even though the goods are unsold by the wider group and the profit of 40 is thus not included in the consolidated financial statements – as discussed below, adjustments are made in the consolidated financial statements to eliminate the intra-group profit.

When to consolidate

General approach

The Companies Act, IFRSs, UK accounting standards and, for AIM companies, the AIM Rules are all relevant in this area. The way in which they interact is as follows. Whether a British company (other than a small company) has to pre-pare consolidated financial statements is determined by s. 399 of the Companies Act 2006; at its balance sheet date is the company a parent? If so, consolidated financial statements are required. Parent companies that are themselves sub-sidiary undertakings are exempt from this requirement if they satisfy various conditions, one of which precludes listed companies from taking advantage of the exemption. However, the exemption is widely used lower down a listed group, allowing many sub-groups not to have to prepare consolidated financial statements. Parent companies that are small companies can choose whether to prepare consolidated financial statements, although listed and AIM-traded companies, amongst others, do not meet the definition of a small company.

When the parent is required to prepare consolidated financial statements by reference to the Act, there are three possibilities:

- AIM companies and companies that, on their balance sheet date, are listed are required to apply EU-adopted IFRSs for their consolidated financial statements. Where this is the case, Schedules 1 and 6 (and 2 and 3 for banking and insurance companies) to SI 2008/410, which set out detailed accounting rules, do not apply, although other provisions of the Act and SI, such as the requirements for a directors' report, directors' remuneration report and for the financial statements to be audited, do still apply.
- If the parent is not listed nor an AIM company, but it opts to apply IFRS, the above bullet again applies.

71

- If the parent is not listed nor an AIM company, and it opts to stay on UK GAAP, Schedules 1 and 6 (and 2 and 3) to SI 2008/410 continue to apply, together with the other provisions of the Act and SI.

What to consolidate

The spectrum of interests in other companies

An entity may have interests in a number of other entities. The labels given to the varying degrees of interest are as follows;

- investment;
- associate;
- joint venture; and
- subsidiary.

How each of them is included in group financial statements depends upon the category into which they fall.

A group is made up of the parent entity and each of its subsidiaries. It is these entities that are 'consolidated'. Associates and joint ventures are dealt with later in this chapter and investments are dealt with in chapter 17.

Definitions of parent and subsidiary undertaking

Within the Act there are references to 'subsidiary undertakings' and to 'subsidiaries'. 'Subsidiary undertaking' is more widely defined and is used to determine whether consolidated accounts are required. IAS 27 uses the term 'subsidiary', but it is equivalent to that in the Act of subsidiary undertaking. In the vast majority of cases an entity will meet both the definition of a subsidiary undertaking in the Act and subsidiary in IAS 27, but on the periphery one but not the other definition may be met, which in extreme cases can cause problems.

Generally speaking, if one entity controls another entity, the latter is likely to be a subsidiary undertaking of the former. Even if it does not meet the definition of subsidiary undertaking, it is still likely to be consolidated under SIC 12 (IFRS) or FRS 5 (UK GAAP) – see below.

IAS 27 takes a principled approach, defining a subsidiary as 'an entity, including an unincorporated entity such as a partnership, that is controlled by another entity (known as the parent)' and defining control as 'the power to govern the financial and operating policies of an entity so as to obtain benefits from its activities'. Elaboration of the definition of control is then to be found within the body of IAS 27 – for example, para. 13 explains that there is a rebuttable presumption of control where more than one-half of the voting power of an entity is owned, directly or indirectly, through subsidiaries.

Control is defined as the *power* to govern the financial and operating policies of an entity so as to obtain benefits from its activities. Accordingly, the standard explains that owning options that are convertible into ordinary shares should be taken into account if they are exercisable at the time.

Most frequently in practice it is owning all or a majority of the ordinary shares in a company that gives rise to the parent/subsidiary relationship. However, it is not necessary to own a majority of an entity in order to control it and thus for it to be a subsidiary.

Control and ownership may not converge, but a parent-subsidiary relationship may still exist. For example, where A owns 49 per cent, 25 per cent or even none of B, but in practice controls it, B will be A's subsidiary undertaking. In such circumstances there are often other arrangements, such as management fees, or special dividend rights, that give A a greater economic interest than the holding (or lack of holding) would suggest.

The IASB issued a statement acknowledging that IAS 27 captures the concept of de facto control. Assume that A owns 48 per cent of B, a listed company in which no other shareholder owns more than 5 per cent of its equity shares. If the other shareholders have not formed any group or groups to vote collectively and the other shareholder representation at general meetings, in person or in proxy, has not been more than 30 per cent of the total voting rights for many years, then A will have de facto control over B because A can control the majority of effective votes at general meetings.

In UK GAAP, FRS 2 is based on the Act, supplementing the rules and definitions in the Act. Thus the effect of applying the definition of subsidiary in IFRS and UK GAAP is very similar.

Exclusions from consolidation

In IFRS, there are no grounds on which a subsidiary should be excluded from consolidation, although where a subsidiary is held for resale IFRS 5 'Non-current assets held for sale and discontinued operations' applies and requires a different form of consolidation.

The position under UK GAAP is shown in Box 8.2.

Special purpose entities and quasi-subsidiaries

The discussion so far in this chapter has been about consolidation of subsidiary undertakings. SIC 12 'Consolidation – special purpose entities' requires that if a special purpose entity (SPE), which can be a company, trust, partnership, unincorporated entity or multi-user structure such as a protected cell company, does not meet the definition of a subsidiary, it should nevertheless be consolidated by an entity where the substance of the arrangement is that the entity controls the SPE. The SPE might be set up, for example, to operate automatically with no decisions needing to be taken (an 'autopilot' mechanism); this might fall outside the definition of subsidiary in IAS 27, but is, to all intents and purposes, no different from a subsidiary. In such a situation, SIC 12 would

---

Box 8.2 *Possible ground for exclusion of a subsidiary under UK GAAP*

	Act	*FRS 2*
Disproportionate expense or delay in obtaining necessary information	Permits exclusion (s. 405(3)(b))	Does not permit exclusion (para. 24)
Severe long-term restrictions over the rights that make it a subsidiary undertaking	Permits exclusion (s. 405(3)(a))	Requires exclusion (para. 25(a))
Held exclusively for resale	Permits exclusion (s. 405(3)(c))	Requires exclusion (para. 25(b))
Inclusion of subsidiary undertaking is not material	Permits exclusion (s. 405(2))	Permits exclusion (accounting standards need not be applied to immaterial items)

---

require the accounting treatment in the consolidated accounts to be the same as if it were a subsidiary. Prior to the introduction of SIC 12, groups were designing entities that were in practice controlled by and for the benefit of the group, but which, in order to keep certain items off balance sheet, did not meet the definition of subsidiary; SIC 12 was therefore written specifically as an anti-abuse measure.

In terms of UK GAAP, FRS 5 introduced a class of entities called quasi-subsidiaries to fulfil the same purpose, although the Act's definition of subsidiary undertaking has subsequently been widened, thus resulting in fewer quasi-subsidiaries now.

Exemption re holding company income statement

In addition to the consolidated financial statements, the directors of a parent company are required to produce the individual company financial statements for the parent. Thus, the published report and accounts includes both information about the group and the parent company itself. For example, there has to be published the balance sheet of the parent company as well as the balance sheet of the group, and many note disclosures have to be given for both the parent company and the group. However, under s. 408, a parent company is permitted not to publish its single entity 'profit and loss account', so long as the profit or loss for the financial year is disclosed as a single figure.

The exemption applies regardless of whether the consolidated financial statements are prepared in accordance with IFRSs as adopted by the EU or UK GAAP.

In all cases, the entity statement should still be prepared, and approved by the board; the exemption is merely from publication.

Techniques of consolidation

The techniques of preparing consolidated financial statements involve, especially for a large and complex group, details that are beyond the scope of this book. This section restricts itself to an overview of the techniques.

Changes in composition of a group

From time to time, a group may acquire new subsidiaries or dispose of them. On the purchase of a new subsidiary, the question arises as to whether acquisition accounting or merger accounting should be used. This used to be a major and controversial question. However, in 2004, merger accounting was banned in international standards (although not for group reconstructions), following on from similar changes to US standards. It is still available in UK GAAP, although its days are numbered if UK GAAP is to be converged with IFRS. Acquisition and merger accounting are discussed more fully in chapter 11.

In the context of both acquisitions and disposals, the results, assets and liabilities are included in the consolidated financial statements while the company in question is a subsidiary of the parent. The date on which an entity becomes or ceases to be a subsidiary hinges on when control is gained or lost.

Full v. proportional consolidation

Subsidiary undertakings are consolidated in full, even if they are not wholly owned. This is because the concept underlying consolidation is control, not ownership. Hence if a subsidiary undertaking is held 60 per cent by its parent and 40 per cent by another party, the parent will consolidate 100 per cent of its assets and liabilities and 100 per cent of its revenues and expenses, and therefore its profit. It will then record the 40 per cent that it does not own as 'minority interest' or 'non-controlling interest'.

There is another approach, called 'proportional consolidation', whereby the parent consolidates the percentage that it owns – in the above example, 60 per cent – of the assets and liabilities, revenues and expenses. In this way, no minority interest adjustment arises. This method is not permitted for accounting for subsidiaries under IFRS or UK GAAP. However, it does have a place in international accounting standards (IAS 31) in accounting for some joint ventures. For example, if the above company, held 60/40 per cent by two parties, was structured as a joint venture, and assuming it was not a subsidiary of the 60 per cent investor, then each party, if using proportional consolidation under IAS 31, would include their respective percentages of each line item in their consolidations.

Minority interests or non-controlling interests

As noted above, minority interests (also called 'non-controlling interests') arise when a subsidiary is not wholly owned. A minority interest arises both in respect of the balance sheet and the income statement. With respect to the balance sheet, it represents the proportion of the net assets of fully consolidated subsidiaries that are owned by third parties (i.e. not owned by the parent shareholders). The minority interest is thus distinct from the equity interest of the holders of the parent's equity, but can be regarded as a different type of ownership interest – a partial interest of some shareholders in the net assets of certain subsidiaries. Traditionally in the UK, minority interests have generally been presented in the balance sheet after liabilities in arriving at net assets, although an alternative presentation, adjacent to shareholders' funds, has been, and still is, permitted. Since 2003, IFRS has mandated that the minority interest must be presented 'within equity', albeit separate from 'issued capital and reserves attributable to owners of the parent'. That is, under IFRS, net assets represents the total net assets of the group and does not include a deduction for the share of those net assets owned by the minority interests.

In the income statement and statement of comprehensive income, the minority interest represents the part of the group results that is not attributable to the parent shareholders. One hundred per cent of the results of subsidiary undertakings are consolidated (both in arriving at profit/loss and for the other comprehensive income), but, using the figures above, only 60 per cent of the results are attributable to the parent shareholders. Mirroring the balance sheet treatment, the profit figure and the figure for total comprehensive income are before any adjustment to reflect minority interests in those items. The profit and the total comprehensive income are then analysed, on the face of the income statement and statement of comprehensive income, but technically separate from the statements, into the amount attributable to minority interest (being 40 per cent of the results of that subsidiary undertaking) and the amount attributable to the owners of the parent.

Elimination of intra-group transactions

The overall objective of consolidated financial statements, as noted above, is to present financial statements as if the group were a single entity. Hence there is no place for numbers representing intra-group transactions. Put another way, a sale from one subsidiary to another is a non-event for the group as a whole. Such transactions, therefore, need to be eliminated in preparing consolidated financial statements. This involves removing the relevant sales figure from the selling company and the equivalent expense figure in the buying company. Where there is a profit to the selling company, that has to be eliminated if the purchasing company retains the asset at the year end; this is because no profit has been earned on an external transaction. It is also necessary, in preparing the consolidated financial statements, to eliminate items on the balance sheet such as balances owing from one group company to another, as they are not assets and liabilities from a group point of view.

Associates and joint ventures

Definitions of associate and joint venture

A business relationship with another company or group may be referred to colloquially as a 'joint venture' (JV). This of itself does not automatically trigger accounting for that other company or group as a joint venture. The appropriate accounting will be determined by which definition in IFRSs is met.

Associates and JVs are defined by IAS 28 and IAS 31 respectively. IAS 28 defines an associate as 'an entity, including an unincorporated entity such as a partnership, over which the investor has significant influence and that is neither a subsidiary nor an interest in a joint venture'. Significant influence is defined in IAS 28 as 'the power to participate in the financial and operating policy decisions of the investee but is not control or joint control over those policies'.

IAS 31 defines a joint venture as 'a contractual arrangement whereby two or more parties undertake an economic activity that is subject to joint control'. IAS 31 sub-divides joint ventures into three categories: jointly controlled operations; jointly controlled assets; and jointly controlled entities.

Associates and JVs are therefore quite different from each other. For example, a typical JV might involve three parties with 33.3 per cent of the JV each. An associate, on the other hand, may involve an investment in the range 20 to 50 per cent, but the other shareholdings would typically be diverse or, at least, not held by other JV parties. These contrast with a subsidiary undertaking where the investor controls alone the investee.

Where a company holds a stake in the range 20 to 50 per cent in another that is neither a joint venture nor a subsidiary, that is normally accounted for as an associate. It is assumed at this level that the investor has 'significant influence' over the investee. For example, an associate holding would normally be accompanied by a seat on the board of the investee. However, the 20 per cent threshold is an indication rather than a rule. For example, a holding of 18 per cent could give rise to significant influence if accompanied by a seat on the board. A holding of 22 per cent might not give rise to significant influence if there was a dominant majority shareholder holding between 51 and 78 per cent.

The definitions of associate and joint venture applying for UK GAAP purposes are to be found in FRS 9 and the Act. They are similar to those in IFRS, but not identical. For example, FRS 9's definition is more restrictive as it requires that the investor must *actually exercise* significant influence for an associate relationship to exist, whereas under IAS 28 an investor only has to have the *power to participate* in the financial and operating policy decisions of the investee, regardless of whether that power is actually exercised. Consequently, some associates under IAS 28 would not be classified as such under FRS 9.

Accounting treatment of associates in consolidated financial statements

Equity accounting is the form of accounting for associates within consolidated financial statements under both IFRS and UK GAAP. Nevertheless, there are differences in how this is presented in arriving at profit/loss.

Under IFRS, the investing group's share of its associate's profit, being profit after tax, is included as one line in arriving at the investing group's profit or loss; IAS 1 suggests that this should be after finance costs but before tax, but in practice the share of profits could be presented higher up the income statement if justified, although it must still be the group's share of after-tax profits wherever included.

Under UK GAAP (FRS 9), the group's share of the associate's operating profit is added after the operating profit of the group (that is, the operating profit of the parent and its subsidiary undertakings). Because the associates' profit added in is operating profit, it follows that any subsequent line items in the income statement, such as interest and tax, need to include the relevant share of the associates' interest and tax. The overall effect is rather like proportional consolidation (that is, including the relevant proportion in each line item), but only from the operating profit line downwards.

In the consolidated balance sheet, the group's interest in associates under IFRS is shown as a single line item among non-current assets. At the point of acquisition, the carrying value is cost. This grows to reflect the investing group's share of profits retained in the associate itself and the investing group's share of any other changes in the associate's equity, for example, revaluation gains on property. The balance sheet treatment under UK GAAP is the same, albeit the group's interest in the associates is included within fixed asset investments.

Accounting treatment of JVs in consolidated accounts

In IFRS, accounting for JVs is set out in IAS 31 and depends on the nature of the JV. For the mainstream case of a jointly controlled entity, the choice is between equity accounting (as outlined above) and proportional consolidation, although an exposure draft proposes dropping the option to use proportional consolidation (and renaming jointly controlled entities as joint ventures). For the other two categories – jointly controlled operations and jointly controlled assets – the investing group accounts for its assets, liabilities, income and expenses and its share of any jointly owned assets, liabilities, income and expenses.

In UK GAAP, the accounting treatment of JVs is set out in FRS 9 and is basic equity accounting, as described above for associates under UK GAAP, augmented by additional disclosure in the primary statements, and the result is called the 'gross equity method'. FRS 9 requires that 'in the consolidated profit and loss account the investor's share of its joint ventures' turnover should also be shown – but not as part of group turnover ... [and] in the consolidated balance sheet the investor's share of the gross assets and liabilities underlying the net equity amount included for joint ventures should be shown in amplification of that net amount' (para. 21).

The additional disclosures are required because the view is that joint ventures are more important than associates, and hence the figures for turnover, gross assets and gross liabilities need emphasis. Nevertheless, this does not amount to full consolidation; neither, technically, does it amount to proportional consolidation, although it edges close to it.

9

Presentation of financial statements

Introduction

The Companies Act requires the directors to prepare financial statements and various reports each year and to send them to shareholders. The total package, including the full financial statements, rather than summary financial statements, tends to be known as either the 'Report and Accounts' (taking this name from the days when the Act required only the directors' report and the annual accounts) or the 'Annual Report' (reflecting the fact that the various reports, financial statements and other information together form one report to shareholders). In this chapter we look at the components of the financial statements, or accounts. Other parts of the Report and Accounts, such as the Operating and Financial Review and the Directors' Remuneration Report, are discussed in chapter 20. Some argue that 'accounts' refers to the primary statements, while 'financial statements' refers to the primary statements together with the notes thereto, but often the two terms are used interchangeably. We use the two terms interchangeably within this book.

IFRSs are intended to be applied worldwide and thus are not developed around any legislation, as each country has its own national legislation, whereas, for example, UK accounting standards were originally developed against the background of British legislation. Accordingly, much of what is outlined in this chapter is laid down by accounting standards, mainly IAS 1, for IFRS accounts, whereas it comes from a mix of accounting standards and legislation for UK GAAP accounts.

Under IAS 1(2007), a complete set of financial statements comprises:

- a balance sheet as at the end of the period;
- a statement of comprehensive income for the period (which is an income statement followed by the other comprehensive income and can be presented as one statement or two);
- a statement of changes in equity for the period;
- a cash flow statement for the period;
- notes, comprising a summary of significant accounting policies and other explanatory information; and
- comparative information in respect of the previous year.

Rather than 'balance sheet' and 'cash flow statement', IAS 1 uses 'statement of financial position' and 'statement of cash flows' respectively. However, it goes on to say that 'An entity may use titles for the statements other than those used in this Standard', which applies to all the statements, including the statement of comprehensive income.

The content is very similar in UK GAAP, with an income statement (referred to in UK legislation as a profit and loss account) and balance sheet, being required by the Act, and a cash flow statement and statement of total recognised gains and losses (detailing the other comprehensive income to use the IFRS terminology), being required by accounting standards, and notes being required by a combination of the Act and accounting standards.

Statement of comprehensive income

Overview

The statement of comprehensive income was introduced into IAS 1 in its 2007 revision. The statement combines two earlier statements: the income statement; and the statement of recognised income and expense (SORIE). The statement of comprehensive income can be presented as one statement (in which case IAS 1 (2007) refers to it as the statement of comprehensive income) or as two. If two statements are presented, they will be the income statement and what was previously called the statement of recognised income and expense, but is now called the statement of comprehensive income by the IASB.

Under the previous version of IAS 1, a SORIE was not mandatory unless a particular option with regard to accounting for the cost of pensions was adopted. In practice, most UK companies adopted this method of pension cost accounting and so did present a SORIE. Accordingly, if, as we expect most UK companies to do, the two-statement approach is adopted, the resulting statements will be an income statement and a SORIE/statement of comprehensive income.

Disclosure on the face of the income statement

Traditionally, the income statement, which reports profit for the year and its key components, has been the element of a set of financial statements on which the most attention has been focused and in the main this will continue to be so.

IAS 1 (2007) stipulates the minimum content that must be included on the face of the income statement. The items are as follows:

- revenue (previously referred to as turnover in the UK);
- finance costs (this means the gross interest payable and other finance costs; if a company wishes to disclose net finance costs on the face of the income statement, this has to be in addition to, rather than as a replacement for, gross finance costs);

- share of the profit or loss of associates and joint ventures accounted for using the equity method (this is discussed in chapter 8);
- tax expense;
- a single amount comprising the total of (1) the post-tax profit or loss of discontinued operations and (2) the post-tax gain or loss recognised on the measurement to fair value less costs to sell or on the disposal of the assets or disposal group(s) constituting the discontinued operation; and
- profit or loss.

Additionally, the profit or loss attributable to minority interest (or non-controlling interest) and the profit or loss attributable to the owners of the parent have to be shown on the face of the income statement as allocations of the profit or loss for the period. This disclosure is required whether the one- or two-statement approach is adopted.

Where relevant to an understanding of the entity's financial performance, IAS 1 (2007) requires additional line items, headings and subtotals to be presented on the face of the income statement. This is relevant regarding disclosure of what, in the UK, we are used to calling 'exceptional items' (see section headed 'Exceptional items' below).

Companies in the UK have become accustomed (under FRS 3) to disclosing operating profit on the face of the income statement. Many companies have continued this practice under IFRS, justifying it under the above provision, namely that it is relevant to an understanding of the company's results. The IASB, in its 'Basis of conclusions' in respect of IAS 1, recognises that many entities wish to disclose operating profit and calls for such entities to ensure that they do not omit any items from its calculation that are operating in nature, for example, expenses that are unusually large one year compared to other years, such as restructuring expenses. Thus, companies are not in breach of any standards if they disclose operating profit on the face of the income statement, providing they include all operating items when calculating it.

Disclosure on the face of the income statement or in the notes

Further details are required to be disclosed, but these can either be on the face of the income statement or in the notes to the accounts.

Expenses have to be analysed by function (cost of sales, distribution costs and administrative costs, with, as a minimum, cost of sales having to be disclosed separately from other expenses) or by nature (depreciation and amortisation, employee benefits, etc.). The choice of income statement formats in Schedule 1 to SI 2008/410 available to companies continuing to apply UK GAAP (and that applied prior to IFRS) offer the same choice of expense analysis, thus, in the main, companies continue their presentation under IFRS that they used under UK GAAP prior to 2005. The analysis by function is the more popular in the UK.

Exceptional items

Although this term is widely used in the UK, it is not used in IFRSs. FRS 3 defines exceptional items as 'material items which derive from events or transactions that fall within the ordinary activities of the reporting entity and which individually or, if of a similar type, in aggregate, need to be disclosed by virtue of their size or incidence if the financial statements are to give a true and fair view'. IAS 1 does, however, state that when items of income or expense are material, their nature and amount shall be disclosed separately, either on the face of the income statement or in the notes. Examples of circumstances where such disclosure may need to be given are listed in IAS 1 and include restructuring expenses and impairment write-downs. This IAS 1 disclosure is similar, if not quite equivalent, to FRS 3's disclosure of exceptional items and a number of UK companies have continued to use the term 'exceptional items' in their IFRS financial statements. Where the term 'exceptional item' is used in IFRS financial statements, it should be defined in those financial statements, preferably in the accounting policies.

Discontinued operations

To be of most use to the readers of a set of financial statements, those financial statements need to explain not only the profit or loss for the year but also individual components making up that number. This year, but not last year, was there a large profit on the sale of a building? This is likely to be separately disclosed as discussed above (under 'exceptional items'). Were all aspects of the business profitable or were some in a loss situation? This information is likely to be provided by segmental analysis in a note.[1] These and other disclosures are helpful to readers trying to forecast future results. The presentation and disclosure of discontinued operations similarly enables users to focus on the results of the business lines that are expected to continue.

Discontinued operations are separate major lines of business or geographical areas of operations that an entity has disposed of or is disposing of.

Each line item on the face of the income statement, from revenue down to, and including, the tax charge, includes only the relevant amount for continuing operations in IFRS reporting. The profit or loss after tax for discontinued operations, aggregated with the profit/loss on disposal, impairment write-down, etc. in respect of the discontinued operations is included on the face of the income statement, below the results from continuing operations, either as one line and analysed in the notes, or with full analysis on the face of the income statement.

By contrast, under UK GAAP each line item on the face of the income statement includes the relevant amount for total operations, whether continuing or discontinued, although the total has to be analysed into the two components.

1 See ch. 20.

Box 9.1 *Extract from Income statement for the year ended 31 December 2008*

	Before exceptional items	Exceptional items (note 2)	Total
	2008	2008	**2008**
	£'000	£'000	**£'000**
Revenue	49,464	–	**49,464**
Cost of sales	(33,755)	(2,791)	**(36,546)**
Gross profit	15,709	(2,791)	**12,918**
Distribution expenses	(5,060)	–	**(5,060)**
Administration expenses	(3,221)	(2,964)	**(6,185)**
Operating profit	7,428	(5,755)	**1,673**

As a minimum, the analysis of turnover and operating profit (into continuing and discontinued operations) has to be on the face of the income statement. The analysis of the other operating items, for example, cost of sales, can either be in the notes or on the face of the income statement. In addition, there are some differences in the definition of discontinued operations between UK GAAP and IFRS, mainly with respect to the timing of when an operation may fall to be classified as discontinued.

Columns and boxes

When FRS 3 was introduced into UK GAAP in 1992 it outlawed extraordinary items, which had been until then presented after profit after tax. Examples of items that might have been treated as extraordinary prior to FRS 3 include restructuring costs, profits or losses on sale or closure of businesses, bid-defence costs and the costs of the impact of natural disasters. These are items that we now readily accept as being part of profit before tax and even, particularly under IFRS, part of operating profit, but on the introduction of FRS 3 this was quite a sea change. Companies therefore tried to present their financial statements in a manner that made the impact of these items transparent. The use of additional columns and boxes on the face of the income statement became a common way of showing additional information (alternative performance measures). Providing this is done carefully, such presentation is also acceptable under IFRS. Two examples illustrating this, showing the income statement down to operating profit only, are shown in Boxes 9.1 and 9.2. Clearly, the comparatives would have to be presented in a manner consistent with the current year. It is inappropriate to use columns, as in Box 9.1, for the current year and not also for the comparative year if there were exceptional items in that comparative year.

Box 9.2 *Extract from Income statement for the year ended 31 December 2008*

	2008 £'000
Revenue	49,464
Cost of sales	(36,546)
Gross profit	12,918
Distribution expenses	(5,060)
Administration expenses	(6,185)
Operating profit before exceptional items	7,428
Operating exceptional items	(5,755)
Operating profit	1,673

The additional items, for example, the 'before exceptional items' column, should not receive greater prominence than the items required to be disclosed, for example, the 'total' column. See chapter 6 for a summary of the guidance regarding presenting alternative performance measures.

Earnings per share and dividends per share

Basic and diluted EPS, together with basic and diluted EPS from continuing operations, are required by IAS 33 to be presented on the face of the income statement or, if the one-statement approach is adopted, of the statement of comprehensive income of a listed company. EPS is a key statistic with much attention focused on it by analysts and users of accounts and thus by boards themselves in explaining their results. As a result of all the attention and because extraordinary items are no longer allowed (in IFRS or UK GAAP), a number of variants to basic and diluted EPS have been developed. EPS is discussed in chapter 10.

IAS 1 calls for the amount of dividends recognised as distributions to owners during the period, and the related amount per share, to be disclosed either in the statement of changes in equity or in the notes.

Prior to 2005, in the UK, the presentation for the income statement showed the profit for the year and how much of that the directors were paying out as a dividend to shareholders (the amount of dividends paid and proposed in respect of the year) even though the final decision in respect of the amount of the proposed final dividend was not made during the year itself. In reality, however, a dividend is paid out of distributable profits available at the time, no matter whether they arose in that or an earlier year. Thus, in a year of loss or significantly reduced profits due, say, to a one-off event, directors are still able to pay a dividend even though the profits for the year may be lower, or even non-existent, providing sufficient profits have been retained in earlier years. In addition, under pre-2005 accounting, the proposed dividend was included in the balance sheet as a liability. Standard-setters, however, struggled with the concept of including a liability in the balance sheet that did not exist at the balance sheet date. UK GAAP changed in 2005, to align with IFRS.

Under both UK GAAP and IFRS, only dividends paid or declared by the balance sheet date are recognised in the financial statements. Declared for these purposes means that the dividend has been appropriately authorised and is no longer at the discretion of the entity. For interim dividends this means that unless they are paid by the balance sheet date they are not reflected in the financial statements and unless final dividends have been authorised by shareholders in a general meeting on or before the balance sheet date (which, generally, they are not), they also are not reflected in the financial statements. For a company with a December year end paying dividends as follows:

2007	£m
Interim dividend paid September 2007	2.6
Final dividend authorised in general meeting in April 2008 and paid in May 2008	3.4
2008	
Interim dividend paid September 2008	2.8
Final dividend authorised in general meeting in April 2009 and paid in May 2009	3.8

the 2008 financial statements will include £6.2 million as dividends paid in the year in its statement of changes in equity, being the £3.4 million final dividend for 2007 and the £2.8 million interim dividend for 2008, and will merely disclose the £3.8 million proposed final dividend for 2008. Accordingly, the IAS 1 disclosure would require the £6.2 million in aggregate and as a per share amount to be disclosed either in the statement of changes in equity or in the notes.

Many UK companies also disclose the total paid and proposed 'in respect of 2008', that is, the £6.6 million (being £2.8 million + £3.8 million) as an aggregate and as a per share amount. Care is needed in doing this to ensure that the IAS 1 disclosure is also given and that there is no confusion between the different amounts.

Statement of comprehensive income or statement of recognised income and expense

In the two-statement approach, the second statement is the same as the statement of recognised income and expense (SORIE, pronounced 'sorry') under IAS 1 before its 2007 revision. However, the statement is now called a statement of comprehensive income, which is the same name given to the statement in the one-statement approach.

What is in this second statement? It begins with profit or loss (i.e. the number from the foot of the income statement) and then displays the components of other comprehensive income. Consequently, the total at the foot of the statement, total comprehensive income, is the same whether it is the foot of the second statement in the two-statement approach or it is the foot of the one-statement in the one-statement approach.

Total comprehensive income is all changes in equity (or net assets) other than changes resulting from transactions with owners in their capacity as owners. In essence, the idea is to bring together all the changes in net assets recognised in the financial statements during the year that result from the performance of the entity – that is, profits and losses that are shown in the income statement (or in the income statement part of the statement of comprehensive income), but also items such as revaluation gains that, whilst not shown in the income statement, are nonetheless part of a wider notion of economic performance. In contrast are transactions between the entity and its owners in their capacity as owners. Capital injections, such as a rights issue, and dividends to shareholders would therefore be excluded, but a sale of goods to an owner at normal market price would not be excluded as this, albeit a transaction with an owner, is not in its capacity as owner.

The statement of comprehensive income will show:

- profit or loss for the period;
- each component of other comprehensive income classified by nature;
- share of the other comprehensive income of associates and joint ventures accounted for using the equity method; and
- total comprehensive income.

Examples of other comprehensive income that will be displayed in the statement of comprehensive income include:

- revaluation gains or losses on property, plant and equipment;
- revaluation gains or losses on available-for-sale investments;
- actuarial gains and losses on defined benefit pensions;
- foreign currency gains and losses on translating the net assets of foreign subsidiaries; and
- gains and losses on hedging instruments in a cash flow hedge, e.g. on a floating to fixed rate interest rate swap.

Total comprehensive income attributable to (1) minority interest (or non-controlling interest) and (2) owners of the parent must be disclosed in the statement.

The tax relating to *each* component of other comprehensive income has to be disclosed either in the statement of comprehensive income or in the notes.

As with the income statement, IAS 1 requires:

- additional line items, headings and subtotals to be presented on the face of the statement where relevant to an understanding of the entity's financial performance; and
- that when items of income or expense are material, an entity shall disclose their nature and amount separately.

The above two points are more relevant in the context of the income statement (or income statement part of the statement of comprehensive income), but have been drafted to apply equally to the presentation of the other comprehensive income.

An example of a statement of comprehensive income is as follows:

	2009 £'000	2009 £'000
Profit for the year		849
Gain on revaluation of properties	22	
Exchange differences on retranslation of overseas subsidiaries	67	
Cash flow hedges	(9)	
Loss on available-for-sale investments	(25)	
Actuarial losses on defined benefit pension plans	(86)	
Tax relating to components of other comprehensive income	9	
Other comprehensive income for the year net of tax		(22)
Total comprehensive income for the year		827
Total comprehensive income attributable to:		
Owners of the parent		793
Minority interest		34
		827

The statement of comprehensive income in the two-statement approach and, thus, the SORIE are very similar to the UK GAAP statement of total recognised gains and losses (STRGL, pronounced 'struggle') which has been common in the UK since its introduction by FRS 3 in 1992.

Balance sheet

The 2007 version of IAS 1 refers to the balance sheet as the statement of financial position. However, this term does not have to be used by entities in their financial statements.

Current and non-current assets and liabilities have to be presented separately on the face of the balance sheet under IFRS unless a presentation based on liquidity provides information which is reliable and more relevant, as might be the case for a financial institution, in which case all assets and liabilities have to be presented in order of liquidity. For these purposes, IAS 1 (2007) requires an entity to classify an asset as current when:

- it expects to realise the asset, or intends to sell or consume it, in its normal operating cycle;
- it holds the asset primarily for the purpose of trading;
- it expects to realise the asset within twelve months after the reporting period; or
- the asset is cash or a cash equivalent (as defined in IAS 7), unless the asset is restricted from being exchanged or used to settle a liability for at least twelve months after the reporting period.

It similarly requires an entity to classify a liability as current when:

- it expects to settle the liability in its normal operating cycle;
- it holds the liability primarily for the purpose of trading;
- the liability is due to be settled within twelve months after the reporting period; or
- the entity does not have an unconditional right to defer settlement of the liability for at least twelve months after the reporting period.

The minimum that must appear on the face of the balance sheet, in addition to the above, is:

(a) property, plant and equipment;
(b) investment property;
(c) intangible assets;
(d) financial assets (excluding amounts shown under (e), (h) and (i));
(e) investments accounted for using the equity method;
(f) biological assets;
(g) inventories;
(h) trade and other receivables;
(i) cash and cash equivalents;
(j) the total of assets classified as held for sale and assets included in disposal groups classified as held for sale in accordance with IFRS 5;
(k) trade and other payables;
(l) provisions;
(m) financial liabilities (excluding amounts shown under (k) and (l));
(n) liabilities and assets for current tax, as defined in IAS 12;
(o) deferred tax liabilities and deferred tax assets, as defined in IAS 12;
(p) liabilities included in disposal groups classified as held for sale in accordance with IFRS 5;
(q) minority interest (or non-controlling interest), presented within equity; and
(r) issued capital and reserves attributable to owners of the parent.

As with the income statement and statement of comprehensive income, additional line items, headings and subtotals can be presented on the face of the balance sheet where relevant.

Amplification of the information above is required either on the face of the balance sheet or in the notes, for example, analysing property, plant and equipment into the different classes, such as land and buildings, machinery, motor vehicles, etc. Where a line item in the balance sheet includes amounts expected to be recovered or settled more than twelve months after the reporting period as well as within this period, the amount expected to be recovered or settled more than twelve months after the reporting period has to be disclosed.

Balance sheet format 1 in Schedule 1 to SI 2008/410 sets out, for a UK GAAP balance sheet, a list of items that must be included on the face of the balance sheet. The items listed are very similar to those set out in IAS 1, but the main difference is that while the order is prescribed for UK GAAP, it is not for an IFRS reporter. There is a second format permitted for UK GAAP reporters, but most British companies adopted format 1.

The Act requires the directors to approve the accounts and for a director to sign those accounts, on the company's balance sheet, on behalf of the board; this is so for IFRS as well as UK GAAP accounts. Every copy of the balance sheet that is published must state the name of the director who signed the accounts on behalf of the board. This requirement relates to the *company* balance sheet. In the past, the company and group balance sheets were often presented on the same page, but this happens less frequently now for listed companies (see below). Where the two are presented on separate pages, it has become common practice for a director to sign the consolidated balance sheet in addition to the company balance sheet.

Cash flow statement

As illustrated in chapter 1, net cash flow during a year does not equate to the profit or loss for that year; they are different concepts and they give the reader two different views of the same underlying events. Considerable importance is placed on cash flow statements as well as on income statements. In particular, the cash flow statement is often seen as a 'sense check' on the income statement. It is quite normal for a company to sell goods and services on credit, and that means, in accounting terms, that revenue is often recognised in the income statement before the cash flow is recognised in the cash flow statement. However, where revenue is recognised in the income statement but the transaction does not generate cash flows for a significant period, it might suggest that revenue is being booked too early. For example, the Review Panel, in its press release on the case of Wiggins Group Plc, stated with respect to revenue recognition that:

'In reviewing the company's 1999 accounts the Panel noted that the turnover and profits recognised under this policy were not reflected in similar inflows of cash; indeed, operating cash flow was negative and the amount receivable within debtors of £46 m represented more than the previous two years' turnover of £44 m. As a result, the Panel enquired into the detailed application of the policy . . .'

In this particular case, the directors were persuaded to change their accounting and revised accounts were issued. Of course, revenue that does not result in cash flows for a significant period will not always mean that the revenue recognition is inappropriate and it is here where narrative reporting is also essential.[2]

IAS 7 'Statement of cash flows' requires an entity to present its cash flows under three headings: operating; investing; and financing. Probably in an anti-avoidance move, operating is the default category. Along with cash flows arising from the entity's 'principal revenue-producing activities', any cash flows not meeting the definition of investing activities or financing activities must also be classified as operating.

Cash flows are defined as inflows and outflows of cash and cash equivalents. Cash is cash in hand together with demand deposits and cash equivalents are short-term, highly liquid investments that are readily convertible to known amounts of cash and which are subject to an insignificant risk of change in value. Normally, for an investment to qualify as a cash equivalent, it will have a short maturity, say, three months or less from the date of acquisition.

In UK GAAP, the cash flow statement has nine headings under which the cash flows are classified: operating activities; dividends from joint ventures and associates; returns on investments and servicing of finance; taxation; capital expenditure and financial investment; acquisitions and disposals; equity dividends paid; management of liquid resources; and financing. Although the original cash flow statement introduced into UK GAAP showed the inflow and outflow of cash and cash equivalents, since 1996 the statement has shown only the movement of cash. For these purposes cash is defined as cash in hand and deposits repayable on demand (24 hours or less) with any qualifying financial institution, less overdrafts from any qualifying financial institution repayable on demand. In the UK GAAP statement, cash flows of what are 'cash equivalents' for IFRS purposes are reported within the 'management of liquid resources' section.

Accounting policies

There will sometimes be more than one acceptable method of treating a transaction or event in a set of financial statements. Sometimes, there are choices set out within an accounting standard. For example, IAS 16 on property, plant and equipment allows companies to measure assets at cost or on a valuation

2 See ch. 20.

basis (in each case, subject to depreciation). FRS 15 allows the same choice in UK GAAP. In other cases, different treatments arise in practice in areas that are unregulated by formal GAAP. Some companies are more aggressive than others in terms of recognising revenue from transactions, or in terms of carrying forward costs. However, in practice the scope to take different judgements now lies in a fairly narrow band: the basic requirement laid down in IAS 1 that financial statements shall 'present fairly the financial position, financial performance and cash flows', i.e. that they show a true and fair view, together with the guidance in IAS 8 'Accounting policies, changes in accounting estimates and errors', guide directors to select policies that achieve this outcome. Similarly, the requirement that UK GAAP financial statements show a true and fair view narrows down the policies from which companies can choose.

Partly because there are choices of policies, and partly for clarity for the reader even where there is no choice, companies are required by IAS 1 to disclose 'the measurement basis (or bases) used in preparing the financial statements' and 'the other accounting policies used that are relevant to an understanding of the financial statements'. FRS 18 similarly calls for material accounting policies to be disclosed.

In its report setting out its preliminary findings in respect of IFRS implementation by UK listed companies in their annual accounts, the Review Panel noted that:

> 'there was also evidence of "boiler-plating" in the accounting policies selected for disclosure. For example, accounting policy descriptions were given which, on enquiry, were found to be irrelevant since there were no underlying accounting transactions falling within their scope. This issue arose, in particular, in relation to the descriptions of accounting policies for hedging instruments which appeared to have been copied from IAS 39, "Financial Instruments: Recognition and Measurement", whether or not such hedges were used in practice'.

It is important, therefore, not to provide a list of accounting policies that covers every possible eventuality even though there is no intention of some of them ever needing to be applied. Instead, it is important to select for disclosure only those that are relevant in interpreting the accounts and to explain company-specific aspects; the Review Panel also noted, in the same report, that:

> 'Standardised disclosures have limited use especially where the policy is prescribed by IFRS. Descriptions of accounting policies are more useful when they identify issues relevant to a company's individual circumstances. For example, revenue recognition policies may need to describe the methods applied to determine the stage of completion of transactions involving the rendering of services (IAS 18, "Revenue"). As the methods used will vary according to the nature of the circumstances it is helpful if the policy includes specific relevant details'.

These points were reiterated by the Review Panel in its annual report for 2007.

Notes

Numerous notes are required expanding upon the information in the primary financial statements. For example, an analysis of the figure for property, plant and equipment is required showing the movements during the year for each class of property, plant and equipment. If a particularly large charge is made in arriving at profit/loss one year that is not expected to remain at such a scale in future years, an explanation is required to be disclosed. Particularly extensive note disclosures are required in respect of financial instruments, employee benefits (especially defined benefit pension plans) and share-based payment arrangements.

A couple of important disclosures required by IAS 1 that are not explicitly required in UK GAAP are:

- assumptions about the future and other major sources of estimation uncertainty at the balance sheet date that have a significant risk of resulting in a material adjustment to carrying amounts of items in the balance sheet within the following year, together with the nature and carrying amount of the balance sheet items; and
- other judgements taken in preparing the financial statements that have the most significant impact on the amounts recognised in the financial statements.

In its annual report for 2007, the Review Panel noted that these two requirements 'attracted more Panel questions and comment than any other aspect of IFRS or, indeed, any other standard'. The Panel particularly pointed out that satisfying the disclosure requirements of an IFRS or IAS on a particular topic does not negate the need to consider whether these two requirements of IAS 1 may require further disclosures.

Individual entity and consolidated financial statements: combined or separate

As stated above, directors have to present consolidated financial statements for the group headed by the company (unless there is an exemption from doing this, such as the company is an intermediate parent company meeting the various other specified exemption conditions) and single entity financial statements for the company. Although most emphasis is placed on the consolidated financial statements, both have to be prepared and presented. An exemption from presenting the parent company income statement is available as explained in chapter 8 above. Prior to 2005, both sets of financial statements (consolidated and single entity) were prepared under UK GAAP and were presented as an integrated set of financial statements. For example, only one set of accounting policies would typically be included. Another example is that the balance sheets were often presented side by side on the same page.

From 2005, some companies have continued with this presentation as they have moved the parent company, as well as the consolidated, financial statements to IFRS. Many UK companies, for the time being at least, have chosen to retain UK GAAP for their parent company, single-entity financial statements, thus necessitating presentation of two quite different sets of financial statements within the same 'package'. Integrated presentation is thus not possible in these instances; the two sets of financial statements must be presented separately from one another. In such instances the consolidated financial statements are usually presented first and would include the group-only accounting policies. The single-entity financial statements of the parent company will be presented on separate pages and will require, inter alia, its accounting policies to be presented in full.

10

Earnings per share

Introduction

Listed companies that are budgeting future results or considering strategies, such as acquisitions, often consider the implications for earnings per share (EPS) as part of their analysis. Of course, it is unrealistic to think that the performance of a company or group for a whole year can be summed up in a single figure, and informed readers of financial statements look to a wider range of indicators. Nevertheless, the figure for EPS is generally regarded as an important measure in the published financial statements of listed companies.

Earnings per share is, in simple terms, a company's earnings (profit after tax, cost of preference shares and minority interests) divided by the number of shares in issue. In most cases, additional complexities arise and these are dealt with by the accounting standard IAS 33, which lays down rules primarily stipulating how the denominator, that is the 'number of shares' part of the calculation, is determined. Two companies both reporting under IFRS may choose different accounting policies for a particular issue, for example, in accounting for their defined benefit pension schemes: one may choose to amortise the actuarial variation in excess of the corridor in arriving at profit/loss, whereas the other may choose to recognise the full actuarial variation as other comprehensive income (see chapter 16 on pensions). If everything else were identical, the two companies would nevertheless produce very different profit figures for the year. Accordingly, even though identical guidance is followed in the calculation of EPS, the two companies would produce very different EPS numbers.

Summary

IAS 33 requires both basic and diluted EPS to be calculated for total profit, profit from continuing operations and profit from discontinued operations. Each of these figures must be presented on the face of the income statement (or statement of comprehensive income in the one-statement approach), with the exception of basic and diluted EPS in respect of discontinued operations, which may alternatively be presented in the notes to the financial statements. A number of other disclosures are required in the notes which, in the main, elaborate on the calculations.

The bulk of the standard contains guidance on how to calculate EPS. In a nutshell, the profit for the year (total, continuing or discontinued) is divided by the weighted average number of ordinary shares outstanding during the year to give basic EPS. Basic EPS is therefore a measure of how much profit is attributable to each ordinary shareholder. The calculation uses the weighted average number of shares, rather than the number of shares in issue at the year end, in order to reflect the average amount of equity finance available during the year.

Diluted EPS takes the profit figure used for basic EPS and adjusts it as though certain contracts to issue shares had actually been fulfilled and the shares issued. For example, if a company has issued convertible debt, the finance charge deducted in arriving at profit for the year (and which would be used to calculate basic EPS) is added back because, had that debt been converted into shares, there would not have been a finance charge. Similarly, the weighted average number of shares is also increased as though the shares had been issued.

The standard is mandatory for companies whose ordinary shares or potential ordinary shares, e.g. convertible debt, are publicly traded or are in the process of becoming so. In addition, any entity not otherwise within the scope of the standard but voluntarily choosing to disclose EPS in its IFRS financial statements must calculate and present EPS in accordance with IAS 33.

Basic EPS

Basic EPS is a measure of how much of the profit, or loss, for the year is attributable to each ordinary shareholder. It is calculated as follows:

$$\frac{\text{Profit or loss attributable to ordinary equity holders in the parent company}}{\text{Weighted average number of ordinary shares in issue during the year}}$$

The starting point for the profit figure is the profit, or loss, at the foot of the income statement (or income statement part of the statement of comprehensive income). Dividends and other appropriations, e.g. amortisation of issue discount, in respect of preference shares classified as equity, net of any tax effect, are deducted from it. Any minority interests are also deducted.

For preference shares that are classified as liabilities, their finance cost will have been expensed (through the interest line of the income statement) in arriving at profit/loss and thus no adjustment is needed when calculating basic EPS.

For a company with only one class of ordinary shares and either no preference shares or only preference shares that are classified as liabilities, the profit figure to use will be found on the face of the income statement (or statement of comprehensive income in the one statement approach) in the analysis of the profit into that attributable to the owners of the parent and that attributable to the minority interest. It is the amount described as attributable to the owners of the parent company that is used in calculating basic EPS.

For any calculation of basic EPS, whether there is one class of shares (or more than one), the number of shares used in the calculation is the weighted average number of shares (in that class if there is more than one class) in issue during the year. Generally, shares are included from the date that their consideration is receivable. For example, ordinary shares being issued for cash are included from the date that the cash is receivable and ordinary shares issued upon conversion of debt are included from the date that interest on the debt ceases to accrue. The principle behind this is that if a company has more capital, it has more earning potential. Consider a simple example. E Plc issues 1,000 £1 ordinary shares on the first day of the year for £10,000. These shares remain in issue throughout the year. In addition, half way through the year a further 1,000 shares are issued, again, for £10,000. Assuming no other capital, that the company earns £2,800 in the first half of the year, £5,600 in the second half of the year and that all of the profit for the first half year was paid out as a dividend at the end of the half year. EPS is calculated as follows:

$$\frac{£8400}{15000} = 56 \text{ pence per share}$$

The 15,000 denominator is calculated as $(^6/_{12} \times 10,000) + (^6/_{12} \times 20,000)$, reflecting the fact that 10,000 shares were in issue for the first six months and 20,000 shares were in issue throughout the second half of the year.

If instead of using a time-weighted denominator, the number of shares in issue at the end of the year was used, the EPS would be 42 pence per share (being £8,400 / 20,000). This would not, however, be a fair basis from which to predict the likely EPS of the following year. Assume that all of the second half's profits were paid out by dividend at the end of year 1 and that in year 2 the company's profits were £5,600 for each half year (and that, again the first half's profits were paid out at the end of that half year), the profit for year 2 would be £11,200. This would give an EPS of 56 pence per share (being £11,200 / 20,000 shares). In other words, by using a weighted average number of shares, the EPS is the same in both years, whereas the absolute profits in both years are different, reflecting the fact that the company's ability to generate profits increases as its capital increases.

Basic EPS for continuing and discontinued operations is calculated in exactly the same way, but (instead of using total profit) using the profit attributable to the continuing and discontinued operations respectively.

Diluted EPS

Diluted EPS is required to be disclosed, in addition to basic EPS, where the company has issued a financial instrument or entered into a contract: (1) which may entitle the holder to ordinary shares in the company; and (2) where those shares would have reduced EPS from continuing operations had they been issued during the year.

Detailed guidance on how to calculate diluted EPS is given in IAS 33. First, a company has to identify its 'potential ordinary shares': these are the financial instruments that it has issued and contracts that it has entered into which may result in the company giving ordinary shares in the company to the holder of the instrument/contract, for example, convertible debt. Second, the company has to identify which, if any, of these are dilutive; they will be dilutive if 'their conversion to ordinary shares would decrease earnings per share or increase loss per share from continuing operations'. Finally, the company calculates diluted EPS (for total profit, profit from continuing operations and profit from discontinued operations) using those potential ordinary shares that have been found to be dilutive.

How is diluted EPS calculated once a company has worked out which potential ordinary shares are dilutive? The idea behind diluted EPS is to disclose what EPS would have been had the dilutive potential shares been converted to shares either on the first day of the year or, if later, the date of issue of the potential ordinary shares. Thus, the starting point is the calculation of basic EPS; both the earnings number and the weighted average number of shares are then adjusted as if the dilutive potential ordinary shares had been converted to shares. The earnings number is adjusted to eliminate the post-tax effects of the dilutive potential ordinary shares and the number of shares is increased by the weighted average number of shares that would have been issued. Consider a company that had issued convertible loan stock two years ago, none of which had yet been converted to shares. Its profit for the year will have been reduced by the finance charge in respect of the liability element of this stock, but had the stock been converted to shares on the first day of the year there would have been no finance charge during the year. Hence, if the stock is dilutive the finance charge is added back to the profit used to calculate basic EPS. Any other consequential adjustments to profit that would have arisen had the stock been converted are also made. Thus, if the tax charge would have been higher (because the finance charge would not have been made and so taxable profits higher), an adjustment is also made for this impact. The weighted average number of shares is also increased by the number of shares that would have been issued had the stock been converted to shares on the first day of the year.

The standard sets out rules on how various different potential ordinary shares, such as share options and contingently issuable shares (shares that will be issued if certain conditions are met) are to be treated.

Adjusted EPS

In the UK, the demise of extraordinary items in the early 1990s led to an array of income statement presentation. In particular, many companies included their exceptional items in a separate column or in a box on the face of the income statement (see chapter 9). A logical extension of this was to disclose EPS, basic and diluted, not just for total profit (as was the requirement at the time under UK GAAP), but also for the profit excluding exceptional items. Other companies used columns to highlight the results of their discontinued operations (a presentation which is no longer appropriate under IFRS). Again, it was a logical extension to disclose EPS for continuing operations as well as for total profit (which is now a requirement under IFRS).

IFRS similarly permits adjusted EPS to be disclosed, although mandates that the disclosure be 'in the notes to the financial statements', and requires a reconciliation from the profit figure used in the calculation of adjusted EPS to a line item disclosed in the income statement/statement of comprehensive income. Adjusted EPS must be calculated using the weighted average number of shares determined in accordance with IAS 33 and basic and diluted adjusted EPS must be presented with equal prominence. Similarly, the adjusted EPS figures should not be more prominent than the GAAP figures.

11

Mergers and acquisitions

Introduction

Accounting for acquisitions and mergers has long been a controversial area of accounting. In particular, there have been disputes about whether the technique of merger accounting should be permitted, and about the nature and accounting treatment of goodwill.

Changes in US accounting rules in this area shortly before the IASB was formed led to changes in IFRS; IFRS 3 'Business combinations' was published in March 2004 and is the extant standard on this topic (with a revised version shortly to supersede it – see below). In a nutshell, merger accounting is no longer permitted in IFRS, although the scope of IFRS 3 does not extend to group reconstructions where the use of merger accounting has been, and continues to be, prevalent in the UK. Goodwill is no longer amortised; IFRS 3 requires goodwill to be carried at cost less any accumulated impairment losses.

IFRS 3 was the output of Phase I of the IASB project on business combinations. Phase II, which was a joint project with the FASB (the US standard setter), sought to improve and align further the accounting for business combinations. Phase II was recently completed and a revised version of IFRS 3 was published in January 2008. It is effective for business combinations for which the acquisition date is on or after the start of the accounting period beginning on or after 1 July 2009. For a company with a calendar reporting period, it is effective for business combinations made on or after 1 January 2010. Some of the changes to IFRS 3 are controversial and reflect a desire for the standard to move away from the parent entity perspective to the economic entity concept. Much of the standard nevertheless remains the same and in this chapter we highlight separately the key changes introduced in Phase II.

UK law sets out some details about acquisition and merger accounting, although, with the exception of the provisions about share premium, merger relief and group reconstruction relief, these do not apply to entities applying IFRS.

Current UK GAAP rules are found in FRS 6 'Accounting for acquisitions and mergers', FRS 7 'Fair values in acquisition accounting' and FRS 10 'Accounting for goodwill and intangibles'. Under these, merger accounting is still permissible in limited circumstances as well as in group reconstructions and, when acquisition (rather than merger) accounting is applied, goodwill is carried at cost and amortised unless it is regarded as having an indefinite useful economic life, in which case it is not amortised, but is reviewed annually for impairment.

Overview of acquisition and merger accounting

Introduction

The generic term applied where one company, or group of companies, acquires or merges with another company or group of companies is a 'business combination'. Once a business combination has taken place, say, Fast Growing Group Plc acquires Newcomer Plc, this must be reflected in the financial statements. Assuming that Fast Growing Group Plc bought all the issued shares of Newcomer Plc, the business combination will be accounted for in the group financial statements of Fast Growing Group Plc using either acquisition or merger accounting, except that in IFRS merger accounting is no longer allowed.

In the international arena, the terms 'purchase method' and 'acquisition accounting' are both used, with the original version of IFRS 3 using the former, while the 2008 revised version of IFRS 3 uses the latter. Since 'acquisition accounting' is the term used in the revised version, we will use this term throughout this chapter.

Summary of acquisition accounting

Key features of acquisition accounting (under IFRS and UK GAAP) are as follows:

- One of the companies is treated as the acquirer for accounting purposes.
- The assets and liabilities of the acquired company are restated to reflect fair values at the date of acquisition.
- The numbers of one or both of the combining companies (but typically those of the acquired company) are restated, where necessary, to harmonise accounting policies for the enlarged group.
- The income statement/statement of comprehensive income for the year of acquisition comprises the results for the whole of the current year for the acquiring group together with the results for the post-acquisition period only of the acquired company. The comparative figures are those of the acquiring group only. The same principle is used for the cash flow statement.
- The balance sheet at the start of the year of acquisition is that of the acquiring group only. The balance sheet for any date after the acquisition includes also the net assets of the acquired company.
- Goodwill arises and is recognised in the group balance sheet; it is generally positive, but can be negative.

- The fair value of the net assets acquired is brought into the consolidated balance sheet in place of the capital and reserves of the acquired company at the date of the acquisition. It follows from this that the group reserves at any year end after acquisition comprise the reserves of the acquiring group and its share of the post-acquisition retained reserves of the acquired company. The pre-acquisition reserves of the acquired company remain in that entity, but do not form part of the consolidated reserves of the enlarged group.

It will be noted that the acquisition accounting presentation shows growth as a result of the combination. Thus an acquisitive group can, in its headline figures, give the appearance of growth even though the underlying businesses may be stagnant. However, various required disclosures (under IFRS and UK GAAP) show whether growth is organic or bought-in.

In an acquisition, the acquirer (Fast Growing Group Plc) pays to buy the shares of the acquired company, the acquiree (Newcomer Plc). Having bought all of the shares in another company, the acquirer now controls the business(es) of that other company and needs to account for it/them. It accounts for them in its consolidated financial statements as it does all the other businesses that it controls, that is, it brings in each asset and liability of the business on a line-by-line basis. As its name suggests, the thinking underlying acquisition accounting is that the acquirer has purchased these businesses (and thus the underlying assets and liabilities) and must account for this as it would the acquisition of any asset. Since, in its group financial statements, it brings in each asset and liability of the acquired entity (rather than simply bringing in the shares that it has bought), it needs to work out how much of the total payment was for each asset and liability. The fair values of the assets and liabilities of the acquiree on the date of acquisition are calculated and it is assumed that these are what the acquirer would have paid for them individually and so it is at these amounts that they are brought into the consolidated financial statements on acquisition.

In addition, the acquirer is required to calculate what it paid for the shares. Where cash was paid, it is a case of simply adding up how much cash was paid out. If the acquirer paid partly in cash and partly in something else, or wholly by some other means, it is necessary to work out how much that was worth so that the accounting entries can be made. For example, if shares were given, their value has to be determined. Where the cash is paid out at a later date, rather than immediately, the cash to be paid out is discounted back to its value at the date of acquisition. In this way, the fair value of what was paid is calculated.

Where all of the acquiree's shares were purchased, the difference between the total paid out (the fair value of what was given to the vendor) and the sum of the fair value of the individual assets and liabilities acquired is goodwill, positive or negative.

So, for example, assume that:

- FGG acquires 100 per cent of N;
- N's net assets at book value are 70, but when stated at fair value are 90;
- FGG pays shares worth 115 plus 10 in cash; total consideration 125.

The (positive) goodwill is $125 - (90 \times 100\%) = 35$.

As we saw in chapter 8, it is not necessary to own 100 per cent to acquire a subsidiary. Now, for example, assume that:

- FGG acquires 80 per cent of N;
- N's net assets at book value are 70, but when stated at fair value are 90;
- FGG pays 93 in shares plus 10 in cash; total consideration 103.

Under the current version of IFRS 3 (and UK GAAP), the (positive) goodwill is $103 - (90 \times 80\%) = 31$.

On acquisition, FGG would still record the fair value of N's assets and liabilities in full, namely, 100 per cent of each asset and liability. A minority (or non-controlling) interest is then presented, which in IFRS financial statements must be presented in equity, equal to 20 per cent of N's net assets just recognised in FGG's group financial statements, i.e. the minority interest recognised on the date of acquisition is 18. In UK GAAP financial statements, the minority interest is presented either in equity or as a deduction from net assets.

A choice is allowed in the revised version of IFRS 3: either the goodwill and minority interest are calculated as above; or the goodwill can be 'grossed-up' to include the minority's share. For example, assume that, as before:

- FGG acquires 80 per cent of N;
- N's net assets at book value are 70, but when stated at fair value are 90;
- FGG pays 93 in shares plus 10 in cash; total consideration 103.

In addition, assume that:

- the remaining shares representing 20 per cent of N are valued at 22 (less per share than the 80 per cent stake acquired as the 80 per cent stake included a premium for obtaining control).

Under the alternative option, the (positive) goodwill is $(103 + 22) - (90 \times 100\%) = 35$.

The minority (or non-controlling) interest is then presented, in equity, on the date of acquisition as 22 (not the 18 under the earlier option). This alternative, 'grossing up', option is derived from US GAAP and we believe that it is unlikely to be widely adopted among UK companies that follow IFRS.

From a practical point of view, the step up in asset values to fair value, which is a fundamental part of acquisition accounting, leads to increased charges for depreciation and greater risk of impairments. Additionally, goodwill arises; in service and technology company acquisitions this can be a very large component of the overall value. Any impairment (or, in UK GAAP, amortisation) of goodwill hits reported profits. Furthermore, goodwill on the balance sheet increases the reported capital employed, which worsens the return on capital employed ratio; on the other hand, it improves gearing.

Summary of merger accounting

The key features of merger accounting (UK GAAP only) are as follows:

- Neither company is treated as the acquirer for accounting purposes.
- There is no restatement of the carrying values of the assets of either merging company to reflect fair values.
- No goodwill arises (although any goodwill already in the balance sheet of either party to the merger as a result of previous acquisitions remains there).
- The income statement is presented on an aggregated basis, as if the two companies had always been merged. The same principle is used for the cash flow statement.
- The balance sheets, both pre and post the combination, are aggregated in a similar way, as if the two companies had always been combined.
- The numbers of one or both of the combining companies are restated, where necessary, to harmonise accounting policies for the enlarged group.
- The reserves of the two companies are combined to form the group reserves; there is no elimination of pre-acquisition reserves.
- Despite the notions of equality, as a practical matter one company – either one of the two merging companies, or a new holding company superimposed – becomes the top company in the group's legal structure, and is the one that issues shares to the former shareholders of the other company(ies).

It will be noted that, in the financial statements of the year of a merger, the merger accounting presentation shows no growth as a result of the combination. This is because comparative figures are restated as if the two companies had always been merged. Any growth in the numbers would reflect growth in the underlying businesses.

For third-party transactions, merger accounting is not commonly used in UK GAAP as the criteria are restrictive and is not used at all in IFRS. However, it is used in accounting for group reorganisations, such as when a 'newco' is inserted or a group of subsidiaries is moved from one part of a group to another.

Application of IFRS 3

The current international standard on business combinations is IFRS 3. For business combinations for which the acquisition date is on or after the first day of the first accounting period starting on or after 1 July 2009, a revised version of IFRS 3 (referred to here as IFRS 3 (2008)) will apply. Key changes to be introduced by IFRS 3 (2008) are highlighted. For companies with a 31 December year end, IFRS 3 (2008) will apply to acquisitions made on or after 1 January 2010.

Merger accounting banned

Unlike the predecessor standard (IAS 22), IFRS 3 bans the use of merger accounting: all business combinations (excluding group reconstructions, which are outside the scope of IFRS 3) should be accounted for as acquisitions. That is, an acquirer should be identified for accounting purposes even if the two parties are of similar size and describe the combination as a merger.

Merger accounting has, except in the context of group reconstructions, been quite rare in recent years, and it has gradually become discredited. This is largely because it is almost impossible to develop criteria that effectively distinguish genuine mergers. The view, particularly of the standard-setters, is that, even when restrictive criteria are used, some combinations that meet the criteria are in fact acquisitions in substance and an acquirer is identifiable. Perhaps there are genuine mergers, but they are so rare in the business environment, and so difficult to identify, that it is not worth having a different method of accounting just to get the accounting right for those few, if the result is getting the accounting wrong for some of the combinations that should properly be presented as acquisitions. Thus, IFRS 3 bans merger accounting. However, IFRS 3 does not include group reconstructions in its scope and thus merger accounting principles continue to be used in intra-group transactions, in the short term at least.

Acquisition accounting under IFRS 3

In an acquisition, one party gains control over the other. Control is a question of fact – does one party have the power to govern the financial and operating policies of the other? There is a presumption that acquisition of more than one-half of the voting rights of another entity confers control.

The key features of acquisition accounting generally are set out above under 'Summary of acquisition accounting' and apply equally to IFRS 3 (both the current version and IFRS 3 (2008)) and UK GAAP. There are, however, two key differences between IFRS 3 and UK GAAP and these are in the areas of goodwill and intangibles.

The first difference is that IFRS 3 requires that more separate intangibles be identified than previous standards, and than UK GAAP, and this has the effect of reducing the residual amount attributed to goodwill. Recognising intangibles is discussed later – see goodwill and other intangibles.

Second, there is a different approach to amortisation of goodwill. Goodwill is not amortised at all under IFRS 3. It is tested for impairment annually. This means that if the goodwill is shown to have at least retained its value, there is no charge in arriving at profit/loss. However, if there is shown to have been an impairment, there is an immediate charge to write down the goodwill to its recoverable amount. Under UK GAAP, although goodwill is in some circumstances subject to an annual impairment review in place of annual amortisation, in practice this route is less common than annual amortisation over a twenty-year life.

IFRS 3 (2008) introduces an alternative way of calculating goodwill from that in the current version of IFRS 3 and UK GAAP – see above under 'Summary of acquisition accounting'.

Fair value of the consideration given

The cost of acquisition of the shares in the new subsidiary has to be measured at fair value for group accounts purposes.

Most commonly, the consideration given for the acquisition of a new subsidiary will include cash paid or securities issued by the acquiring company, such as its equity or loan stock. When securities are issued, their fair value needs to be established. If they are quoted securities, this is given by their market value. If they are not quoted, a range of valuation techniques is available. The question arises as to what date should be used. Where control is achieved in a single transaction, rather than a holding being gradually built up over a period, the price used is that on the date of acquisition. Using one date or another can make a big difference. This was the subject of a Review Panel press release in 2006, albeit under UK GAAP, in which it was announced that the directors of the particular company had agreed to change the accounting and value the shares on a different date (when the value was 7.25 pence per share) to the one they had originally used (when the value was 12.475 pence per share). The exception to using acquisition date price is where the share price on that date has been affected by the thinness of the market.

Where the payment involves a contingent element, the treatment differs between IFRS 3 and IFRS 3 (2008).

Contingent consideration often forms part of consideration paid – for example, additional cash consideration will be paid if profits post-acquisition exceed a specified amount. Where such payment is probable and can be measured reliably, the fair value of such amount (e.g. discounted to reflect the time value of money) is included as part of the cost of consideration under IFRS 3, whereas under IFRS 3 (2008) the fair value of the amount is included irrespective of whether its payment is probable. In the post-acquisition period, adjustments are made to the estimate of contingent consideration payable and, under IFRS 3, these are adjusted against goodwill. IFRS 3 (2008), on the other hand, requires such adjustments (that are beyond one year from the acquisition date) to be charged or credited in arriving at profit/loss.

Under the current version of IFRS 3, acquisition expenses, such as legal fees and necessary due diligence, are added to the fair value of the consideration paid to give the total cost of acquisition. IFRS 3 (2008), however, precludes

virtue of its relative size. If FRS 6's criteria are met, merger accounting is mandatory.

Legislative requirements – acquisition and merger accounting

The detailed legal rules relating to accounting for acquisitions and mergers are set out in Schedule 6 to SI 2008/410 (and are taken from Schedule 4A to the Companies Act 1985). These apply to groups preparing accounts under UK GAAP, but not to those preparing accounts under IFRS.

The Schedule describes the acquisition method of accounting and stipulates the key elements of accounting, such as bringing in the acquired entity's results from the date of acquisition and including its net assets at their fair value at the date of acquisition. The Schedule's requirements are consistent with those in FRS 6, although they contain less detail.

Set out in Schedule 6 to SI 2008/410 (previously introduced into Schedule 4A to the Companies Act 1985 by the Companies Act 1989) are four conditions that must be met if merger accounting is to be applied. The first three conditions reflect what was thought to represent a merger at the time they were written, that is, that very little cash leaves the group, and the conditions are, not surprisingly, legalistic. The third condition is particularly onerous, requiring that the fair value of any consideration that is not equity shares does not exceed 10 per cent of the *nominal* value of the equity shares issued. Recently, a number of companies have used the true and fair override in group reconstruction scenarios to use merger accounting where this condition has not been met. The fourth condition is that adoption of the merger method of accounting accords with generally accepted accounting principles or practice. Hence if merger accounting is banned by a future accounting standard, the fourth condition will be failed, and hence merger accounting will not be permitted by legislation either.

If the four conditions are met and merger accounting is being applied, as with acquisition accounting, the Schedule sets out the key elements of merger accounting. Again, these are consistent with FRS 6's requirements.

Group reconstructions

FRS 6 explicitly provides that:

> 'A group reconstruction may be accounted for by using merger accounting, even though there is no business combination meeting the definition of a merger, provided:
>
> (a) the use of merger accounting is not prohibited by companies legislation (4A Sch 10);
> (b) the ultimate shareholders remain the same, and the rights of each such shareholder, relative to the others, are unchanged; and
> (c) no minority's interest in the net assets of the group is altered by the transfer'.

111

Future developments in UK GAAP

At the point that the revised version of IFRS 3 was issued, the ASB had not incorporated the original version into UK GAAP. It was waiting for the completion of Phase II of the IASB's project, namely IFRS 3 (2008), before taking any steps to alter UK GAAP, so that there could be one, not two, changes on this topic. Now, however, the ASB plans to retain FRSs 6, 7 and 10 until it has decided its strategy for convergence with IFRSs generally.

Share premium, merger relief and group reconstruction relief

The requirements relating to share premium, merger relief and group reconstruction relief are set out in ss. 610 to 616 of the Act. These are discussed briefly below. It is important to stress that the rules operate independently of the accounting method adopted in the consolidated financial statements. Similarly, they will apply irrespective of whether the financial statements are prepared in accordance with UK GAAP or IFRS. Their operation in individual circumstances depends upon the precise wording of the legislation.

The rules that follow apply to the issuing company's single entity financial statements.

The basic rule relating to setting up a share premium account is that if a company issues shares for an amount, cash and/or non-cash, that is greater than the nominal value of the shares, the amount in excess of the nominal value is credited to a share premium account. For example, if a company issues 100 shares, each with a nominal (or par) value of £1, for cash of £1,000, the company credits £100 to the share capital account and £900 to the share premium account. A share premium account is not distributable and there are restrictions on what it may be used for.

'Merger relief', as set out in s. 612 of the Act, is something of a misnomer. It might better be called relief from the need to set up a share premium account – which is exactly what it is. Merger relief arises in an entity's financial statements; it is not a consolidation issue. Moreover, it does not arise only when merger accounting is used in the related consolidated financial statements. In other words, it can be used in conjunction with using acquisition accounting on consolidation. Equally, it applies regardless of whether IFRS or UK GAAP is applied in the individual entity financial statements.

In summary, if company A, by issuing its equity shares, acquires 90 per cent or more of the equity share capital of company B, and A's shares are issued at a premium, the general requirement of s. 610 of the Act to set up a share premium account does not apply.

Note that there is nothing that says that the whole of the 90 per cent should be acquired in one tranche. For example, A might already hold 70 per cent of B as a result of an earlier (cash or shares) transaction. However, if A then issues equity to acquire the next 20 per cent of B's equity, relief under s. 612

arises and applies to the shares issued by A to acquire that 20 per cent, i.e. no share premium is recorded in respect of A's shares that are issued to acquire that last 20 per cent of B. Section 612 is mandatory, that is, there is no choice; no share premium is recorded. It does not specify what should be done instead. There are two possibilities. One is that the shares issued are still accounted for at fair value (or, under IAS 27, at some other balance); but the amount that would have been credited to the share premium account is instead credited to another reserve, generally called a 'merger reserve'. The other possibility is that under s. 615 the premium is disregarded completely, and the shares issued are simply recorded at their nominal value.

In addition to merger relief, the Act also provides, in s. 611, 'group reconstruction relief', which applies in certain intra-group transfers. This is similar to merger relief in that it is a relief from the need to set up a share premium account, but the details are different and more complex; in particular a share premium account can still be required under this section in some circumstances (although not necessarily for the full amount). The overall effect of group reconstruction relief is that where an asset is transferred within a (qualifying) group its carrying value in the acquiring company is generally not lower than it had been in its previous place in the group structure. However, the wording of s. 611 differs from that of s. 612. In particular, the generally accepted view is that relief under s. 611 is optional, although where s. 611 relief applies s. 612 relief is not available.

The final piece of the jigsaw is s. 615 of the Act. Under this section, if share premium relief or group reconstruction relief applies, and as a result an amount is not credited to the share premium account, it may be disregarded for the purposes of determining, in the acquiring company's single entity balance sheet, the carrying value of the investment in the acquired company.

For example, assume that shares are issued to acquire another company and merger relief under s. 612 is available. The nominal value of the shares issued is £100,000 and the fair value is £800,000. The £700,000 is not credited to the share premium account. Neither does it need to be taken into account for determining the carrying value of the investment. Since the s. 615 relief is optional, a company has the choice of recording the transaction either as shown in Box 11.1, or, using s. 615 relief, as shown in Box 11.2.

Whilst this is a matter of choice, most practitioners would take the approach in Box 11.2. A lower carrying value for the investment is helpful in that it gives

---

Box 11.1 *Recording investment at fair value*

Dr Investment in new subsidiary	£800,000
Cr Shares issued	£100,000
Cr Merger reserve	£700,000

> **Box 11.2** *Recording investment using s. 615 relief*
>
> | | |
> |---|---|
> | Dr Investment in new subsidiary | £100,000 |
> | Cr Shares issued | £100,000 |

the company less exposure to impairments. That is, without s. 615 relief the investment would be recorded initially at its full cost of £800,000. If it lost, say, £150,000 in value, it would need to be written down to a revised carrying value of £650,000. However, with the benefit of s. 615 relief, the investment could lose up to £700,000 of its value before it became necessary to make an impairment write-down.

The accounting treatment in the consolidated financial statements follows the acquisition accounting rules in IFRS 3 or the acquisition or merger accounting rules of the Act and FRS 6, irrespective of whether s. 615 relief is taken in the parent's entity financial statements.

12

Interaction of accounting with tax

Introduction

Company financial statements and corporate tax are closely related in a number of ways. First, although assessment of corporation tax is based on complex rules of tax law and practice, the starting point is the pre-tax profit shown in the company's annual statutory financial statements. Tax is levied at the entity, not consolidated, level so it is the individual company financial statements that are of relevance when preparing the tax computation. Second, financial statements need to reflect a company's obligations to pay tax. The most obvious example of this is the tax payable in respect of each year. However, in addition, accountants have developed accounting for 'deferred tax', the effect of which is that, generally, the tax effects of transactions are recognised in arriving at profit/loss in the same period that the transaction itself is recognised in arriving at profit/loss. Similarly so for other comprehensive income. Additionally, there is the question of how the move to IFRS at individual entity level affects tax assessment; although the group accounts of listed companies have now moved to IFRS, many individual entity accounts within those groups are still prepared using UK GAAP. These issues are discussed in turn. This chapter seeks to give an introductory guide to accounting aspects of the issues; it is not a guide to tax law or practice.

Accounting profit and its adjustment

Accounting profit – specifically, the profit before tax figure in the income statement/statement of comprehensive income – is the starting point for assessment of corporation tax. However, a number of adjustments are made. Examples of adjustments are:

- Depreciation of non-current (or fixed) assets that is charged in arriving at profit is added back, as it is not allowable for tax purposes. In its place there is a system of capital allowances, designed to give tax relief for certain types of capital expenditure. The amount and timing of capital allowances is based on tax law, which reflects the government's desire to give companies incentives to invest. Except by coincidence, capital

Box 12.1 *Example tax computation*	
	£
Profit before tax per the statutory accounts	1,000
Add: depreciation	200
Add: entertaining expenses	30
Less: tax-free grants	(60)
Less: capital allowances	(250)
Profit for tax purposes (i.e., taxable income)	920

allowances do not equate to accounting depreciation in any particular year, although in aggregate over the life of the asset the two will generally coincide. An example of the relationship between capital allowances and accounting depreciation is shown below, under the heading 'Deferred tax'.

- Certain types of expenditure are disallowable for tax purposes, for example, fines and some types of entertaining expenses. Where such costs are charged in arriving at accounting profit, they are added back for tax purposes.
- Some items of income, such as certain government grants, may not be taxable.
- Some items of expenditure that are charged in arriving at accounting profit are allowable for tax, but in different periods. For example, defined contribution pension costs are charged in arriving at accounting profit on an accruals basis, but are allowed for tax purposes when paid. This gives rise to a temporary (or in UK GAAP terminology, timing) difference, which again is reflected in deferred tax.

Hence an adjustment of accounting profit for tax purposes might look like that shown in Box 12.1.

If the accounting profit were the exact basis for tax purposes, one would expect tax payable of 30% × £1,000 = £300. However, tax payable in fact would be 30% × £920 = £276. The reduction of £24 is a mixture of items that are permanently different for accounting and tax purposes, such as entertaining and grants, and items that feature for both accounting and tax purposes, but whose timing is different, such as depreciation and capital allowances. Note that 28 per cent is currently the full rate of corporation tax; for many years prior to 1 April 2008 it was 30 per cent. A small companies rate, currently 21 per cent and expected to be 22 per cent from 1 April 2009, is payable on low profits. For simplicity, the worked examples that follow generally use 30 per cent.

Accounting for current and deferred tax

Current tax

In IFRS, there is one accounting standard, IAS 12 'Income taxes', which deals with both current and deferred taxes, although the main focus of that standard is on deferred tax.

Current tax is the tax charged on the profits for the year. There are very few rules about accounting for current tax and in general these are uncontroversial. Current tax is charged as an expense, or income in some loss-making situations, in arriving at profit/loss; it is charged in the income statement unless the tax in question relates to a gain or loss that is recognised outside profit or loss. If a gain or loss is recognised in other comprehensive income, the related tax is also recognised in other comprehensive income[1] and if a gain or loss is recognised directly in equity the related tax is also recognised directly in equity. UK GAAP contains similar rules, albeit these are set out in a separate accounting standard, FRS 16 'Current tax'.

Deferred tax

Accounting for deferred tax is a much more complex issue than accounting for current tax. The basic premise is that accounting only for current tax understates a company's liabilities (or assets), as there may be additional liabilities (or assets) that crystallise in future years yet that originate from the transactions and events of the earlier year. An example may clarify.

A company might operate a bonus scheme for senior employees; under the scheme it has accrued for bonuses of £100,000 in its financial statements for the year ended 31 December 2008. However, it will not pay those bonuses to employees until October 2009. Because the bonus is paid more than nine months after the end of the year in which it is accrued, the £100,000 expense reduces the taxable profits for 2009, not 2008. Thus, the bonus is charged as an expense when calculating the accounting profits for 2008, but only reduces the current tax charge for 2009, so a temporary, or timing, mismatch arises. In 2009, the company's tax charge will be lower by £30,000 (30 per cent of £100,000) as a result of the bonus payment.

Accounting rules require companies to recognise deferred tax liabilities and assets, such as the £30,000 in the above example. The impact on the income statement/statement of comprehensive income of the bonus and its tax effects can be shown in tabular form in Box 12.2.

The end result is that the accounting profit is reduced by the bonus accrual, net of tax, in 2008 even though the company does not receive the tax benefit (by means of paying less tax to HM Revenue & Customs) until 2009.

1 See ch. 9.

Box 12.2 *Impact on the income statement/statement of comprehensive income of the bonus (paid more than 9 months after the year to which it relates) and its tax effects*

	2008 £	2009 £
Bonus accrual	(100,000)	–
Current tax charge	–	30,000
Deferred tax	30,000	(30,000)
Net impact on profit	(70,000)	–

The IFRS rules are found in IAS 12 'Income Taxes'; it is a complex standard to read and digest, containing many rules. However, the end result of applying the standard is that, generally, the tax consequences of a transaction or event are recognised in the same period and place (part of profit/loss, other comprehensive income or directly in equity) as the transaction or event itself.

IAS 12 takes a balance sheet approach; its fundamental principle is that if the recovery of an asset (for example, the cash flows that it will generate from use or sale) or the settlement of the carrying amount of a liability would make future tax payments larger or smaller than they would be if such recovery or settlement were to have no tax consequences, then deferred tax is recognised.

To put this principle into action, IAS 12 requires an entity to calculate 'temporary differences' by comparing the book value of its assets and liabilities with their 'tax base'. The tax base of an asset or liability is defined as 'the amount attributed to that asset or liability for tax purposes'. In the main, the tax base of an asset is the amount that will be deductible for tax purposes against any taxable economic benefits that will flow to an enterprise when it recovers the carrying amount of the asset; and the tax base of a liability is the carrying value of the liability less any amount that will be deductible for tax purposes in respect of that liability in future periods. In the above accrued bonus example, therefore, at the balance sheet date for the 2008 accounts (31 December 2008), the book value of the liability is £100,000 and the tax base of this liability is nil (being the carrying value of the liability of £100,000 less the amount that will be tax deductible in 2009, also £100,000), thus there is a 'temporary difference' of £100,000 and deferred tax is calculated by multiplying this amount by the tax rate. Using a tax rate of 30 per cent, a deferred tax asset of £30,000 is recognised. Reverting back to IAS 12's principle, the settlement of that accrued liability will lead to a lower tax charge for 2009, thus, at 31 December 2008, there is a deferred tax asset of £30,000.

Consider another example: a company buys a new machine for £1,200 in year 1. For accounting purposes, the machine is assessed as having a useful life of six years, with no scrap value at the end of that six years. Hence it is

---

Box 12.3 *Accounting depreciation and tax capital allowances in respect of a new machine*

Year	Accounting		Tax	
1	Cost	1,200	Cost	1,200
	Depreciation	(200)	Capital allowances	(240)
	NBV	1,000	WDV	960
2	Depreciation	(200)	Capital allowances	(192)
	NBV	800	WDV	768
3	Depreciation	(200)	Capital allowances	(154)
	NBV	600	WDV	614
4	Depreciation	(200)	Capital allowances	(123)
	NBV	400	WDV	491
5	Depreciation	(200)	Capital allowances	(98)
	NBV	200	WDV	393
6	Depreciation	(200)	Capital allowances	(393)*
	NBV	NIL	WDV	NIL

* Whether capital allowances in year 6 are the remaining £393 in the form of a balancing allowance on sale for zero or are 20 per cent of £393, with the remainder to be allowed over future years, depends on a number of factors. We assume £393 for ease of illustration.

---

depreciated on a straight-line basis over six years. For tax purposes, we assume it will attract capital allowances at 20 per cent on a reducing-balance basis. Therefore, the pattern of book depreciation and capital allowances over the six years' life is as shown in Box 12.3.

At the first balance sheet date, there is an asset with a carrying value of £1,000 and under IAS 12 the asset's tax base is £960, thus there is a 'temporary difference' of £40 and deferred tax is calculated by multiplying this amount by the tax rate. A deferred tax liability of £12 is recognised if the appropriate tax rate is 30 per cent. Explaining this against the standard's principle is slightly different: first, we have to assume that the asset will generate income (directly, or indirectly in conjunction with other assets) of at least £1,000 – if this is not true then the asset should be written down as impaired. Thus the asset will generate taxable income of at least £1,000. However, the asset will only lead to *taxable* income being reduced in future years by £960, as this is the balance of capital allowances that is left. Consequently, taxable income will be a net £40 higher and so (using a 30 per cent tax rate) tax of £12 will be payable as a result of recovering the asset's balance sheet carrying value. Accordingly, a deferred tax liability of £12 must be recognised in the balance sheet.

Box 12.4 sets out the calculation of temporary differences and thus the deferred tax.

The impact on profit/loss of the asset only is set out below (Box 12.5).

Box 12.4 *Calculation of temporary differences and deferred tax*

Year	Depre- ciation	Net book value	Capital allowances	Tax written down value	Temporary difference (NBV less tax WDV)	Tax (30%) on the temporary difference	Change in tax on TD over the year
1	200	1,000	240	960	40	12	(12)
2	200	800	192	768	32	10	2
3	200	600	154	614	(14)	(4)	14
4	200	400	123	491	(91)	(27)	23
5	200	200	98	393	(193)	(58)	31
6	200	–	393	–	–	–	(58)

Box 12.5 *Impact on profit/loss of the asset*

Years	1 £	2 £	3 £	4 £	5 £	6 £
Depreciation	(200)	(200)	(200)	(200)	(200)	(200)
Current tax	72	58	46	37	29	118
Deferred tax	(12)	2	14	23	31	(58)
Net effect on profit	(140)	(140)	(140)	(140)	(140)	(140)

Box 12.6 *Example adjustments*

Add: entertaining expenses	30
Less: tax-free grants	(60)

Other sources of temporary differences are the different tax and accounting treatment of pension costs and share-based payment. In each case, they are accounted for in one period, but the tax consequences arise, to some degree at least, in other periods. However, certain differences – such as entertaining expenses (which do not attract tax relief) – are permanent in their impact.

The table in Box 12.1, in which the accounting profit was adjusted for tax purposes, included the adjustments shown in Box 12.6.

The first item in Box 12.6 is non-deductible for tax purposes and the second is non-taxable. Under UK GAAP, they are called 'permanent differences' and this phrase is likely to continue to be used colloquially within the UK under IFRS; there is no formal term in IAS 12 for such items. IAS 12 refers to temporary differences, both positive and negative, but in this case there is no difference. The items will never be taxable or deductible, and they cause the company's effective tax rate (the tax charge expressed as a percentage of profit before tax) to be different from the standard rate of, say, 30 per cent. Deferred tax accounting has no role here: there is no liability or asset; the effective tax rate will correctly be less than the standard tax rate. That is, in this example it will be less, as the tax-free income exceeds the disallowable expenses. In a different example, the effect could be the other way round.

The UK GAAP rules are found in FRS 19 'Deferred tax'. This refers to 'timing differences' and permanent differences and, although it takes a different approach to IAS 12, it gives the same answer in the two examples above. Indeed, the end outcome of applying FRS 19 is similar to IAS 12, with certain exceptions, including:

(i) Revaluation gains. Under IAS 12, if an entity revalues an asset upwards from, say, 100 to 150, deferred tax is recognised on the increase in value of 50 (assuming that the increase of 50 is expected to lead to an equivalent amount of taxable income and, as is generally the case in the UK, the asset's tax base is unaffected). On the other hand, FRS 19 argues that there is no liability to pay additional tax on the gain in excess of cost until the asset is sold at such higher amount; the revaluation of itself does not cause any future tax liabilities to arise, and thus no deferred tax should be recognised, unless, by the balance sheet date, there is a binding sale agreement.

(ii) Fair value adjustments in acquisition accounting. When accounting, in group financial statements, for the acquisition of a new subsidiary the net assets of the acquired subsidiary are stated at their fair values. Where the fair values differ from the tax base of the items, as will often be the case, IAS 12 requires deferred tax to be recognised on the difference, whereas FRS 19 generally does not.

(iii) Discounting. UK GAAP allows discounting of deferred tax liabilities. This is not commonly applied, but can make a big difference where, as for example in some utility companies, the liabilities stretch out over a long period.

The UK GAAP view is that deferred tax should only be recognised in respect of inevitable consequences of transactions or events that have already occurred.

HM Revenue & Customs and the move to IFRS

As noted above, the starting point for tax assessment is the profit shown in the company's annual statutory financial statements. Until 2005, for UK companies, this was always the profit as calculated under UK GAAP. In 2005, listed companies changed the accounting in their consolidated financial statements to IFRS; and they, together with other companies, had the choice of remaining with UK GAAP or moving to IFRS at the entity financial statements level. The choice of moving to IFRS can be taken at any point, although, in the main, once taken, cannot be reversed. One of the big factors for a company in deciding whether to move to IFRS at the entity level is the effect that such a move might have on tax assessments.

When IFRS was introduced, HM Revenue & Customs (HMRC) issued a policy statement which said that the measures it was introducing were 'to ensure that companies choosing to adopt IAS to draw up their accounts receive *broadly equivalent* tax treatment to companies that continue to use UK Generally Accepted Accounting Practice (UK GAAP)' (emphasis added). This statement is, at best, an oversimplification. What it seems to mean in practice is that: (1) where there is a specific tax rule affecting an item, that rule continues to apply; but (2) where tax follows GAAP, and profits under IFRS are higher (or lower) than under UK GAAP, tax assessments will also be higher (or lower) in an equivalent manner.

As an example of (1), revaluation gains on investment property are recognised in arriving at profit/loss under IFRS, whereas they are recognised outside of profit/loss under UK GAAP. IFRS profits are higher than under UK GAAP for such companies at times of a rising property market. However, there is a specific tax rule and such gains are not taxable until sale, so the move to IFRS does not affect the timing of when the tax is payable.

Simply put, (2) means that if profits under IFRS are higher (or lower) than under UK GAAP, the tax payable is likely to be higher (or lower), although there are some specific exclusions, such as the investment property example above. This could arise either: (a) in terms of timing – where revenue or expenses are recognised earlier (or later) than under UK GAAP; or (b) in terms of permanent differences – where an item is recognised as income (or expense) under IFRS, whereas it is not so recognised, or not recognised at the same amount, under UK GAAP.

For example, if a receipt of £300 is recognised in arriving at profit/loss over a three-year period under UK GAAP, but under IFRS is recognised as revenue immediately, then on a move to IFRS the tax treatment would, in a simple case, follow the accounting, and the tax payable of £90 (£300 × 30%) would be accelerated into year 1, rather than spread over the three years.

There are in place rules that seek to stop companies from taking advantage of using a mixture of IFRS and UK GAAP within a group. If one company in a group uses IFRS and has a transaction with another company in the group that uses UK GAAP, and if the transaction has, as a main benefit, the conferring of a tax advantage as a result of different accounting treatments, the IFRS company will have to use UK GAAP for the transaction for tax purposes. Indeed, BERR[2] has legislated to make it rare for some companies in a group to use UK GAAP and others to use IFRS; all UK subsidiaries within a group should use the same

2 Formerly the DTI.

accounting standards – either IFRS or UK GAAP – unless there is a 'good reason' for a group company to use a different basis (s. 407 CA 2006). BERR has given some examples of genuine cases where mixed GAAP within a group would be acceptable. An example of an acceptable use is where a group using IFRS acquired a subsidiary that had not been using IFRS; in the first year of acquisition, it might not be practical for the newly acquired company to switch to IFRS straight away. However, tax is not among the examples given.

13
Assets

Introduction

The key questions that arise in relation to assets are: what is the definition of an asset; which assets are recognised on balance sheet; when are they first recognised; how are the assets that are recognised on balance sheet measured; and whether the assets should be written down for impairment. There are also questions of how assets should be classified and presented on balance sheets, and questions of depreciation. These issues are considered in turn.

Definition of an asset

In a formal sense, the IASB's Framework for the Preparation and Presentation of Financial Statements[1] defines an asset as 'a resource controlled by the entity as a result of past events and from which future economic benefits are expected to flow to the entity'. The Framework explains[2] that:

> 'The future economic benefit embodied in an asset is the potential to contribute, directly or indirectly, to the flow of cash and cash equivalents to the entity. The potential may be a productive one that is part of the operating activities of the entity. It may also take the form of convertibility into cash or cash equivalents or a capability to reduce cash outflows, such as when an alternative manufacturing process lowers the costs of production'.

Less formally, an asset is something of value that a company controls.

Recognition of assets

From the definition, it might appear that all a company's assets are recognised on the balance sheet. In fact, they are recognised only if they meet the recognition criteria: it is probable that the entity will get the economic benefits of the asset and that the asset can be measured reliably. For this reason, and in some cases because the asset in question is not controlled by the company, assets such as a company's reputation, its skilled workforce, training, advertising and its self-developed brands – valuable though they may be – are not recognised on balance sheet.

1 See para. 49(a).   2 See para. 53.

Expenditure on research is not recognised on balance sheet as an asset; it is not possible at the research stage of a project to demonstrate that it is probable that economic benefits will flow to the entity. This may be so also in the early stages of the development phase of the project. However, once it is probable that the development project will generate economic benefits for the entity and various other specified criteria are met, an asset is recognised.

Measurement of assets

Traditionally, accounting has been strongly based on historical cost. As noted in chapter 7 at p. 63, one of the recent developments in accounting is the increased use of fair value or a similar valuation basis, resulting in a mixed measurement model. The use of fair value rather than cost varies depending on the type of asset, and also varies to some degree as between IFRS and UK GAAP. For example, property, plant and equipment may be measured in both IFRS and UK GAAP at either cost or valuation.[3] For investment properties, however, while there is the same choice in IFRS,[4] valuation is compulsory under UK GAAP.[5] For investments and other financial assets, the picture is more complex, as it depends into which of the four categories of financial asset[6] the item is classified under IAS 39 and FRS 26. Goodwill is accounted for at cost under both IFRS and UK GAAP. In slight contrast, whilst other intangibles are nearly always carried on a cost basis, they can in principle be carried on a valuation basis, but the criteria are strict and as a result that treatment is rare. Under IAS 41, biological assets are carried at an amount based on fair value. In general, current assets are carried at the lower of cost and net realisable value, for example, inventories, although some current assets, such as financial assets held for trading and derivatives, are carried at fair value.

Impairment of assets

Whether an asset's carrying value is based on cost or fair value, there is an underlying principle that it should not be carried on a balance sheet at more than its 'recoverable amount'. That is, in stating an asset on a balance sheet at a particular amount, there is an implication that it is worth that amount or more. In this context, 'worth' could mean that the asset could be sold for at least that amount, or it could refer to the fact that it (or it together with other assets) will generate cash flows over a period of at least that amount in present value terms (see below).

More formally expressed, recoverable amount is the higher of:

- fair value less costs to sell (UK GAAP term – net realisable value (NRV)); and
- value in use.

3 IAS 16; FRS 15.   4 IAS 40.   5 SSAP 19.   6 See ch. 17.

The fair value less costs to sell, or NRV, is 'the amount obtainable from the sale of an asset . . . in an arm's length transaction between knowledgeable, willing parties, less the costs of disposal'.[7]

Value in use is 'the present value of the future cash flows expected to be derived from an asset'.[8] 'Present value' refers to the time value of money. For example, if an asset will generate £105 in one year's time and interest rates are 5 per cent, the present value of that cash flow is £100. This process is also called 'discounting'.

The notion of recoverable amount being the higher of two measures as set out above reflects commercial reality. That is, if an asset has a 'fair value less costs to sell' of £80, but a value in use of £100, a rational management would keep the asset rather than sell it. Hence the recoverable amount is £100. Thus, if the asset's carrying value (for example, for property, plant and equipment, cost or value less accumulated depreciation – see below) is less than £100, no impairment write down is required; but if the carrying value is above £100, the asset has to be written down to £100. If the asset's carrying amount were between £80 and £100, say, £95, the asset would not be written up to £100 (assuming that it had not previously been written down for impairment); it simply would not be impaired – its carrying amount is expected to be recovered in full.

The rules on impairment of assets – when impairment testing should be carried out; the methodology; and when, and to which asset, an impairment write down is required – are complex. It should be recognised, however, that impairment testing is an imprecise art. An asset's 'fair value less costs to sell' might be easily established, although that will depend on the type of asset. However, an asset's value in use is at best an estimate and is only as good as the forecast of future cash flows that the asset will generate – such a forecast is necessarily uncertain, especially when the time horizon extends to a long period. Having said that, it is important for companies to test assets for impairment at appropriate times, as otherwise they risk being carried on balance sheets at unjustifiable amounts. This is one of those occasions when accountants speak of the numbers being 'roughly right rather than exactly wrong'.

Impairment, as discussed above, primarily applies to non-current (or fixed) assets, although the same underlying principle – that an asset should not be carried at above its recoverable amount – applies to all assets. In the case of some current assets, for example, inventories, the principle is achieved by using as the measurement basis the lower of cost and net realisable value.

Classification and presentation of assets

Under IFRS, unless a presentation based on liquidity is more relevant, current and non-current assets have to be presented separately on the face of the

7 IAS 36, para. 6.   8 IAS 36, para 6.

balance sheet. In UK GAAP, the terms 'current' and 'fixed' are used. With minor differences, the effect is similar.

As a minimum the following different types of asset have to be presented on an IFRS balance sheet:

(a) property, plant and equipment;
(b) investment property;
(c) intangible assets;
(d) financial assets (excluding amounts shown under (e), (h) and (i));
(e) investments accounted for using the equity method;
(f) biological assets;
(g) inventories;
(h) trade and other receivables;
(i) cash and cash equivalents; and
(j) the total of assets classified as held for sale and assets included in disposal groups classified as held for sale in accordance with IFRS 5 'Non-current Assets Held for Sale and Discontinued Operations'.

Classification as between current and non-current is determined by IAS 1 (2007), para. 66, which states that:

'An entity shall classify an asset as current when:

(a) it expects to realise the asset, or intends to sell or consume it, in its normal operating cycle;
(b) it holds the asset primarily for the purpose of trading;
(c) it expects to realise the asset within twelve months after the reporting period; or
(d) the asset is cash or a cash equivalent (as defined in IAS 7) unless the asset is restricted from being exchanged or used to settle a liability for at least twelve months after the reporting period.

An entity shall classify all other assets as non-current.'

Although item (c) in the definition refers to twelve months, the reference in (a) to an entity's normal operating cycle is not limited to twelve months and thus assets could be presented as current even though they are not expected to be converted to cash form within one year of the balance sheet date.

For UK GAAP, the Companies Act defines fixed assets as those 'which are intended for use on a continuing basis in the company's activities' and current assets as 'assets not intended for such use'. Again, the definition of current assets is not limited to one year.

Depreciation

Some non-current (or fixed) assets last for a long period of time and maintain their value, whereas others lose value as time passes. For example, a non-current investment may, if well selected, hold or increase its value over a long period. The same applies, generally, to land. In contrast, a building, a piece of plant or IT equipment may lose its value over a period. For this latter category of assets, depreciation is relevant. The term 'depreciation' is used in connection with property, plant and equipment (tangible fixed assets). Depreciation is a common phenomenon in everyday life: many non-accountants are expert at the depreciation of cars, for example. Depreciation, for accounting purposes, is defined as: 'the systematic allocation of the depreciable amount of an asset over its useful life', where depreciable amount is 'the cost of an asset, or other amount substituted for cost, less its residual value'.[9] The UK definition is similar.

The key point that the definitions make clear is that depreciation is an exercise in allocation of cost (less residual value) over accounting periods. It does not seek to reflect interim valuations of assets. For example, a company might own a car costing £10,000 and expect to keep it for four years, at the end of which period its expected residual value will be £4,000. If so, the depreciable amount would be £6,000 and the depreciation charge against profits, on a straight-line basis, would be £1,500 each year for the four years. Thus, at the end of the first year, the car would be carried in the balance sheet at a net book value (NBV) of £8,500. This is so, even though the second-hand value of the car is very likely to be less than £8,500. The car is not impaired (see above) as the company expects to carry on using it profitably over the next three years, at the end of which it will be sold for an estimated £4,000.

Like many aspects of accounting, depreciation involves estimates. The useful life of the asset and its residual value at the end of that life can only be estimates. For that reason, IAS 16 and FRS 15 require companies to keep under review their estimates: for example, if an asset looks likely to last longer than originally expected, the depreciation profile should be slowed down. Despite such adjustments, it is quite common for an asset, when sold, to realise an amount more or less than its residual value. Any such difference is reported in the income statement (or income statement part of the statement of comprehensive income) as a profit or loss on sale.

Amortisation

Goodwill and other intangibles are covered by their own accounting standards: IAS 38 and IFRS 3 in IFRS; and FRS 10 in UK GAAP. Accountants use the term 'amortisation' for intangibles, rather than depreciation, although the meaning is the same.

Under IFRS, goodwill is not amortised, but is tested annually for impairment. Other intangibles are amortised in the main, but non-amortisation (replaced with annual impairment testing) is required if an indefinite life can

9 IAS 16, para 6.

be demonstrated. For example, patents and copyrights are generally amortised, whereas some brands are not.

While in principle intangibles are subject to amortisation under UK GAAP, there are exceptions. FRS 10 envisages a minority practice under which goodwill and intangibles need not be amortised if the facts of the case demonstrate an indefinite life. This requires a true and fair override of the CA 2006 (UK GAAP financial statements only) in the case of goodwill; and for both goodwill and intangibles the amortisation is replaced by annual impairment testing.

Disclosure

Various details of assets have to be given in the notes to the financial statements, but for the most part these merely provide additional details about items that are recognised on balance sheet. Examples include movements on property, plant and equipment and intangible assets, and details about investments. There is also a requirement[10] to disclose certain contingent assets; these are not recognised on balance sheet.

10 IAS 37, para. 89; FRS 12, para. 94.

14
Liabilities

Introduction

As noted in chapter 1, a balance sheet can be considered, in summary form, as follows:

$$\text{Assets } \textit{less} \text{ liabilities} = \text{shareholders' equity}$$

Shareholders' equity is called 'capital and reserves' in the Companies Act format, and was generally called 'shareholders' funds' under UK GAAP.

Hence liabilities are one of the major components of a balance sheet. The key questions that arise in relation to liabilities are: what is the definition of a liability; how are they distinguished from shareholders' equity; which liabilities are recognised on the balance sheet; when are they recognised; and how are the liabilities that are recognised on the balance sheet measured. There are also questions of how liabilities should be presented on balance sheets, and questions of disclosure, including disclosure of contingent liabilities. These issues are considered in turn.

Definition of a liability

During the 1980s and, to a lesser extent, earlier, some companies had sought to distort their accounting by setting up liabilities – in particular provisions for items such as restructuring costs – on a large-scale but discretionary basis. For example, a company might have had a more profitable year than expected, but would know that it was likely to incur costs in future years in restructuring its business. It would, therefore, set up, at the end of the profitable year, a provision for these future costs, thereby reducing the profits of that year. When the costs were subsequently incurred, they would be set against the provision rather than reducing the profits of that later (perhaps less profitable) year. However, this technique fell into disrepute as it amounted to little more than profit smoothing, and failed to represent the results of the year in question.

Standard-setters sought to remedy this and, in the 1990s, IAS 37 (IFRS) and FRS 12 (UK GAAP), both entitled 'Provisions, Contingent liabilities and Contingent assets', were developed as part of a joint project. Consequently, not only are the two standards consistent, but in many places contain exactly the same wording.

A liability is defined in the IASB's Framework for the Preparation and Presentation of Financial Statements and IAS 37 'Provisions, Contingent Liabilities and Contingent Assets' as 'a present obligation of the entity arising from past events, the settlement of which is expected to result in an outflow from the entity of resources embodying economic benefits'. A similar definition is found in UK GAAP (the ASB's Statement of Principles and FRSs 5 and 12).

The IASB's and ASB's definitions take a much more precise and restrictive approach than previously to what can be regarded as a liability.

The definitions start by saying that, in order for there to be a liability, there must already be an *obligation*. This means that the entity is not free to avoid the outflow of resources. If a company merely had an idea that it might undertake a restructuring in a year's time, that would not count as a liability, as the company could abort or change its plans – it is not committed to that course of action and can avoid the costs involved if it so chooses. Embodied in the definitions also is that, for a liability to exist at the balance sheet date, the obligation to transfer economic benefits must have resulted from a past transaction or event. So, for example, an obligation under a warranty would be recognised only to the extent of goods actually sold at the end of the accounting year.

The definition of a liability applies in a number of contexts. In this chapter, we consider the general case of creditors and provisions. In chapter 17, we consider capital instruments issued by a company such as various types of debt instrument, preference shares and ordinary shares. Careful analysis is sometimes needed to establish which of those should be accounted for as liabilities and which as shareholders' equity.

Recognition of liabilities

A liability might exist in terms of the definition (see above), but that does not automatically mean that it should be recognised on balance sheet. This point is well explained in the accounting standard on provisions (IAS 37 'Provisions, Contingent Liabilities and Contingent Assets' and the similarly titled FRS 12). This clarifies that by 'provisions' it means 'liabilities of uncertain timing or amount'. However, much of its thinking applies to all liabilities. IAS 37 states that:

> 'A provision shall be recognised when:
>
> (a) an entity has a present obligation (legal or constructive) as a result of a past event;
> (b) it is probable that an outflow of resources embodying economic benefits will be required to settle the obligation; and
> (c) a reliable estimate can be made of the amount of the obligation.
>
> If these conditions are not met, no provision shall be recognised.'[1]

1 IAS 37, para. 14.

From this quotation, it is clear that where an obligation exists, it is recognised only if there is a probable transfer to another party of economic benefits. For example, a company might guarantee the borrowings of a second company. A guarantee is a legal obligation. However, if the second company is financially sound, it is unlikely that the first company will have to pay up under its guarantee. Hence no liability is recognised by the first company.

Furthermore, obligations are recognised only if a reliable estimate can be made of the amount of the liability. For example, a company might have potential obligations in relation to claims from customers or employees in respect of damage of some kind. It may be that a payment is considered 'probable', but, in the early stages of the case, it may be very difficult to estimate the liability with sufficient reliability for inclusion in the balance sheet. These circumstances are expected to be extremely rare, although if an obligation is not recognised, it is still appropriate to give note disclosure (see below).

Liabilities are recognised not only in respect of legal obligations, but also in respect of *constructive obligations*. These are obligations that derive:

> 'from an entity's actions where:
>
> (a) by an established pattern of past practice, published policies or a sufficiently specific current statement, the entity has indicated to other parties that it will accept certain responsibilities; and
>
> (b) as a result, the entity has created a valid expectation on the part of those other parties that it will discharge those responsibilities.'[2]

Examples of constructive obligations include those arising as a result of environmental damage and reorganisations. In the former case, while the law requires some environmental damage to be rectified, there may be other examples where there is no legal requirement to rectify, but the company has an announced policy and an established practice of rectifying damage of that kind. This creates an expectation among third parties that the company will continue to follow its policy and practice, and this gives rise to the need to record a constructive obligation on the balance sheet. In the case of restructuring or reorganisation of a business, similar principles apply. However, here, because restructuring is a common example, and perhaps because of earlier abuses in this area, IAS 37 and FRS 12 are more specific:

> 'A constructive obligation to restructure arises only when an entity:
>
> (a) has a detailed formal plan for the restructuring identifying at least:
>> (i) the business or part of a business concerned;
>> (ii) the principal locations affected;
>> (iii) the location, function, and approximate number of employees who will be compensated for terminating their services;
>> (iv) the expenditures that will be undertaken; and
>> (v) when the plan will be implemented; and

2 IAS 37, para. 10.

(b) has raised a valid expectation in those affected that it will carry out the restructuring by starting to implement that plan or announcing its main features to those affected by it.'[3]

The aim, in connection with constructive obligations, is that a company should record a liability where it is for all practical purposes obliged to incur the expenditure in question. Perhaps it is not legally committed to incur the expenditure; but if it did not incur it, it would be damaged from a reputational point of view. For example, if a company announced a restructuring in sufficiently specific terms to meet para. 72 (quoted above), it could in theory revoke its decision and say to employees that it had changed its mind, and their jobs are to be maintained after all. However, this is not the situation in which most companies would wish to find themselves.

Measurement of liabilities

Accounting has largely moved away from prudence towards neutrality of measurement. Hence liabilities should be measured at the best estimate of the amount that will be required to settle them at the balance sheet date. This amount is generally determined by estimating the expected outflows, without adding a further amount (sometimes called a 'cushion'), and discounting them to establish a 'present value', reflecting the time value of money. The equivalent applies in the context of normal creditors – that is, those where, unlike provisions, the amount and timing are known. If an amount owed to a creditor does not bear interest and is not payable for, say, two years, it similarly should be recorded at its present value to reflect the time value of money. For example, if interest rates were 10 per cent, £110 payable in one year or £121 payable in two years would be equivalent to £100 payable today. Discounting should be done where the effect is material. In general, discounting starts to become material if the period involved is more than one year, although this also depends on the absolute amount.

Presentation of liabilities on balance sheets

As explained above in chapter 9, unless a presentation based on liquidity is more relevant and is reliable, current and non-current liabilities have to be presented separately on the face of the balance sheet under IFRS. An entity has to classify a liability as current when:

- it expects to settle the liability in its normal operating cycle;
- it holds the liability primarily for the purpose of trading;
- the liability is due to be settled within twelve months after the reporting period; or

3 IAS 37, para. 72 (FRS 12, para. 77).

- the entity does not have an unconditional right to defer settlement of the liability for at least twelve months after the reporting period.

Whichever method of presentation is adopted, current/non-current or liquidity, where a category includes amounts payable both within and beyond twelve months after the balance sheet date, the amount that is payable more than twelve months after the balance sheet date must be disclosed. This disclosure does not have to be on the face of the balance sheet.

Current liabilities are defined more narrowly in UK GAAP. The determining factor is whether the liability is to be settled within twelve months of the balance sheet date; if it is, the liability is current.

Under IAS 1, the minimum that must appear on the face of the balance sheet in respect of liabilities is:

- trade and other payables;
- provisions;
- financial liabilities (excluding amounts shown under trade and other payables and under provisions);
- liabilities for current tax, as defined in IAS 12 'Income Taxes';
- deferred tax liabilities, as defined in IAS 12; and
- liabilities included in disposal groups classified as held for sale in accordance with IFRS 5.

As may be noted from this balance sheet presentation, provisions are shown separately from trade and other payables, short and long. This is because provisions are, relative to these payables, uncertain as to timing or amount.

Current liabilities, as seen from the above definition, are generally regarded as being involved in the operating cycle of the business. Non-current liabilities, on the other hand, are viewed as part of a business's longer-term financing. A business needs a certain amount of long-term finance; part of this is provided in the form of shareholders' equity, and often part in the form of long-term liabilities. The relationship between these is known as 'gearing'. Consider the summarised balance sheet in Box 14.1 and assume that non-current liabilities comprise solely debt.

Gearing for this company can be expressed in a number of ways: there is no single agreed definition. A popular measure is long-term debt (40) expressed as a percentage of shareholders' equity (80), i.e. 50 per cent. An alternative is to express the extent to which total long-term capital is provided by debt, i.e. $40/120 = 33.3$ per cent.

Disclosure, including contingent liabilities

Various details of liabilities have to be given in the notes to the accounts, but, for the most part, these merely provide additional details about items that are recognised on balance sheet, such as bank loans. In this respect, no further

---

Box 14.1 *Summarised balance sheet*

Non-current assets		100
Current assets		70
Total assets		170
Shareholders' equity		80
Non-current liabilities	40	
Current liabilities	50	
Total liabilities		90
Total equity and liabilities		170

comment is needed. However, there is a further class of disclosures that warrant comment, namely those in relation to contingent liabilities.

A contingent liability is defined as:

'(a) a possible obligation that arises from past events and whose existence will be confirmed only by the occurrence or non-occurrence of one or more uncertain future events not wholly within the control of the entity; or

(b) a present obligation that arises from past events but is not recognised because:

(i) it is not probable that an outflow of resources embodying economic benefits will be required to settle the obligation; or

(ii) the amount of the obligation cannot be measured with sufficient reliability.'[4]

Part (a) of the definition deals with those liabilities that are genuinely contingent, that is, whether the liability arises depends on whether an uncertain future event occurs. Part (b) deals with matters that are not contingent in the same way. Rather they are actual liabilities (such as an existing guarantee) where an outflow of resources is not likely; or they are those very rare cases where there is an actual liability, but it is not recognised on the balance sheet because it is not possible to measure it with sufficient reliability. Despite these differences, the accounting implications are the same, namely that contingent liabilities should not be recognised on balance sheet. However, certain details should be given about contingent liabilities in the notes to the accounts:

'Unless the possibility of any outflow in settlement is remote, an entity shall disclose for each class of contingent liability at the end of the reporting

4 IAS 37, para. 10; FRS 12, para. 2 is similar.

period a brief description of the nature of the contingent liability and, where practicable:

(a) an estimate of its financial effect, measured under paragraphs 36–52;
(b) an indication of the uncertainties relating to the amount or timing of any outflow; and
(c) the possibility of any reimbursement.'[5]

---

5 IAS 37, para. 86; FRS 12, para. 91 is similar.

15
Leases

Introduction

The accounting standard dealing with this topic is IAS 17 'Leases'. Its UK GAAP counterpart, SSAP 21 'Accounting for leases and hire purchase contracts', is very similar, taking the same overall approach, although there are some differences between the two standards – see 'Leases under UK GAAP' below.

IAS 17 was issued in 1982 and SSAP 21 two years later. These were the first international and UK accounting standards explicitly to require the substance, rather than the legal form, of a transaction to be reflected in the accounting treatment. A decade later in the UK, FRS 5 set out a much more comprehensive role for substance over form. This has no IFRS equivalent; hence substance over form, while referred to in the frameworks of both bodies, is a stronger notion in UK GAAP than in IFRS. Nevertheless, this does not detract from the stance taken in IAS 17.

In a nutshell, IAS 17 and SSAP 21 both divide leases into two categories, finance leases and operating leases, with different accounting treatments for each. With a finance lease, a lessee is in substance buying the asset and paying on deferred terms in the same way as it would if it took out a loan to buy the asset and was then repaying the loan. Accordingly, the standards require the asset to be capitalised by the lessee (and depreciated over its useful economic life or, if shorter, the lease term) and the related obligation to be recognised on the lessee's balance sheet as equivalent to a loan. For other leases (operating leases), the argument is that the asset has not in substance been purchased by the lessee and thus the asset and related financing obligation are not recognised on its balance sheet. Instead, the lease payments are charged in arriving at profit/loss, generally on a straight-line basis, over the lease term. Lessor accounting mirrors that of the lessee. That is, a lessor removes the asset from its balance sheet when it leases the asset out under a finance lease and leaves the asset on its balance sheet when it leases the asset out under an operating lease.

SIC 15 'Operating leases – incentives' contains rules on accounting for operating leases when incentives, such as upfront cash payments, reimbursement of expenses or rent-free periods, are provided to induce a lessee to enter into a lease. In essence, the incentives are amortised over the lease term. SIC 27 'Evaluating the substance of transactions involving the legal form of a lease' sets out guidance on when IAS 17 should determine the appropriate accounting treatment of a lease and when, instead, a series of transactions, involving one or more leases, should be viewed as a whole.

IFRIC 4 'Determining whether an arrangement contains a lease' sets out guidance for determining when IAS 17 should be applied to a transaction involving the right to use an asset in return for a series of payments even though there is no lease in legal terms.

Both the IFRS and UK GAAP accounting treatments are set to change, as there is a project under way to alter radically the accounting treatment for operating leases.

This chapter will run through the accounting treatment (including disclosure) under current IFRS, then current UK GAAP and will finish by looking at future developments.

Leases under IFRS

Definitions

The definitions in IAS 17 of a finance lease and an operating lease are short. They are as follows:

> 'A finance lease is a lease that transfers substantially all the risks and rewards incidental to ownership of an asset. Title may or may not eventually be transferred.'

> 'An operating lease is a lease other than a finance lease.'[1]

IAS 17 explicitly states that hire purchase contracts are within the definition of a lease, thus they will be accounted for as finance leases or operating leases depending upon which definition is met. Generally, hire purchase contracts meet the definition of a finance lease.

Treatment of operating leases

Underlying the accounting for an operating lease is the premise that the lessor not only retains legal ownership of the asset, but also beneficial ownership. Accordingly, the lessor continues to recognise (or, in the case of an asset specially purchased for the transaction, starts to recognise) the asset on its balance sheet and recognises rental income. Alternatively, the lessor might lease the asset in from another party on an operating lease, thus having an operating lease both in and out. If so, the lessor will follow the lessee accounting for its lease in from the other party and will recognise rental income (in the same way that it would if it owned the asset) for its lease out. For an operating lease, the lessee does not recognise the asset on its balance sheet, but simply

---

1 IAS 17, para. 4.

Box 15.1 *E plc*
Amount charged in arriving at profit/loss

Year 1	£16,000
Year 2	£48,000
Year 3	£32,000
Total	£96,000

---

records a rental expense over the lease period. For both the lessee and lessor, the accounting treatment is to recognise the rentals in arriving at profit/loss on a straight-line basis over the lease term, even if the payments are not made on such a basis, unless another systematic and rational basis is, for a lessee, more representative of the time pattern of the lessee's benefit from the use of the asset and, for a lessor, more representative of the time pattern over which the benefit derived from the leased asset is diminished. The accounting treatment is illustrated in the following example.

E Plc leases a piece of equipment from O Limited for two years starting 1 September in year 1. Rentals of £12,000 are payable quarterly in advance. E has a calendar accounting period. At the end of the first accounting period, E will have paid £24,000 (£12,000 on 1 September and £12,000 on 1 December). However, the amount charged in the first and subsequent accounting periods is as shown in Box 15.1.

These figures reflect the normal principles of accruals accounting. For example, in year 1 the lessee, E, has had the benefit of the equipment for four months, and so charges four months' rentals (£12,000 × 4/3 = £16,000) in arriving at profit/loss for the year.

SIC 15 'Operating leases – incentives' clarifies that the above rule about straight-line charging (subject to another systematic and rational basis not being more appropriate) applies even where the lessor pays a large up-front incentive to the lessee or where there is an initial rent-free period. The incentive, whatever form it takes, is simply regarded as a negative rental when calculating the total rentals to be spread over the lease term.

Treatment of finance leases

A lease meets the definition of a finance lease if it transfers substantially all the risks and rewards of ownership of the asset to the lessee. This sets the tone for the accounting. Although the lessor retains legal title to the asset (except possibly at the end of the lease when a purchase option may be exercised by the lessee), beneficial ownership has transferred to the lessee on inception of the lease, and both lessee and lessor account as though the lessor has sold the asset to the lessee and the lessee has a loan from the lessor for the capital sum. Thus, at the start of the contract, the lessee recognises in its balance sheet

---

Box 15.2 *X plc*
Finance lease accounting

| *On day 1* | Dr Property, plant and equipment | £100,000 | | | | |
| | Cr Liabilities | | | | | £100,000 |

In years 1 to 5

	Year 1	Year 2	Year 3	Year 4	Year 5	Total
Dr income statement* – interest expense	£5,606	£4,521	£3,369	£2,146	£848	£16,490
Dr finance lease obligation – reduction of liability	£17,692	£18,777	£19,929	£21,152	£22,450	£100,000
Cr cash – payment of cash	£23,298	£23,298	£23,298	£23,298	£23,298	£116,490
Dr income statement* – depreciation expense	£20,000	£20,000	£20,000	£20,000	£20,000	£100,000
Cr property, plant and equipment – provision for depreciation	£20,000	£20,000	£20,000	£20,000	£20,000	£100,000

* or income statement part of the statement of comprehensive income

---

both the asset and a liability for the same amount. The excess of the rental payments over the capital sum recognised on day 1 is recorded as an interest expense in arriving at profit/loss over the life of the lease. The total amount recognised as interest is allocated to each accounting period at a constant rate on the outstanding balance. The asset is accounted for as any other asset, thus it is depreciated over its useful economic life (or, if shorter, the lease term) and is reviewed for impairment if there is an indicator of impairment.

Consider the following example. On 1 January, X Plc entered into a lease with Y Limited under which X leases a machine from Y for five years at an annual rental of £23,298, payable in quarterly instalments. The machine's expected residual value at the end of the five years is nil and its fair value on day 1 is £100,000. The lease is a finance lease and the lessee will account for it as shown in Box 15.2.

Box 15.2 shows that the lessee records as expenses in arriving at profit/loss both: (1) interest on the liability; the interest is higher in the early years ('front loaded') as it is a constant percentage on the amount of principal outstanding; and (2) depreciation on the asset, as if it were owned; we assume straight-line

---

Box 15.3 *Y Limited*
Finance lease accounting

On day 1	Dr receivable	£100,000
	Cr asset	£100,000

Box 15.4 *Y Limited*
Finance lease accounting

In years 1 to 5

	Year 1	Year 2	Year 3	Year 4	Year 5	Total
Dr cash – received from lessee	£23,298	£23,298	£23,298	£23,298	£23,298	£116,490
Cr income statement* – interest income	£5,606	£4,521	£3,369	£2,146	£848	£16,490
Cr receivable – collection of principal	£17,692	£18,777	£19,929	£21,152	£22,450	£100,000

* or income statement part of the statement of comprehensive income

---

depreciation for this purpose. Hence the total charge is front loaded (£25,606 in year one reducing to £20,848 in year 5). Over the five years, the aggregate of the two charges equates to the total cash paid in rentals.

The lessor's accounting mirrors the above in aggregate, although there can be differences in the allocation of interest to the accounting periods. Boxes 15.3 and 15.4 illustrate the accounting.

The day 1 accounting entries in Box 15.3 reflect the lessor no longer having the original asset, but disposing of that in favour of an amount receivable from the lessee. Then, during years 1 to 5, the lessor receives cash which he or she allocates to interest income and collection of principal, as illustrated here.

Lessors are required under IAS 17 to allocate the interest income to the different accounting periods so as to give a constant periodic rate of return on their 'net investment' in the lease. The net investment in the lease represents the present value of both the payments due under the lease and the estimated residual value, guaranteed and unguaranteed. Given that in this example we assumed the residual value was nil, the interest is allocated in the same way by both lessee and lessor.

Consider now a lessor that manufactures assets at a cost of £800 each and either sells them for £1,000 (immediate payment) or leases them out. Where the lease is a finance lease, the accounting logic is that the lessor has sold the asset to the lessee. Accordingly, under IAS 17 the lessor can book the gross selling profit of £200 at the start of the lease period and allocate the lease interest income over the remainder of the lease period as above. If, on the other hand, the lease is an operating lease, no gross selling profit can be recognised, as the accounting reflects the view that the lessor still owns the asset.

Classification of leases into finance or operating

One of the most critical questions in lease accounting presently is whether the lease is an operating lease or a finance lease. For lessees, classification as an operating lease is normally favoured as the accounting for this does not give rise to a liability on the balance sheet and thus does not adversely affect the gearing ratio.

Supplementing IAS 17's definition of finance and operating leases is guidance, set out in paras. 10 to 12 inclusive of the standard, which is of such importance to this topic that it is reproduced in full:

'10. Whether a lease is a finance lease or an operating lease depends on the substance of the transaction rather than the form of the contract. Examples of situations that individually or in combination would normally lead to a lease being classified as a finance lease are:

(a) the lease transfers ownership of the asset to the lessee by the end of the lease term;

(b) the lessee has the option to purchase the asset at a price that is expected to be sufficiently lower than the fair value at the date the option becomes exercisable for it to be reasonably certain, at the inception of the lease, that the option will be exercised;

(c) the lease term is for the major part of the economic life of the asset even if title is not transferred;

(d) at the inception of the lease the present value of the minimum lease payments amounts to at least substantially all of the fair value of the leased asset; and

(e) the leased assets are of such a specialised nature that only the lessee can use them without major modifications.

11. Indicators of situations that individually or in combination could also lead to a lease being classified as a finance lease are:

(a) if the lessee can cancel the lease, the lessor's losses associated with the cancellation are borne by the lessee;

(b) gains or losses from the fluctuation in the fair value of the residual accrue to the lessee (for example, in the form of a rent rebate equalling most of the sales proceeds at the end of the lease); and

(c) the lessee has the ability to continue the lease for a secondary period at a rent that is substantially lower than market rent.

12. The examples and indicators in paras. 10 and 11 are not always conclusive. If it is clear from other features that the lease does not transfer substantially all risks and rewards incidental to ownership, the lease is classified as an operating lease. For example, this may be the case if ownership of the asset transfers at the end of the lease for a variable payment equal to its then fair value, or if there are contingent rents, as a result of which the lessee does not have substantially all such risks and rewards.'

One of the examples of a situation that would normally lead to a lease being classified as a finance lease is a lease where 'at the inception of the lease the present value of the minimum lease payments amounts to at least substantially all of the fair value of the leased asset'. In practice, this is one of the main determinants of a finance lease. Fundamental to this analysis are the 'minimum lease payments'. These are defined as shown in Box 15.5.

Box 15.5 *Items included in minimum lease payments*

	Lessee	Lessor
Rentals over the 'lease term'	✓	✓
Residual amounts guaranteed by lessee*	✓	✓
Residual amounts guaranteed by a party related to lessee, e.g. by parent or fellow subsidiary of lessee*	✓	✓
Residual amounts guaranteed by party NOT related to lessee*	✗	✓

* Alternatively, if there is an option to purchase the asset for a price that is expected to be below the fair value at the time such that it is reasonably certain, at the start of the lease, that the lessee will exercise the option, the option exercise proceeds are used in place of residual value guarantees (as these would not be expected to come into play).

It can be seen that the definition for the lessor is similar to that for the lessee, but with an additional component; this difference in definition can lead to different classification. Consider an asset with a useful economic life of six years. A lessor enters into a lease under which a lessee will lease it for three years, the present value of the lease payments being, say, 65 per cent of the asset's fair value on day 1. The lease will probably be classified as an operating lease by the lessee (because 65 per cent is not 'substantially all' and for the purpose of this example it is assumed that the other indicators also point to classification as an operating lease). If, however, the lessor also enters into an agreement with a third party (unrelated to both lessee and lessor) under which the third party agrees to purchase the asset from the lessor at the end of the three years for a fixed sum if the lessor chooses to offer it to the third party, the present value of the fixed sum being 35 per cent of the asset's fair value on day 1, the lessor would classify the lease as a finance lease (assuming that the third-party guarantor was financially capable of fulfilling his or her obligations under the guarantee).

'Lease term' can also be critical to the classification of a lease. The 'lease term is the non-cancellable period for which the lessee has contracted to lease the asset together with any further terms for which the lessee has the option to continue to lease the asset, with or without further payment, when at the inception of the lease it is reasonably certain that the lessee will exercise the option'[2]

Paramount in the earlier guidance is that the substance of the lease is the deciding factor in classification as finance or operating lease. Where, for example, the minimum lease period is equal to the asset's useful economic life, the substance is that the lessee has the use of the asset for its entire useful economic life and thus should treat the lease as a finance lease and account as though it had purchased the asset. The present value of the lease payments may be less than the fair value of the asset; in effect this means that it is simply a bargain purchase for the lessee, rather than that it is not a finance lease.

Other than for some investment properties, a lease of land and buildings has to be divided into two components – a lease of the land and a lease of the buildings – and each categorised separately. Land generally has an indefinite life and, unless title to the land passes to the lessee at the end of the lease, most leases of land are categorised as operating leases. However, the lease of the building may be classified as a finance lease notwithstanding that the lease of the land is an operating lease.

The lease agreement may cover more than simply the lease of an asset. For example, it may also provide for maintenance of the asset over the lease period. In analysing a lease to determine its classification, it is only the payments relating to the use of the asset that are taken into account. Other payments, such as for maintenance, are excluded from any numerical analysis and are accounted for separately.

Sale and leaseback transactions

IAS 17 specifically addresses sale and leaseback transactions.

If an asset is sold by an entity, but leased back on a finance lease, the entity (the seller/lessee) has not in substance disposed of the asset; it has disposed of legal title, but the substance is that it has obtained financing secured on the asset. Hence, under a sale and finance leaseback, the cash received is treated as financing, rather than as disposal proceeds; and any apparent profit or loss is deferred and amortised over the shorter of the lease term and the useful economic life of the asset (assuming, in the case of a loss arising, that the asset is not impaired).

2 IAS 17, para. 4.

Where an asset is sold and leased back under an operating lease, the appropriate accounting treatment under IAS 17 is to record the sale of the asset and then separately to account for the operating lease. Hence the asset no longer appears on the selling company's balance sheet – beneficial, as well as legal, title having now passed to the lessor. IAS 17 specifies that the profit/loss arising on sale is recognised immediately, providing the sale price was fair value.

Disclosures

IAS 17 requires various disclosures to be made in the financial statements. In the main, for lessees, the requirements call for disclosure of the impact that the leases entered into by the lessee have on the financial statements. Two disclosures that relate to future expenditure are as follows:

- For operating leases, the total of the future minimum lease payments under non-cancellable leases that are payable: (1) in the following year; (2) in years two to five, inclusive, after the reporting period; and (3) more than five years after the reporting period.[3]
- For operating and finance leases, the basis on which contingent rent payable is determined.[4]

Similarly, for lessors the disclosures generally amplify how the leases have affected the amounts in the financial statements. Two disclosures that give an indication of future income are as follows:

- For operating leases, the total of the future minimum lease payments under non-cancellable leases that are receivable: (1) in the following year; (2) in years two to five, inclusive, after the reporting period; and (3) more than five years after the reporting period.[5]
- For finance leases, the unearned finance income.[6]

Leases under UK GAAP

The relevant standard is SSAP 21 'Accounting for leases and hire purchase contracts'. It is much like IAS 17, classifying leases into finance leases and operating leases, using similar criteria for classification and with the resulting accounting treatment also being very similar. There are, nevertheless, a number of key differences, as follows:

- Under IAS 17 a lessor recognises interest income in respect of a finance lease so as to give a constant periodic rate of return on the lessor's *net investment* in the lease, whereas under SSAP 21 the requirement is to allocate the interest income so as to give a constant periodic rate of

---

3 IAS 17, para. 35(a).   4 IAS 17, paras. 31(e)(i) and 35(d)(i).
5 IAS 17, para. 56(a).   6 IAS 17, para. 47(b).

return on the lessor's *net cash investment* in the lease. Although the total income recognised over the lease term is unaffected, this can lead to large differences in individual years where the tax allowances and incentives relating to leases (which affect the net cash investment, but not the net investment) are substantial.

- Leases of land and buildings have to be separated under IAS 17 into two components: a lease of the land and a lease of the buildings, with each component being accounted for separately. Because land in the main lasts forever, any lease term (say ninety-nine years) for such land is usually regarded as not being a significant part of the life of the land. Hence, the land element will generally be classified as an operating lease. The buildings element will be classified as either a finance lease or an operating lease in the normal way. The two components need not be separated out under SSAP 21 and are generally considered jointly. It is therefore more likely that finance leases will arise in respect of the buildings under IAS 17 than under SSAP 21.

- If, at the inception of the lease, the present value of the minimum lease payments amounts to at least substantially all of the fair value of the leased asset, this would be indicative that the lease is a finance lease under both IAS 17 and SSAP 21. 'Substantially all' is, however, not expounded in IAS 17, whereas in SSAP 21 it is explained, within the formal definition of a finance lease, as normally being 90 per cent or more. Although expressed only as a guide, the reference to 90 per cent is often referred to by UK GAAP preparers as 'the 90 per cent test' or 'the 90 per cent rule'. Under SSAP 21 and FRS 5, entities are supposed to consider wider issues when classifying leases – typically looking at exactly the sorts of things listed in IAS 17, which includes a numerical analysis – but the practice has developed of putting emphasis on looking at whether the present value of the minimum lease payments is above or below 90 per cent, particularly where other indicators do not give a clear guide as to the appropriate classification.

SIC 27 'Evaluating the substance of transactions involving the legal form of a lease' sets out guidance on when IAS 17 should determine the accounting treatment of a lease and when, instead, a series of transactions, involving one or more leases, should be viewed as a whole. Although FRS 5 'Reporting the substance of transactions' does not directly address when SSAP 21 applies and when a series of transactions should be considered as a whole, its principles are consistent with SIC 27.

IFRIC 4 'Determining whether an arrangement contains a lease' sets out guidance for determining when IAS 17 should be applied to a transaction involving the right to use an asset in return for a series of payments even though there is no lease in legal terms. There is no direct equivalent in UK GAAP, although FRS 5 may lead to similar results.

Accompanying SSAP 21 are lengthy Guidance Notes dealing with some of the practical issues and problem areas arising. For lessors, the Finance and Leasing Association (FLA) SORP 'Accounting issues in the asset finance and leasing industry' provides additional guidance and recommendations. There are no equivalents in IFRS.

The way forward

The IASB has a fundamental project underway to develop new guidance on lease accounting. At the heart of the project is the premise that all lease obligations should be recognised on a lessee's balance sheet. In essence, if it goes ahead all leases will be accounted for in a way similar to the way in which finance leases are currently accounted for. It is the 'right-of-use' model: the 'asset' recognised on balance sheet will be the right to use the physical asset for the duration of the lease. The devil is, however, in the detail and a number of practical issues are giving rise to considerable problems as the standard-setters try to take this project forward.

16
Pensions

Introduction

Pensions have become a considerable economic and political problem. Deficits have risen due to increased longevity, lower interest rates and poor investment performance, relative to a decade ago. Pensions accounting questions arise in two contexts: in relation to the financial statements of pension schemes themselves and in relation to the treatment of the cost of pensions in the financial statements of the sponsoring companies. It is with the latter question that this chapter is concerned. The current accounting rules are set out in IAS 19 'Employee benefits' and FRS 17 'Retirement benefits'.

In addition, various disclosures have to be made about the pension accruing to the individual directors of quoted companies; these are dealt with in chapter 20 under 'Directors' Remuneration Reports'.

Defined contribution and defined benefit schemes

Fundamentally, pension schemes take one of two forms.

Defined contribution schemes

A defined contribution (DC) scheme, or plan, is defined as one 'under which an entity pays fixed contributions into a separate entity (a fund) and will have no legal or constructive obligation to pay further contributions if the fund does not hold sufficient assets to pay all employee benefits relating to employee service in the current and prior periods'.[1] So, for example, the employee might pay 5 per cent of pensionable pay into the fund each year and the employer might pay 8 per cent of pensionable pay. A fund is a separate legal entity that looks after the money on behalf of the employees. The money in the fund is invested by the fund's managers. The pension paid to the employee once he or she has reached retirement age is based solely on the size of the fund into which those contributions have grown. If, say, the investment performance has been poor, and as a result the pension is lower than expected, that is that: there is no obligation on the company to pay additional amounts.

1 IAS 19, para. 7.

The accounting treatment of a defined contribution scheme is straightforward and is the same under IFRS and UK GAAP. The employer's contributions payable to the fund in respect of a year should be charged as an expense in arriving at profit/loss for that year. Note the word 'payable', not paid. This is an accruals basis, not simply a cash basis. For example, taking a December year-end company, if the contributions in respect of December salaries are not paid over to the fund until January, that amount should nonetheless be charged as an expense in the year to 31 December.

Defined benefit schemes

Defined benefit (DB) schemes, or plans, are 'post-employment benefit plans other than defined contribution plans'.[2] That is, if the obligation of the company is anything other than limited to the contributions that are defined (for example, 8 per cent of salary, as above), the scheme is DB. The most common example of a DB scheme is a 'final salary' scheme. Typically, an employee is promised a pension based on his or her final salary. For example, based on forty years' employment, the pension might be 40/60ths of final salary, or of the average salary in the three years' service immediately prior to retiring.

The obligations of an employer in respect of a DB scheme are complex and open-ended. The scheme ideally needs to be fully funded by the date of the employee's retirement, meaning that it contains a fund sufficient to pay, say, 40/60ths of salary. However, whether it will have a fund of sufficient size depends on investment performance, interest rates, mortality, employee behaviour (the extent to which people leave or stay until retirement, for example) and other variables. Actuaries are employed to make estimates periodically of the progress of a plan and to recommend what level of future contributions is necessary.

As is well known, many DB schemes have in recent years swung from surplus into significant deficit, even to the extent that these deficits have in some cases overshadowed the fortunes of the company itself. This is especially so in some traditional industries (e.g. engineering, steel) where the scheme reflects the former size of the company's workforce. Scheme deficits have also become significant barriers to company takeovers.

It will not be surprising that accounting for DB schemes is complex and controversial.

Accounting for defined benefit schemes

To reflect, in the financial statements of the sponsoring company, only the contributions payable to the fund in respect of the year in the case of a DB

---

2 IAS 19, para. 7.

scheme would not properly reflect the uncertainties and obligations to which the employer is subject. For example, in earlier years some schemes found that they were in significant surplus and the actuary was able to recommend a 'contribution holiday', that is, that the company did not need to pay any contributions to the fund for, say, three years. However, to charge nil as pensions expense in arriving at profit/loss would not reflect the underlying expense and obligation to which the company was subject because the employees continue to work for the business and over the year they earn the right to a larger pension than at the start of the year.

The original approach to this, in both international and UK GAAP, was, as with many accounting topics at the time, to take an income statement approach. This resulted in a reasonably smooth pensions charge against profits in each year. Gradually, this approach became discredited and, indeed, the focus on the income statement at the expense of the balance sheet generally fell out of favour. Both IFRS and UK GAAP changed and IAS 19 and FRS 17, the relevant standards, take a balance sheet approach to accounting for defined benefit pension schemes.

When DB pensions are looked at from the perspective of the balance sheet, the question is: what assets and liabilities does the sponsoring company have at the end of its year? To answer this, we have to look at the fund itself. If the fund has a deficit, it is argued that the company has an obligation to fund that deficit. If the fund has a surplus, the company can, to an extent, benefit from that surplus. Hence, in simple terms, a deficit on the fund is shown as a liability of the company; and a surplus in the fund is shown as an asset of the company (although this is restricted to the extent that the company is able to recover the surplus either through reduced contributions in the future or through refunds from the scheme).

IAS 19

IAS 19 is the international standard on pension costs. In fact it is called 'Employee benefits' and deals with a wider range of benefits than just pensions. For example, it also deals with short-term benefits such as holiday pay and bonuses, and with long-term benefits payable during employment. However, its principal focus is pensions and other retirement (or, as it calls them, post-employment) benefits.

Under IAS 19 the scheme assets in the fund are stated at fair value (i.e. market value where there is a market, e.g. listed investments and government bonds) and the scheme liabilities are stated at an estimate of the present value of the obligation to pay pensions in the future for current and past employees. The obligation is discounted using current interest rates and uses an estimate of future salaries. The actuarial method adopted for this purpose is the projected

> **Box 16.1** *Example: assumptions*
>
> | | |
> |---|---|
> | Scheme assets, 1 January 2009 | 3,000 |
> | Scheme obligations, 1 January 2009 | (4,000) |
> | Deficit, 1 January 2009 | (1,000) |
> | Deficit, 31 December 2009 | (1,500) |
> | Movement (deterioration) in year | (500) |
> | Contributions to scheme during year | 100 |

unit credit method. The net of the assets and liabilities measured in this way is IAS 19's measure of the surplus or deficit in the scheme.

The swing from opening surplus/deficit to closing surplus/deficit can be quite dramatic. Under IAS 19, the difference between the opening and closing surplus/deficit is analysed into a number of components, which are reported in different places in the performance statements. This can best be explained by use of a simplified example, the assumptions for which are set out in Box 16.1.

We see from Box 16.1 that the deficit has increased during the year. This may be due to a fall in the value of investments and/or an increase in the value of the scheme's liabilities to pay pensions. The true deterioration or loss is 600, as the deficit increased by 500 despite 100 of cash being put into the scheme. Box 16.2 shows how the loss of 600 might be analysed; the figures are purely illustrative, but are typical.

In this example, 60 of the loss is recognised in arriving at profit/loss, i.e. is recognised in the income statement (or income statement part of the statement of comprehensive income).

IAS 19 offers a choice with respect to the accounting of the remaining 540:

(i) recognise all 540 as 'other comprehensive income' (this is the option taken by most UK companies);

(ii) recognise in arriving at profit/loss only a part of the actuarial gain/loss, say, 30, calculated in accordance with a predetermined formula (this is known as the 'corridor method'); or

(iii) recognise in arriving at profit/loss any amount between the 30 and 540 in (ii) and (i) above.

Prior to 2004, only options (ii) and (iii) were permitted. Thus, companies had to charge (or credit) actuarial losses (or gains) in arriving at profit/loss. Option (ii), the 'corridor method', was the more popular choice on the part of companies. Basically, with the corridor method, the first chunk of actuarial gains and losses can be ignored for accounting purposes and the remainder (that is, the amount

---

Box 16.2 *Example: analysis of deterioration in deficit of 600 (before taking account of contributions paid)*

Current service cost (1)	(50)
Interest cost (2)	(160)
Expected return on assets (3)	150
	(60)
Actuarial gains and losses (4)	(540)
	(600)

Notes

(1) This represents what, at the start of the year, is the present value of the expected cost of the additional pension benefit to be earned by the employees (which is the additional obligation incurred by the scheme) in the year, without reference to whether the scheme is in surplus or deficit or indeed whether it is funded at all. It is calculated using what, at the start of the year, is the expected final salary. This is charged in arriving at profit/loss for the year, usually as an expense within operating profit.

(2) Say, 4 per cent interest on liabilities of 4,000. The interest cost is calculated by using the discount rate applicable at the start of the period and applying this to the present value of the pension obligation at the start of the year and to material movements during the year, e.g. current service cost, past service cost, transfers in and out of the scheme and pensions paid during the year. For simplicity we have assumed that the movements during the year all occur on the last day of the year.

(3) Say, 5 per cent return on assets of 3,000. This is, again, calculated at the start of the year and reflects the expected return (dividends, interest, other revenue and capital gains) during the year.

Items (2) and (3) are included in arriving at profit/loss for the year. Some companies include these in the interest area of the income statement, while others include them in arriving at operating profit.

(4) This actuarial loss is the remainder of the cost, which typically comprises a loss in value of the investments and/or a loss due to an increase in the value of the scheme liabilities, including factors such as changes in mortality and other assumptions.

(5) This example assumes that the pension entitlements were not changed during the year, e.g. there was no increase in the rate of pension accruing to current and former employees.

---

not recognised in earlier periods that is in excess of 10 per cent of the higher of scheme assets and scheme liabilities) may be spread over a period, being the expected average remaining working lives of the employees. It is widely accepted that this method has no conceptual basis.

In late 2004, the IASB, being uncomfortable with the corridor method, added a third option (option (i) above), namely to allow companies to recognise the actuarial gain or loss outside the calculation of profit/loss; but, where this was done, the actuarial gain or loss had to be recognised in full. This had the effect of introducing into IAS 19 a treatment broadly equivalent to the UK-style FRS 17 accounting and, not surprisingly, many UK companies adopted this treatment when they applied IFRS. Following the 2007 changes to IAS 1, the actuarial gain or loss is recognised in other comprehensive income.

IAS 19 also requires extensive note disclosures, primarily about DB schemes.

Differences between IFRS and UK GAAP

The main difference between IFRS and UK GAAP in accounting for defined benefit schemes relates to the recognition of actuarial gains and losses. Under UK GAAP (FRS 17), the full gain or loss must be recognised immediately via the STRGL, whereas under IFRS, as outlined above, while recognising it immediately in other comprehensive income is one permitted treatment, it is also possible to recognise it in arriving at profit/loss over an extended period and only to the extent that the amount not recognised in earlier periods exceeds 10 per cent of the higher of scheme assets and scheme liabilities. It is also possible under IFRS to recognise it in full in arriving at profit/loss.

The expected return on scheme assets and the interest cost in respect of scheme liabilities are presented adjacent to interest in a UK GAAP income statement, whereas the positioning within the IFRS income statement (or income statement part of the statement of comprehensive income) is not specified by IAS 19. In their IFRS accounts, some UK companies have continued to include these items below operating profit, with interest, while others have included these in arriving at operating profit.

In a UK GAAP balance sheet the surplus or deficit is recognised on balance sheet net of the related deferred tax, whereas with IFRS accounting the related deferred tax is presented as part of the deferred tax balance.

Distributable profits are determined by reference to individual company financial statements and the accounting for a defined benefit pension scheme is one area where there can be a huge impact on distributable profits (see below). Accordingly, the accounting for defined benefit pension schemes within individual company financial statements is critical and, for some groups, is another key area of difference between IFRS and UK GAAP. Consider a group of companies operating a defined benefit scheme where each company within the group pays contributions into the scheme and those contributions are affected by the overall surplus or deficit, but each company is unable to identify its share of the underlying scheme assets and liabilities. Under UK GAAP, each company within the group simply accounts, in its individual company financial statements, for the contributions it has to pay each year; in other words, the accounting is as if the scheme were a defined contribution scheme supplemented with additional disclosures. It is possible, therefore, depending upon the particular arrangements within a group, for all companies within the group to use defined contribution accounting and thus for no individual company to recognise the surplus or deficit in its balance sheet (it is recognised only in the consolidated balance sheet). By contrast, under IFRS, whilst all but one company within the group may be able to use defined contribution accounting in this scenario, IAS 19 explicitly requires one company, the company that is legally the sponsoring

153

employer for the scheme, to recognise the full scheme surplus or deficit in its balance sheet and the full charge, calculated using defined benefit accounting, in its income statement and other comprehensive income. Thus, under IFRS, there can be a big impact on distributable profits. Following changes in tax rules, having effect for periods ended on or after 6 April 2006, it is possible that fewer group schemes will be structured so as to allow for defined contribution accounting within individual subsidiaries, thus reducing the impact of this GAAP difference.

The effect of pensions on realised and distributable profits

The calculation of realised and distributable profits is discussed more generally in chapter 19. Questions about realised profits arise only in the accounts of individual entities; they do not apply to group accounts as it is companies, not groups, that make distributions.

Here we consider the effect of accounting for pension costs on realised profits. The ICAEW, together with the ICAS, published in December 2004 'TECH 50/04 – Guidance on the effect of FRS 17 "Retirement benefits" and IAS 19 "Employee benefits" on realised profits and losses'. This guidance has subsequently been consolidated into TECH 01/08 'Guidance on the determination of realised profits and losses in the context of distributions under the Companies Act 1985'.

The key points with respect to defined benefit pension schemes may be summarised as follows. In order to establish the impact that a surplus or deficit under IAS 19/FRS 17 has on a company's realised profits, it is necessary to:

- identify the cumulative net gain or loss taken to reserves in respect of the pension surplus or deficit; and
- establish the extent to which that gain or loss is realised.

In this context, it does not matter whether the amounts that have ended up in reserves went through profit/loss or other comprehensive income (STRGL for UK GAAP).

The basic guidance[3] is that a cumulative loss in respect of a pension scheme taken to reserves is a realised loss. This is because it results from the creation of, or an increase in, a provision for a liability or loss resulting in an overall reduction in net assets. Similarly, a cumulative net credit in respect of a pension scheme in reserves constitutes a realised profit; but this is only to the extent that it is represented by an asset to be recovered by agreed refunds and the refunds will take the form of qualifying consideration.[4] See chapter 19 at p. 187 for the meaning of 'Qualifying consideration'.

---

3 See para. 8.11 of TECH 01/08.   4 See para. 8.12.

The impact on reserves is the amount of the pension surplus or deficit recognised in the balance sheet adjusted for: (1) the net contributions paid to the scheme; and (2) any asset or liability introduced as a result of a business combination.[5] Although the impact on reserves will not usually be the same as the asset or liability recognised on balance sheet, it will often be obvious that all of the amounts included in reserves are realised.[6]

5 See para. 8.10 and 8.14.   6 See para. 8.18.

17

Financial instruments

Introduction

'Financial instruments' is a broad term, encompassing a wide range of financial assets and liabilities as well as a company's own equity. These terms are defined below. Financial assets include shares and debt instruments held by an investor. By contrast, debt instruments, in the financial statements of the issuer of the debt, are financial liabilities. Although a company's own equity (that is, where it issues its own shares) is excluded from the definition of financial liabilities, it is nevertheless a financial instrument and is discussed below. Financial assets and liabilities also include derivatives and more straightforward instruments such as cash, receivables (debtors) and payables (creditors). Accounting for financial instruments has been one of the most complex and controversial aspects of accounting. The requirement that some financial instruments are stated at fair value is a major source of complexity. The fair value requirement is also controversial, especially where changes in fair values are reported in the income statement, giving rise to earnings volatility. However, there are other problematic aspects, including when and how to use 'hedge accounting' and how debt and equity should be distinguished.

The term 'capital instruments' has been used historically in the UK. This represents all instruments issued by an entity as a means of raising finance, comprising the entity's equity instruments, together with debt instruments such as loans and debentures. However, the term 'capital instruments' is not used in IFRS.

Background

The IFRS requirements relating to accounting for financial instruments are set out in IAS 32 'Financial instruments: presentation' and IAS 39 'Financial instruments: recognition and measurement'.

IAS 32 deals with classification of issued instruments into debt and equity; the classification is, in principle, based on the substance of the instrument, not its legal form. However, in practice, the substance has to be determined by the exact contractual terms. As a result, sometimes the classification can appear to be at odds with a common-sense view of the instrument's substance. IAS 32 also contains rules on when financial assets and financial liabilities can be offset.

IAS 39 deals with the recognition and measurement of financial assets and liabilities generally. It sets out four categories for financial assets and two categories for financial liabilities. These are described below. IAS 39 also contains specific rules for the use of hedge accounting; when financial assets and liabilities should be recognised and de-recognised; and accounting for derivatives and 'embedded derivatives'.

The requirements relating to disclosure of financial instruments are set out in IFRS 7 'Financial instruments: disclosures'. The disclosures themselves are very extensive, running into many pages for large or complex groups.

Definitions

The following definitions apply in IASs 32 and 39 and IFRS 7.

A *financial instrument* is any contract that gives rise to a financial asset of one entity and a financial liability or equity instrument of another entity.[1]

A *financial asset* is, broadly, any asset that is:
(a) cash;
(b) an equity instrument of another entity;
(c) a contractual right:
   (i) to receive cash or another financial asset from another entity; or
   (ii) to exchange financial assets or financial liabilities with another entity under conditions that are potentially favourable to the entity; or
(d) a contract that will or may be settled in the entity's own equity instruments and is:
   (i) a non-derivative for which the entity is or may be obliged to receive a variable number of the entity's own equity instruments; or
   (ii) a derivative that will or may be settled other than by the exchange of a fixed amount of cash or another financial asset for a fixed number of the entity's own equity instruments. For this purpose, the entity's own equity instruments do not include instruments that are contracts for the future receipt or delivery of the entity's own equity instruments.[2]

A *financial liability* is, broadly, any liability that is:
(a) a contractual obligation:
   (i) to deliver cash or another financial asset to another entity; or
   (ii) to exchange financial assets or financial liabilities with another entity under conditions that are potentially unfavourable to the entity; or

1 IAS 32, para. 11.   2 See IAS 32, para. 11 for full definition.

(b) a contract that will or may be settled in the entity's own equity instruments and is:

   (i) a non-derivative for which the entity is or may be obliged to deliver a variable number of the entity's own equity instruments; or

  (ii) a derivative that will or may be settled other than by the exchange of a fixed amount of cash or another financial asset for a fixed number of the entity's own equity instruments. For this purpose, the entity's own equity instruments do not include instruments that are contracts for the future receipt or delivery of the entity's own equity instruments.[3]

An *equity instrument* is any contract that evidences a residual interest in the assets of an entity after deducting all of its liabilities.[4]

Debt and equity

The distinction

The basic classification rule, applying to all issuers of financial instruments, is that an instrument, or its component parts, shall be classified as a financial asset, financial liability or equity instrument in accordance with its substance.[5]

The critical issue in determining whether there is a financial liability is whether there is an obligation to deliver cash or other financial assets, or to exchange financial assets or liabilities on terms that are potentially unfavourable to the issuer. This basic test – is there an obligation? – means that instruments are classified according to their substance. Hence certain redeemable shares are classified as debt; and in certain circumstances something that is legally a debt instrument is classified as equity, that is, if there is no obligation to pay interest and principal.

Where an entity issues a compound instrument, such as convertible debt, it is separated into its component parts; in the case of convertible debt, this would be a debt component and an equity component, being an option over shares, with each being presented separately on the balance sheet.

Types of shares and balance sheet classification

There are many different forms of shares; the most common examples are ordinary and preference shares, including redeemable preference shares and participating preference shares. Prior to 2005, an issuing company following UK GAAP would have accounted for all of these within shareholders' funds, but now under IFRS or UK GAAP they are classified as either financial liabilities or as equity instruments in accordance with their substance, as explained above.

---

3 See IAS 32, para. 11 for full definition.   4 IAS 32, para. 11.   5 IAS 32, para. 15.

Box 17.1

Type of share	Balance sheet classification
Preference shares mandatorily redeemable for a fixed amount and paying a fixed annual dividend	Financial liability
Preference shares mandatorily redeemable for a fixed amount, but with a discretionary dividend	The capital element (present value of redemption amount) would be classified as a financial liability and the dividend element (the balance) would be classified as an equity instrument
A preference share paying fixed annual dividends, but with no redemption option	Financial liability
Participating preference shares where the annual dividend comprises a fixed amount plus an additional amount equal to a proportion of the dividend payable on the ordinary shares, with no redemption option	The fixed dividend element would be classified as a financial liability and the participating dividend component would be classified as equity
Ordinary shares	Equity instruments

IAS 32 explains that preference shares that are redeemable on a fixed date or at the option of the holder contain a financial liability as the issuer has an obligation to transfer a financial asset. The guidance explains that the issuer's potential inability to satisfy the obligation, say, because of insufficient distributable profits or funds, does not negate the obligation and it is the obligation that determines the classification.

Box 17.1 sets out the balance sheet classification of the common types of shares.

A preference share paying fixed annual dividends (i.e. not at the discretion of the directors) but with no redemption option will still be classified as a financial liability because the present value of the dividend payments, which will go into perpetuity and which form the issuer's obligation, will equal the capital value of the shares.

Equity shares in the Companies Act

As stated above, IAS 32 distinguishes debt from equity, and equity is defined as a residual category. It should be noted that the Companies Act 2006 uses the

---

Box 17.2 *Issue of shares – entries in legal accounting records*		
Dr	cash	£250,000	
Cr	share capital account		£100,000
Cr	share premium account		£150,000

Box 17.3 *Issue of shares – entries in legal accounting records*		
Dr	cash	£2,100,000	
Cr	ordinary share capital		£1,000,000
Cr	preference share capital		£400,000
Cr	share premium account		£700,000

term 'equity shares', but its definition is different from, generally being wider than, that in IFRS. Applying to all companies irrespective of whether IFRS or UK GAAP is used for financial reporting, the Companies Act definition (found in s. 548) remains in force. The conditions determining whether merger relief from setting up share premium is available (see chapter 11), for example, refer to equity shares and non-equity shares, as defined by the Act.

Issue of shares

Where shares are issued for more than their nominal value, the amount equal to their nominal value is recorded in share capital and the balance of consideration is recorded in share premium under s. 610 of CA 2006. There are exceptions to the recording of share premium in the form of merger relief and group reconstruction relief – see chapter 11, p. 112. If a company issued 100,000 £1 ordinary shares each for £2.50 cash, the entries in the accounting records would be as shown in Box 17.2.

It is important to stress that these would be the entries in the legal accounting records irrespective of the balance sheet classification of the shares as financial liabilities or equity instruments.

Consider a company which, upon its formation, issues 1,000,000 £1 ordinary shares for £1.50 per share, and 400,000 £1 preference shares for £1.50 per share, paying an annual dividend of 6 per cent and redeemable at £1.50 per share in five years' time. The initial entries in its accounting records are as shown in Box 17.3.

However, assuming the substance of the preference shares is that they are classified as liabilities, the company's balance sheet immediately after its formation will be as shown in Box 17.4.

The Companies Act permits expenses incurred in issuing shares to be deducted from the amount transferred to the share premium account on the

Box 17.4 *Balance sheet*	
Assets – cash	£2,100,000
Liabilities – loan	(600,000)
Net assets	£1,500,000
Share capital	£1,000,000
Share premium	500,000
Total equity	£1,500,000

issue of those shares. These are often referred to as issue costs or transaction costs.

IAS 39 uses the term 'transaction costs', which it defines as those 'incremental costs that are directly attributable to the acquisition, issue or disposal of a financial asset or financial liability. An incremental cost is one that would not have been incurred if the entity had not acquired, issued or disposed of the financial instrument'.

Deducting issue costs is one of very few permitted uses of the balance on the share premium account. Moreover, if the costs are deducted from share premium rather than from retained earnings, they do not reduce distributable profits. These factors sometimes cause considerable attention to be paid to what can and cannot be regarded as an issue cost. It is only the costs that are directly incurred in the issue of the particular instrument that meet the definition, for example, stamp duty payable on the issue, lawyers' fees incurred for drawing up the necessary documentation and underwriting fees.

Categories of financial instrument

Introduction

IAS 39 lays down rules on the recognition and measurement of financial assets and financial liabilities.

Financial assets include: cash, receivables, a holding of shares of another company (although an interest in a subsidiary, associate or joint venture will often be excluded from IAS 39's rules) and derivatives with a positive value. Financial liabilities include debt instruments issued by the entity, bank and other borrowings, payables, financial guarantees and derivatives with a negative value.

Initial measurement

On first being recognised, financial assets and liabilities are measured at fair value, adjusted (other than for trading and derivative assets and liabilities and any other assets and liabilities to be classified as at fair value through profit or loss) by directly incurred transaction/issue costs. Trading and derivative assets

161

and liabilities and any other assets and liabilities to be classified as at fair value through profit or loss are initially measured at fair value without any addition of costs. So if fair value of a trading asset is 10 and costs are 1, a purchase would be recorded as: pay cash 11; create asset 10, report loss 1.

Just as non-trading assets, say, available-for-sale assets, are initially measured at fair value plus costs (gross cost), so non-trading liabilities are initially measured at fair value minus costs (net proceeds).

The rule of initial recognition at fair value (whether or not adjusted for transaction costs) means, for example, that any long-term receivables and payables that are not subject to a market rate of interest need to be discounted so that the net present value – the economic value – is recognised initially. For example, if a company sells goods to a customer for £150,000 receivable in two years' time, the seller should record revenue and an initial receivable of £136,054 (assuming a market rate of interest of 5 per cent). The seller then records interest income of £6,803 and £7,143 in years 1 and 2 respectively.

A similar example relates to a loan obligation. The initial proceeds received will often be equal to fair value. However, if the 'interest' payments are not at a market rate, fair value will be the net present value of the payments to be made over the life of the instrument. The effect of this is that a market rate of interest is imputed and charged to the income statement in arriving at profit/loss, rather than the stated (but off-market) rate.

In practice, if receivables or payables are due within a few months and the interest rate is low, discounting is ignored because it would not have a material effect.

Subsequent measurement

Although initial recognition of financial assets and liabilities is at fair value, the subsequent accounting treatment may or may not be. In order to determine the subsequent accounting, financial assets and liabilities are divided into categories. Financial assets are divided into:

(a) financial assets at fair value through profit or loss;
(b) held-to-maturity investments;
(c) loans and receivables; and
(d) available-for-sale financial assets.

Category (d) is the residual category for all financial assets that do not meet the definitions of the first three categories.

Categories (b) and (c) are accounted for at amortised cost (with the initial carrying amount (fair value plus transaction costs) regarded as cost), while categories (a) and (d) are subsequently accounted for at fair value (with no deduction for transaction costs that would be incurred on their sale). The amortised cost method is described below. Changes in fair value of assets in category (a) are recognised in arriving at profit/loss, whereas changes in fair value for available-for-sale (AFS) assets (category (d)), other than where these are in respect of foreign exchange movements or impairments, are taken to equity and reported as other comprehensive income. However, putting the gains or losses to equity is only a temporary treatment for AFS assets: the cumulative amount of such gains and losses is subsequently recognised in the income statement in arriving at profit/loss on the sale ('derecognition') of the asset.

Financial liabilities are divided into:

(a) financial liabilities at fair value through profit or loss; and
(b) all other financial liabilities.

The first category includes trading liabilities (only likely to be found in financial institutions) and derivatives with a negative value.

Liabilities in category (a) are measured at fair value and those in category (b) are measured at amortised cost.

Fair value through profit or loss

Any financial asset or liability held for trading must be classified as at fair value through profit or loss. A financial asset or financial liability must be classified as held for trading if it is:

'(i) acquired or incurred principally for the purpose of selling or repurchasing it in the near term;
(ii) part of a portfolio of identified financial instruments that are managed together and for which there is evidence of a recent actual pattern of short-term profit-taking; or
(iii) a derivative (except for a derivative that is a financial guarantee contract or a designated and effective hedging instrument).'[6]

In addition, certain financial assets or liabilities can be designated, on initial recognition, as held at fair value through profit or loss (often called 'the fair value option'), but only if recognising it at fair value results in more relevant information, because either:

• it eliminates or significantly reduces a measurement or recognition inconsistency (sometimes referred to as 'an accounting mismatch') that would otherwise arise from measuring assets or liabilities or recognising the gains and losses on them on different bases; or
• a group of financial assets, financial liabilities or both is managed and its performance is evaluated on a fair value basis, in accordance with a documented risk management or investment strategy, and information about the group is provided internally on that basis to the entity's key management personnel, for example the entity's board of directors and chief executive officer.

6 IAS 39, para. 9.

Box 17.5 *X plc*

Year	Charged in arriving at profit/loss	Balance sheet
2005	£5,538	£95,538
2006	£5,755	£99,293
2007	£5,986	£103,279
2008	£6,230	£107,509
2009	£6,491	£112,000
Total	**£30,000**	

Amortised cost

Some financial assets and the majority of financial liabilities are carried at 'amortised cost' using the effective interest method. ('Amortised cost' is a phrase that applies more naturally to assets; it may be easier to think of amortised proceeds in the case of liabilities.) This operates as follows in the case of a liability. The difference between the initial carrying amount (fair value less issue costs) and the total amount of payments that the issuer may be required to make in respect of interest and redemption payments represents the total finance cost. Because transaction costs are deducted from proceeds when calculating the initial carrying amount, this has the effect that the transaction costs are included in the total finance cost. The total finance cost is allocated over the term of the instrument at a constant rate on the carrying amount and, in accordance with IAS 39, is recognised as an interest expense in arriving at profit/loss.

Consider the following example. X Plc issued 100,000 10 pence redeemable preference shares on 1 January 2005 for £1 each. Issue expenses totalled £10,000. The shares pay an annual dividend of 2 pence per share on 1 January every year and are to be redeemed for £1.10 each on 1 January 2010.

On issue, the company receives £100,000 in proceeds from issuing shares. The shares are to be classified as financial liabilities in the financial statements because their substance is debt. The initial carrying value of the liability will be £90,000 (£100,000 minus issue expenses of £10,000). Assuming the company has a 31 December year end, the amount charged as interest in arriving at profit/loss and the balance sheet carrying amount is as shown in Box 17.5. The amount charged in arriving at profit/loss each year is greater than the dividend payable for each year. This excess represents an accrual of the redemption premium together with the spreading of the issue expenses. The total charge over the five years of £30,000 comprises the £10,000 issue expenses, £10,000 aggregate dividend payments and £10,000 redemption premium. The amounts are recognised in the interest line in the income statement (or the income statement part of the Statement of Comprehensive Income). In each case, the balance sheet figures assume that the dividend for the year just ended has not yet been paid. So, for example, the balance sheet liability at 31 December 2009 represents the redemption amount of £110,000 and dividend payable on 1 January 2010 of £2,000.

The amortised cost method works in a similar way in relation to financial assets. That is, the interest income earned on the asset is not just the stated coupon or interest rate, but also takes into account any initial costs and redemption amount – in other words, all the cash flows that relate to the asset are taken together and used to determine the effective interest rate.

Fair value

As noted above, many financial assets and some financial liabilities are required by IAS 39 to be stated at fair value. IAS 39 defines fair value in the same way that other international standards define it for other contexts: 'Fair value is the amount for which an asset could be exchanged, or a liability settled, between knowledgeable, willing parties in an arm's length transaction'.

Fair value is easy to determine for instruments in which there is a deep and liquid market, such as shares listed on a major stock exchange. However, for some financial assets and liabilities, determining fair value has been problematic, especially in the context of the credit crunch from late 2007.

There is extensive Application Guidance in IAS 39 relating to the determination of fair value. Although the detail is beyond the scope of this book, the key points are summarised in para. 48A of IAS 39 as follows:

> 'The best evidence of fair value is quoted prices in an active market. If the market for a financial instrument is not active, an entity establishes fair value by using a valuation technique. The objective of using a valuation technique is to establish what the transaction price would have been on the measurement date in an arm's length exchange motivated by normal business considerations. Valuation techniques include using recent arm's length market transactions between knowledgeable, willing parties, if available, reference to the current fair value of another instrument that is substantially the same, discounted cash flow analysis and option pricing models. If there is a valuation technique commonly used by market participants to price the instrument and that technique has been demonstrated to provide reliable estimates of prices obtained in actual market transactions, the entity uses that technique. The chosen valuation technique makes maximum use of market inputs and relies as little as possible on entity-specific inputs. It incorporates all factors that market participants would consider in setting a price and is consistent with accepted economic methodologies for pricing financial instruments. Periodically, an entity calibrates the valuation technique and tests it for validity using prices from any observable current market transactions in the same instrument (i.e. without modification or repackaging) or based on any available observable market data.'

Some companies and financial institutions have experienced difficulty in determining fair value, and many commentators have criticised them, especially where, in the absence of a market price, a model is used. This has been dubbed 'marking to model' as opposed to marking to market.

Despite this difficulty and controversy, fair value is likely to be retained as the basis for accounting for many financial instruments. The IASB's longer term objective is more extensive use of fair value, although it recognises that this is not a realistic objective in the short term.

Derivatives and embedded derivatives

Many companies use derivatives and, for many financial institutions, they are an integral part of their business. A derivative is a contract between (generally) a company and a financial institution which is to be settled at a future date. Its net value is usually about zero when signed, but moves up and down with the market price of some underlying variable, such as interest rates, the price of oil or the sterling/dollar exchange rate. Two common types of derivative are interest rate swaps and foreign currency forwards.

An interest rate swap serves to change an exposure to (say) floating or variable interest rates to an exposure to fixed interest rates. This is a 'floating to fixed' swap. A company with a floating rate debt obligation might take out a floating to fixed swap if it wanted to reduce or avoid its exposure to variable cash flows, i.e. to 'hedge' them.

In a similar way, a UK company might have $1 million receivable in three months' time arising from a sale denominated in dollars. However, it wants to avoid the exposure to changes in the dollar/sterling exchange rate during that three-month period. It can take out a forward contract to fix the amount of sterling that it will receive in respect of the $1 million. Like the floating to fixed interest rate swap, this forward contract hedges against variable cash flows. These instruments act as cash flow hedges.

A different example is where a company has exposure to variability in the fair value of an asset or liability. It does not want this exposure and so takes out a derivative to reduce or avoid that exposure. A fixed rate loan has stable cash flows, but a variable fair value. Other financial assets and liabilities also have variable fair values. A fixed to floating interest rate swap would act as a fair value hedge of a fixed rate loan. Various other derivatives would act as fair value hedges.

The third example of hedging is where a company has an overseas investment, denominated in (say) Euros. The sterling value of this will fluctuate and the company might want to reduce or avoid that fluctuation. It can do this by taking out a Euro borrowing, or a sterling/Euro derivative such as a forward contract to provide a hedge.

Sometimes derivatives are not freestanding, but are 'embedded' in other instruments or contracts. A host contract such as a borrowing, or a lease, or a purchase contract, might have within its terms a derivative that introduces exposure to (say) the sterling/dollar exchange rate, or to a particular stock exchange index; such a derivative may or may not be closely related to the host contract, and if it is not it needs to be separated from its host contract for accounting purposes.

The basic accounting rule relating to derivatives, as explained above, is that they are initially measured at fair value and subsequently treated as 'at fair value through profit and loss'. That is, they are treated as if they are held for trading or speculation. However, such treatment gives rise to volatility in income. It might be that there are offsetting gains and losses that are also reflected in income, in which case there is a natural hedge. However, if that is not the case, there is an unwanted volatility in income and it is to cater for such situations that hedge accounting has been developed.

Hedge accounting

The normal rules relating to derivatives are that they are treated as at fair value though profit and loss. However, if they are taken out to provide a hedge against another exposure, the accounting would give a more realistic representation of the commercial transaction if the gains and losses on the derivative were treated in a similar way to the losses and gains that they are hedging. This is what hedge accounting seeks to do. Hedge accounting is a collection of methods that break the normal rules of accounting. There are three types of hedge accounting, and these relate directly to the examples given in the above section on derivatives. These are:

- cash flow hedge;
- fair value hedge; and
- net investment hedge.

The mechanics are beyond the scope of this book. However, it is important to note that IAS 39's criteria that have to be met before hedge accounting can be used are restrictive. They include:

- documentation and designation at the time the hedge is taken out; and
- effectiveness testing – prospectively and retrospectively.

Many commercial uses of hedging do not, for various reasons, meet these criteria and so hedge accounting cannot be used. Such instances are sometimes called 'economic hedges', meaning that they are hedges from a commercial point of view, but are not treated as hedges in the accounting. The gains and losses on measuring such derivatives at fair value are therefore reported in arriving at profit/loss.

Recognition and de-recognition

IAS 39 sets out rules relating to when financial assets and liabilities should be recognised – that is, first put on balance sheet; and when they should be derecognised – that is, taken off balance sheet. The rules on recognition are reasonably straightforward: an item is recognised when the company becomes a party to the contractual provisions of the instrument.

The rules on derecognition are somewhat more complex. This is partly because the relevant transactions – such as securitisations – are complex. It is also because the rules are written in something of an anti-avoidance manner, as certain companies have sought to get assets and related obligations off balance sheet. The accounting hurdles, therefore, to achieve validly an off balance sheet treatment, or de-recognition, are high. A detailed treatment of de-recognition is beyond the scope of this book. However, the criteria involved are a mixture of loss of control and loss of the risks and rewards of ownership.

Other matters

Treasury shares

From 1 December 2003, certain British companies have been able to purchase up to 10 per cent of their issued share capital and hold the shares in treasury for subsequent sale, transfer in connection with an employee share scheme or cancellation. Prior to this date, any shares purchased had to be held in a trust or cancelled. The Companies Act rules governing treasury shares (or 'own shares') are to be found in chapter 6 of Part 18 (being ss. 724 to 732) of the Companies Act 2006.

The accounting treatment for treasury shares is to deduct them from shareholders' equity. They are in effect treated as though they had been cancelled and are, for example, disregarded when calculating earnings per share. They are shown as a deduction from shareholders' equity as a whole, but not netted against share capital as such, as the balance sheet figure for share capital represents the nominal value of the shares legally in issue (which, of course, includes the treasury shares held by the issuing company) that have been classified as equity. In law, treasury shares must be purchased out of the distributable profits of the entity that buys them.

There has developed a common practice of listed groups setting up Employee Share Ownership Plan (ESOP) trusts to purchase and hold shares in the listed company for use in ESOPs and Long-Term Incentive Plans (LTIPs), although this practice became prevalent primarily because, as noted above, until December 2003 a company could not purchase and hold shares in itself or its parent. The accounting treatment for such shares in the group accounts of the listed company is the same as for treasury shares, i.e. deduct from shareholders' equity.

Disclosures

IFRS 7 'Financial instruments: disclosures' contains the vast majority of disclosure requirements in respect of financial assets and financial liabilities, and it applies to all entities.

IFRS 7's disclosure requirements are very extensive and are grouped under the following headings:

- significance of financial instruments for financial position and performance;
  - balance sheet –
    - categories of financial assets and financial liabilities;
    - financial assets or financial liabilities at fair value through profit or loss;
    - reclassification;
    - derecognition;
    - collateral;
    - allowance account for credit losses;
    - compound financial instruments with multiple, embedded derivatives;
    - defaults and breaches;
  - statement of comprehensive income –
    - items of income, expense, gains or losses;
  - other disclosures –
    - accounting policies;
    - hedge accounting;
    - fair value;
- nature and extent of risks arising from financial instruments:
  - quantitative disclosures;
  - qualitative disclosures –
    - credit risk;
      - financial assets that are either past due or impaired;
      - collateral and other credit enhancements obtained
    - liquidity risk;
    - market risk – sensitivity analysis;
    - market risk – other market risk disclosures.

Accounting under UK GAAP

The UK standards, FRSs 25, 26 and 29, are based very closely on IASs 32 and 39 and IFRS 7. Accordingly, for companies that apply these FRSs, there is now a large degree of conformity between UK GAAP and accounting under IFRS. FRS 25 is required in UK GAAP. However, the scope of FRS 26 is different from the scope of IAS 39: IAS 39 applies to all entities, whereas FRS 26 is only mandatory for listed entities and other entities, excluding FRSSE entities, that recognise financial instruments in their accounts at fair value. Hence, relatively few UK companies use FRS 26 at present. The FRS 29 disclosures apply to companies that apply FRS 26 except that some subsidiaries are exempt from the requirements of FRS 29, whereas under IFRS the requirements of IFRS 7 apply to all entities.

For those entities not applying FRS 26, rules on accounting for financial liabilities are set out in FRS 4. The rules require the use of 'amortised cost' using the effective interest method as described above under IFRS.

Traditionally, the Companies Act 1985 required disclosures about a company's share capital and debentures. These remain in force and are now required by SI 2008/410 (large and medium companies). It is important to note, however, that the disclosures required about the authorised and issued shares must continue to be given for any instruments that legally are shares whether these are accounted for as equity instruments or financial liabilities.

New disclosures were introduced into the Companies Act 1985 regarding fair values, which are now also in SI 2008/410. All companies other than small companies now have to disclose the fair value of derivatives.

18

Share-based payment

Introduction

This chapter considers the accounting treatment required when a company issues share options or share awards as part of an employee's remuneration package or as consideration for any other goods or services received. It also considers the accounting required when a company issues any other form of consideration, for goods or services, which is calculated by reference to the company's share price, for example, phantom share options issued as part of an employee's remuneration package.

Issuing share options and granting other long-term incentive plans as part of an employee's remuneration package, in particular for executive directors, has long been a common practice in the UK. During the 'dotcom' boom, the practice was extended and it became common, for dotcom companies at least, to issue share options and shares, rather than cash, to non-employees as consideration for goods or services. In terms of employee remuneration, it is also now a widely accepted practice to make payments, as part of a long-term incentive scheme, that are in the form of cash, but which are calculated by reference to the growth in the company's share price.

Controversy, however, has surrounded the appropriate accounting treatment. Many have argued that, for share options and other share awards, there is no cost to the company itself; the 'cost' is to the shareholders who suffer a dilution in their share of the company. Consequently, the proponents of this view argue that the appropriate place to reflect these transactions is in the calculation of earnings per share and that there should be no charge in arriving at profit/loss. However, the predominant view now is that if goods or services have been received their cost should be reflected in the calculation of profit; that is, there should be an expense directly in the income statement. Support for this view is that it gives the same result as if the other party was paid in cash for the goods or services and then that party used the cash to subscribe for shares in the company. This treatment has been required under international accounting standards since 2005 (with no charge required prior to this date). The relevant accounting standard is IFRS 2 'Share-based payment'.

This is now also the required treatment in the UK (with the requirements of FRS 20 being identical to those of IFRS 2), but for the decade earlier a much more limited charge was required, often with employee share options resulting in a nil charge.

In this chapter we outline the requirements under IFRS 2, then look briefly at trusts, which often form part of the practical arrangements to pay employees via shares and share options, and finish by looking at UK GAAP in this area.

Accounting under IFRS

Overview

IFRS 2 'Share-based payment' is the relevant standard and is effective for accounting periods beginning on or after 1 January 2005.

Underlying this standard is the premise that if an entity acquires goods or services, the income statement should be charged with the value of those goods or services as the goods are consumed or the services received. The application of this general principle is, however, limited by the standard to the purchase of goods or services that are part of a 'share-based payment transaction'.

The standard requires that, when an entity receives or acquires goods or services in exchange for issuing shares, share options or as part of some other share-based payment transaction, the entity should recognise the goods when they are obtained and the services as they are received. If the share-based payment has a vesting period, the services will generally be recognised over that period. The amount, which is either the fair value of the goods or services received, the fair value of the equity instruments given or the fair value of the liability incurred (see below), is recognised in arriving at profit/loss unless the goods or services qualify for recognition as assets, e.g. as property, plant or equipment. For equity-settled share-based payment transactions (such as share options), there is a corresponding increase in equity, and for cash-settled share-based payment transactions (such as a phantom share option) a liability is recognised.

What is a 'share-based payment transaction'?

A share-based payment transaction is one where an entity purchases goods or services and pays for them using shares, share options or other equity instruments of the entity or incurs a liability that is determined by reference to the entity's share price or price of other equity instruments of the entity.

The most common examples of share-based payment transactions in a company are the granting of share options to an employee as part of his or her remuneration package or promising shares, or cash equal to the increase in share price, as part of a long-term incentive plan (LTIP). Under a typical executive share option scheme an employee will be granted options on day 1 permitting him or her to buy shares in the company from the company at any point in years 4 to 10, at the day-1 market price, providing he or she is still employed by the company and if predetermined performance criteria – say, the company's EPS outperformed the RPI over years one to three by x per cent – are met. Under an LTIP, an employee will typically receive shares, for no cash payment, after three or four years providing he or she is still employed by the company and if predetermined performance criteria are met, say, the company's total shareholder return (TSR) is ranked in the upper quartile when compared with the TSR of specified comparator companies. Both of these are examples of what the standard terms 'equity-settled share-based payment transactions' as the employee receives equity instruments in the company.

An example of a liability that is determined by reference to the entity's share price would be an LTIP under which an employee receives cash equal to the increase in share price over a specified period, typically three years. For the employee this is equivalent to receiving share options in the entity, exercising them on the first possible day and, on the same day, selling the shares in the market. Consequently, these are sometimes referred to as 'phantom share options' or 'share appreciation rights'. These are an example of what the standard terms 'cash-settled share-based payment transactions' as the employee directly receives cash from the company, which incurs an obligation, on day 1, to pay cash equal to the movement in the company's share price.

Basic principle of the standard

As with the purchase of any goods or services, for example, stationery, hire of plant and machinery and employee services, the standard explicitly requires the entity to charge the income statement with the cost of goods and services acquired as part of a share-based payment transaction as they are consumed. If goods are acquired that qualify for recognition as assets, for example, an item of plant, the cost is capitalised and recognised in the income statement as the item is consumed, for example, in the form of depreciation. All other goods are expensed when acquired. Services are expensed as they are received. Typically, companies enter into these transactions as part of employee remuneration and so the expense is charged in the income statement as the employee's services are received.

Having established this as the overriding principle, the standard contains detailed rules on how to apply this in practice, primarily dealing with how to calculate the amount to charge to the income statement (or capitalise on the balance sheet). Its rules are divided into those applying to equity-settled share-based payments and those applying to cash-settled share-based payment transactions.

Accounting for equity-settled share-based payment transactions

Equity-settled share-based payment transactions are transactions in which the entity uses its own equity instruments as consideration for goods or services,

---

Box 18.1 *Inputs to option-pricing models*

- the exercise price of the option;
- the life of the option;
- the current price of the underlying shares;
- the expected volatility of the share price;
- the dividends expected on the shares (if appropriate); and
- the risk-free interest rate for the life of the option.

---

for example, granting share options to employees as part of their remuneration package.

Under the standard, an equity-settled share-based payment transaction is recorded at the fair value of the goods or services acquired unless that value cannot be estimated reliably, as is deemed to be the case with employees, in which case the entity records the goods or services at the fair value of the equity instruments granted. For employees, the fair value is measured at grant date and for all other transactions it is measured at the date on which the entity obtains the goods or receives the services.

In the vast majority of cases, namely share options and other LTIPs for employees, the transaction is recorded at the fair value of the equity instruments issued (rather than at the fair value of what is received). The standard contains rules on how the fair value of the equity instruments should be calculated. Where a market price is available it should be used, but otherwise, as generally will be the case for share options, the fair value has to be estimated.

For employee share options, the standard mandates the use of an option-pricing model if, as is highly likely, traded options with similar terms and conditions do not exist. Commonly used models are the Black-Scholes-Merton model, the binomial model and the Monte-Carlo simulation. The calculations under these models are quite complex, as the fair value of options depends on a number of factors (see Box 18.1).

For share awards, rather than options, for example, an LTIP under which employees will receive shares (for no payment) in three years' time if certain conditions are met, the standard says that the fair value of the shares, adjusted to reflect the terms and conditions attached to the award, is to be used. In other words, for shares it may not be necessary to use an option-pricing model, but simply to deduct the present value of dividends expected during the vesting period from the market price of shares on the date of grant. However, the existence of market conditions (see below) may necessitate the use of a model in order to incorporate them into the fair value.

The objective in using the estimation techniques is to arrive at the amount that a third party would be willing to pay for the equity instrument when that instrument is granted. IFRS 2 adopts what it calls the 'modified grant date method': under this method, the fair value of the equity instruments (share options, share awards under an LTIP, etc.) are estimated taking into account market conditions only; all other conditions are ignored in arriving at the estimate of fair value. However, the other conditions are reflected in determining how much of this fair value should be expensed in the income statement over the vesting period.

Examples of market conditions are a share price or TSR target. Examples of non-market conditions are EPS targets or a condition requiring an employee to remain in service for a specified period.

Market conditions are reflected in the fair value and hence no subsequent adjustment is required; the fair value is charged over the vesting period, irrespective of whether or when the conditions are satisfied. Non-market conditions, on the other hand, are not reflected in the fair value and thus if a condition is not met causing the option or award not to vest, there will ultimately be no charge, or if the vesting period is variable (dependent on a non-market condition), the charge is ultimately spread over the actual vesting period.

The precise operation of the modified grant date method, initially, can appear to be quite complex, but the example in Box 18.2 should help to clarify the requirements.

Once options have vested, the cumulative charge remains and is not reversed through the income statement, even if the options subsequently lapse unexercised, say, because they are out of the money.

When share options are exercised by employees, the company records the receipt of cash and an increase in equity.

Accounting for cash-settled share-based payment transactions

Cash-settled share-based payment transactions are transactions in which the entity purchases goods or services, paying the supplier, in cash or other assets, an amount that is calculated by reference to the price of the entity's shares or other equity instruments. A common example is a phantom share option scheme (sometimes known as share appreciation rights) under which employees, as part of their remuneration package, are paid a cash bonus after three years, based on the rise in the company's share price over the three years.

Under the standard a cash-settled share-based payment transaction has to be recorded initially at the amount equal to the fair value of the liability incurred (calculated using an option-pricing model). An expense (or asset) is recorded equal to the liability. If the services will be received over a period, say, three years with the phantom share option scheme example above, the expense and liability are recorded gradually over that period. At each subsequent date, up to settlement of the liability, the liability is remeasured to its then fair value. Ultimately, the total expense charged in arriving at profit/loss equals the cash paid out under the scheme.

Box 18.2 *Example: Grant with market and non-market conditions*

At the beginning of year 1, company A grants 500 share options to each of its 100 most senior employees. The share options will vest at the end of year 3, provided that the employees remain in the company's employ, and provided that the company's Total Shareholder Return (TSR) at the end of the three years is in the upper quartile when compared with the TSR of each of twenty named competitors. If the TSR is below the upper quartile, the options lapse.

The TSR requirement is a market condition and the requirement to remain employed in the group is a non-market condition.

On grant date, company A estimates that the share options have a fair value of £20 each, which takes into account the TSR condition, but not the service condition. The company also estimates that 20 per cent of employees will leave before the end of year 3.

By the end of year 1, seven employees have left and the company still expects that a total of 20 employees will have left by the end of year 3.

By the end of year 2, five more employees have left, bringing the total to 12 to date. The entity now expects only three more employees to leave during year 3.

By the end of year 3, a further two employees have left.

APPLICATION OF REQUIREMENTS

Year	Calculation	Remuneration expense for the period £	Cumulative remuneration expense £
1	80 employees × 500 options × £20 × 1/3	266,667	266,667
2	(85 employees × 500 options × £20 × 2/3) – 266,667	300,000	566,667
3	(86 employees × 500 options × £20 × 3/3) – 566,667	293,333	860,000

Notes

The above accounting applies irrespective of whether the TSR requirement, which is a market condition, is met. The requirement to remain in service is a non-market condition and hence it is not reflected in the initial fair value and no charge is made if options lapse as a result of this condition not being met. Hence the ultimate charge only relates to the 86 employees still employed by the company at the end of year 3.

If instead of a TSR condition the options vested only if the company's EPS growth exceeded RPI by 6 per cent over the three years, the accounting would be as above (assuming that £20 is the fair value of the option, ignoring both the EPS and the service conditions) if the EPS condition was expected to be met and ultimately is met. If, on the other hand, the EPS condition (being a non-market condition) was not met, overall there would be no charge and in year 3 the earlier charges would be reversed, thus in year 3 there would have been a credit of £566,667.

Other requirements: IFRIC 8

IFRIC 8 'Scope of IFRS 2' adds an additional layer of complexity into the requirements. Developed to cater for one particular problem which was arising in one part of the world, it has far-reaching implications as its scope has not been limited in any way.

The IFRIC states that if the value of the goods or services initially identified as having been received is less than the fair value of equity instruments issued or liability incurred (in a cash-settled share-based payment transaction), the difference must be recognised as additional goods and services.

Other requirements: IFRIC 11

In the vast majority of cases, a listed company will not restrict participation in a scheme only to employees of the listed company itself; instead, employees from a number of subsidiaries as well as from the top company will participate. IFRS 2, in its scope section, requires the standard to be applied in the financial statements of those subsidiaries that have employees participating in a scheme even though the equity instruments issued are those of the top company. The standard does not specify how this should be applied, but in November 2006 guidance was provided in IFRIC 11 'IFRS 2 – Group and treasury share transactions'.

IFRIC 11 states that where a share-based payment transaction involves equity instruments of the entity's parent, it has to be accounted for as an equity-settled share-based payment transaction if the parent granted the rights (and it is accounted for as equity-settled in the group financial statements). There would thus be a charge to the subsidiary's income statement and the corresponding credit would be to reserves (being a capital contribution from the parent). If instead the entity itself (i.e. the subsidiary) granted the rights, the transaction has to be accounted for as a cash-settled share-based payment transaction.

Disclosure requirements

A large number of disclosures are required by IFRS 2, including, for share options granted during the period, which option pricing model was used and the inputs to that model.

Trusts

Trusts often form part of the practical arrangements for employee remuneration share-based payment transactions. Although companies can now hold some of their own shares in treasury, this is a relatively recent occurrence and prior to 1 December 2003 companies were not allowed to do so. Hence employee share ownership trusts were often set up to hold the shares (although this is complicated somewhat by the fact that legally trusts cannot hold shares;

beneficial ownership lies with the trust, but legally it is the trustees that own the shares). Tax advantages may be other reasons for structuring the practical arrangements through a trust.

Trusts can be used when new shares are issued by the company as well as when existing shares are used to satisfy the exercise of options or when shares are needed under an LTIP.

Although the trust deed will generally require the trustees to act in accordance with the interests of the beneficiaries, most trusts set up as part of a remuneration scheme are set up in such a way that the interests of the group and the duties of the trustees do not conflict. Generally, therefore, a group will control a trust set up to help with the operation of its share option or LTIP scheme and, thus, SIC-12 'Consolidation – Special purpose entities' will require the trust to be included in the group's consolidated financial statements as though it were a subsidiary. Consequently, the assets and liabilities of the trust are included in the group financial statements as though the group owned them. Shares in the company owned by the trust are thus included in the group accounts as though the group directly held them as treasury shares. Accordingly, the shares are deducted from equity. The share option scheme or LTIP will be accounted for in the group financial statements in accordance with the rules of IFRS 2 described above (as clarified by IFRIC 11); this is not affected by the fact that a trust owns the shares needed to satisfy, for example, share option exercises.

Accounting for share-based payment under UK GAAP

In UK GAAP the relevant standard since 2005 is FRS 20 'Share-based payment', which was issued by the ASB following the issue of IFRS 2 by the IASB. The ASB took IFRS 2 and adopted it with minimal changes. IFRIC 8 and IFRIC 11 have also been incorporated into UK GAAP.

Unlike IFRS, there were accounting requirements in UK GAAP prior to FRS 20. These requirements (primarily UITF 13 and 17) were in place and effective for the previous decade. Their scope was not as extensive as FRS 20 and IFRS 2: for example, save-as-you-earn (SAYE) schemes were exempt from the requirements. Under these requirements, the charge in arriving at profit/loss was the difference between the market price of the shares on the date of grant (or cost if the shares to satisfy exercise had been purchased by a trust in the market) and the amount, if any, that the employee had to pay on exercise. Thus, for many executive share option schemes there was no charge in arriving at profit/loss.

19

Realised and distributable profits

Introduction

The issues of which profits are realised and which are distributable are important. These issues arise for an individual company, not for a group: legally it is companies that make distributions, not groups. Thus, for example, in a simple group comprising a parent and its subsidiary, the subsidiary may make a distribution to its parent out of profits available for that purpose. The parent may then, if it has profits available for distribution (and this does not automatically follow simply because a subsidiary has dividended up some of its profits), make a distribution to its shareholders. Therefore, to speak of the group having distributable profits or having made a distribution is not valid. Problems can sometimes arise in a group, for all sorts of reasons, in getting distributions up from a profitable subsidiary to the top parent company so that it has sufficient distributable profits to make a distribution to its shareholders.

Accordingly, the matters discussed in this chapter relate to individual companies and the discussion concerns what amounts are realised and distributable for UK companies only. For companies registered in other countries, the rules may be different from those in the UK, although the basic rules for companies registered in other EU Member States are likely to be broadly similar (although the resulting number may be different due to different GAAPs applying), as the national laws of all Member States are based on the Second EU Company Law Directive of 1976, and it is the law that is the starting point for calculating realised and distributable profits.

'Realised' and 'distributable'

The two terms 'realised' and 'distributable' are related but separate and it is important to distinguish them.

It is appropriate to speak of a specific component of profit or gain as being realised (or not). Taking a simple example, if a company buys an asset for 1,000 and sells it for cash of 1,200, it has made a realised profit of 200. This is because: (1) it is clear that the profit has been made (it can be measured reliably); and (2) it has been received in cash. On the other hand, if the company has a building that cost 1,000 and it is now valued at 1,200, it may recognise that revaluation gain of 200 in its financial statements, but it has not realised the gain (and this applies irrespective of whether the gain was recognised in arriving at profit/loss under IAS 40 on investment properties or was recognised directly in equity). Hence the gain is regarded as an unrealised profit. Had the asset been shares rather than a building, the answer may not have been the same. A fuller analysis of what is realised and unrealised is given below.

Which profits are available for distribution is a matter for a company as a whole, based on the cumulative position with respect to realised profits at the relevant date. It will include, therefore, the aggregate of its transactions and events in the year (such as the examples in the previous para.) and the company's history, for example, whether it has an accumulation of realised profits from previous years. Again, a fuller analysis of this is given below.

General rules on distributions

Before turning to the Companies Act 2006, we should note that, under common law, a company cannot lawfully make a distribution out of capital. In addition, directors have fiduciary duties in the exercise of the powers conferred on them. Directors must therefore specifically consider, inter alia, whether the company would still be solvent following a proposed distribution. Therefore, directors should consider both the immediate cash flow implications of a distribution and the continuing ability of the company to pay its debts as they fall due. Even if a distribution would be in compliance with the Companies Act, the directors must consider the common law position and their fiduciary duties before determining whether to make the distribution.

Part 23 of the 2006 Act sets out rules relating to distributions. First, s. 829 explains the meaning of distribution as 'every description of distribution of a company's assets to its members, whether in cash or otherwise, subject to the following exceptions'. The exceptions are: a bonus issue of shares; a reduction of share capital; a redemption or repurchase of shares out of capital or unrealised profits (in accordance with specific provisions of the Act); and a distribution of assets to members on a winding up.

The most common type of distribution is a cash dividend. A dividend is often paid annually, sometimes supplemented by interim dividends, especially in the case of listed companies. In addition, companies sometimes pay one-off so-called 'special' dividends, perhaps to return a lump sum of cash to shareholders beyond the normal pattern of regular distributions. Moreover, a distribution need not be in cash: it can be a transfer of any asset. For example, one way of effecting a demerger is to make a distribution in specie of either: (1) the assets of the division that is to be demerged; or (2) the shares of the subsidiary that is to be demerged. Another non-cash dividend that companies sometimes make is a 'scrip' dividend; this is where shareholders receive shares in the company equal in value to the cash dividend that they would otherwise receive.

Section 830 defines what may be distributed, starting with the statement that: 'A company may only make a distribution out of profits available for the purpose'. Perhaps the key provision is subsection (2), which states that: 'A company's profits available for distribution are its accumulated, realised profits, so far as not previously utilised by distribution or capitalisation, less its accumulated, realised losses, so far as not previously written off in a reduction or reorganisation of capital duly made'. Simplifying this somewhat, profits available for distribution can be viewed as accumulated net realised profits. Realised profits and realised losses are discussed further on p. 184 below. There are additional provisions for investment companies and insurance companies, but these are not discussed here.

There is, however, an important complication that further restricts distributions by public companies (of which listed companies are a subset). That is that the basic rule in s. 830(2) still applies, but s. 831 adds, in subsection (1):

'A public company may only make a distribution –

(a) if the amount of its net assets is not less than the aggregate of its called-up share capital and undistributable reserves, and
(b) if, and to the extent that, the distribution does not reduce the amount of those assets to less than that aggregate.'

In this context, 'net assets' has its normal accounting meaning of aggregate assets less aggregate liabilities. A company's undistributable reserves are, in simplified form: (1) share premium account; (2) capital redemption reserve; (3) the excess of accumulated unrealised profits over unrealised losses; and (4) any other reserve that the company is prohibited from distributing by its articles or by legislation.

The practical effect of these rules can best be seen in Box 19.1.

So, for example, in company 2, the net unrealised loss of £50 is not relevant for a private company, but restricts distributions for a public company. In company 4, the same principle applies, but the effect is more dramatic: the public company cannot make any distribution despite having net realised profits.

Relevant accounts

The Act states that, in order to determine whether a company has profits available to distribute, and (if it is a public company) whether the additional conditions are satisfied, reference must be made to the *relevant accounts*.[1]

---

1 See s. 836.

Box 19.1 *Examples of distributable profits in private and public companies*

	Company 1		Company 2		Company 3		Company 4	
	£	£	£	£	£	£	£	£
A Share capital		1,000		1,000		1,000		1,000
B Unrealised profits	150		150		150		–	
C Unrealised losses	–		(200)		(200)		(200)	
D Net unrealised profits		150		–		–		–
E Net unrealised losses		–		(50)		(50)		(200)
F Realised profits	300		300		300		300	
G Realised losses	–		–		(120)		(120)	
H Net realised profits		300		300		180		180
I Share capital and reserves		1,450		1,250		1,130		980
Maximum distributable profit:								
Private company (H)		300		300		180		180
Public company (H-E)		300		250		130		Nil

Normally the company's latest audited financial statements that have been circulated to the company's members are its relevant accounts. However, where a distribution would exceed the amount that is distributable according to the latest audited financial statements, *interim accounts* must be prepared in addition to the latest financial statements to see whether the intended distribution can be justified. (The term 'interim accounts' as used here has a different meaning from the interim accounts required to be published regularly under the Listing Rules.) Moreover, *initial accounts* must be prepared and used where a company proposes to make a distribution during its first accounting reference period or before the date on which it circulates its first audited financial statements to its shareholders.

The requirements relating to interim and initial accounts depend on whether the company in question is private or public. If it is private, management accounts together with appropriate adjustments can be used to support a distribution. However, if it is a public company, the requirements are more onerous, as set out in ss. 837 to 839. The main points are that all relevant accounts, including interim and initial accounts, must be properly prepared and give a true and fair view, except that any matters that are not material for determining whether the proposed distribution is lawful may be omitted. Interim and initial accounts have to be filed at Companies House. In addition, with regard to any initial accounts (but not interim accounts), the auditors must have reported whether the accounts have been properly prepared. Annual accounts will, for a public company, be audited in any event. In connection with annual or initial accounts, if the audit opinion is qualified, the auditors must say

---

Box 19.2 *Analysis of change in shareholders' equity during the year*

Profit for the year (from the income statement)	U
Other comprehensive income (e.g. property revaluation)	V
Total comprehensive income	W
Proceeds of new shares issued	X
Dividends paid	(Y)
Increase in shareholders' equity (net assets) in the year	Z

---

whether that qualification is material in determining the legality of the proposed distribution.

Relationship with reporting of performance

The Act's rules about which profits are realised and distributable, although based on accounting numbers, are primarily legal rules concerned with regulating company distributions. They do not necessarily equate to today's notion of either profit or comprehensive income.

As explained more fully in chapter 9, comprehensive income is the sum of the profit (or loss) for the period and the entity's other comprehensive income (or other recognised gains and losses to use UK GAAP terminology). Most of the company's transactions are recognised in arriving at profit for the period; while other comprehensive income comprises all other changes in net assets other than those arising from distributions to or contributions from owners in their capacity as owners. Revaluation gains and losses on PPE such as land and buildings will, for the majority of companies, be part of other comprehensive income, but for a company that chooses to revalue its investment properties under IAS 40 the revaluation gains and losses are reported as part of profit or loss.

Total comprehensive income for the year is a measure that seeks to record performance in its widest sense. It is important to distinguish it from those other items that affect the company's shareholders' equity (or net assets) but which are not economic performance – that is, items such as new capital raised or redeemed, and dividends and other distributions. The distinction is illustrated in Box 19.2.

The line 'total comprehensive income (W)' is the most comprehensive measure of economic performance that accounting achieves. This is not to say that it is perfect. For example, a company may well develop the value of its brands or other intangibles through advertising, but that enhancement in value is not recorded by present-day accounting, largely because the measurement difficulties would render any numbers too unreliable.

Put another way, total comprehensive income is the change in *reported* net assets during the year, excluding contributions from or distributions to shareholders in their capacity as shareholders. It is the change in reported net assets rather than the change in the value of the net assets, as not all assets and liabilities will be recorded and of those recorded not all will be at valuation.

As to which transactions give rise to realised profits, guidance is given in TECH 01/08, which is discussed in the next section. It is important to note that not everything that is recognised in calculating profit or loss for the period is realised and not everything that comprises other comprehensive income is unrealised.

TECH 01/08

Introduction

The 'minor definitions' in Part 23 (Distributions) of the Act (section 853) include the following definition of realised profits and realised losses:

> 'References to "realised profits" and "realised losses", in relation to a company's accounts, are to such profits or losses of the company as fall to be treated as realised in accordance with principles generally accepted at the time when the accounts are prepared, with respect to the determination for accounting purposes of realised profits or losses.'

This somewhat circular definition has been taken by accountants to mean that realised profits and losses are whatever accountants think they are at the time. Guidance from the accountancy institutes helps to determine what this is.

Original guidance was issued in 1982 (TR 481 and 482) and was only superseded in 2003 by TECH 7/03, published by the Institute of Chartered Accountants in England and Wales and the Institute of Chartered Accountants of Scotland ('the Institutes'). TECH 7/03 was based on UK GAAP as it stood at the time of issue. Since then, of course, some companies have chosen to apply IFRS in their company accounts (it is only mandatory in respect of consolidated accounts of listed companies), while for those remaining on UK GAAP the standards that have to be applied have changed, in a number of cases adopting equivalent provisions to those in IFRS. Consequently, further guidance was developed and issued by the Institutes, in the form of TECH 2/07, which supplemented and, in places, superseded TECH 7/03. Two further pieces of guidance were published by the Institutes in 2004, dealing with specific and, at the time, urgent issues.

To make it simpler for users to apply the guidance, the Institutes issued a consolidated version of the four releases in January 2008, superseding the individual documents. Although described as 'guidance', the technical release is regarded by accountants as de facto rules as it is the most authoritative statement in the area. The consolidated guidance is TECH 01/08 'Guidance on the determination of realised profits and losses in the context of distributions under the Companies Act 1985'. The full text is available on the ICAEW website.[2] The guidance in TECH 01/08 applies equally to financial statements prepared under IFRS and UK GAAP.

In the light of its background, it is perhaps understandable that TECH 01/08 is based on the Companies Act 1985. Part 23 of the 2006 Act, which deals with distributions, does not make any significant changes to the law on distributions, although there are some minor changes of drafting. Accordingly, much of the guidance should remain valid. Part 17 of the Act, which deals with a company's share capital, and Part 18, which deals with the acquisition by a limited company of its own shares, also have some bearing on the guidance on realised and distributable profits. The Institutes are developing a revised version of the guidance incorporating references to the Companies Act 2006 and relevant consequential amendments, but at the time of going to press nothing had been issued.

Principles of realisation

TECH 01/08 explains that 'it is generally accepted that profits shall be treated as realised for the purpose of applying the definition of realised profits in companies legislation only when realised in the form of cash or of other assets the ultimate cash realisation of which can be assessed with reasonable certainty'.[3] It continues by stating that 'in this context, "realised" may also encompass profits relating to assets that are readily realisable'. In seeking to apply this, the expression 'readily convertible to cash' is introduced into the determination of realised profits.

Two further principles of realisation are set out in the guidance. First, the guidance notes[4] that: 'In assessing whether a company has a realised profit, transactions and arrangements should not be looked at in isolation'. This is an important point, as it brings into the analysis the principle of substance over form. Paragraph 3.5 adds: 'A realised profit will arise only where the overall commercial effect on the company satisfies the definition of realised profit set out in this guidance. Thus a group or series of transactions or arrangements should be viewed as a whole, particularly if they are artificial, linked (whether legally or otherwise) or circular'. Section 9 of TECH 01/08 deals with intra-group transactions, where this principle is likely to be of particular relevance, and is discussed below.

Second, TECH 01/08 notes[5] that 'a profit previously regarded as unrealised becomes realised when the relevant criteria set out in this guidance are met (for example, a revaluation surplus becomes realised when the related asset is sold for "qualifying consideration"). Similarly, a profit previously regarded as

---

2 www.icaew.co.uk.   3 See para. 3.3.   4 See para. 3.5.   5 See para. 3.6.

realised becomes unrealised when the criteria set out in this guidance cease to be met'.

Definitions

The definition of profit in TECH 01/08 is:

'3.8 "Profit" for the purpose of s. 262(3) [of the Companies Act 1985 – s. 853 of the 2006 Act is the equivalent reference] comprises:

(a) "gains", as defined in the Accounting Standards Board's "Statement of Principles for Financial Reporting" and "income" as defined in the International Accounting Standards Board's "Framework" which both convey (with different wording) increases in ownership interest not resulting from contributions from owners; and

(b) other amounts which are profits as a matter of law, or which are treated as profits, including:

(i) gratuitous contributions of assets from owners in their capacity as such;

(ii) an amount taken to a so-called "merger reserve" reflecting the extent that relief is obtained under ss. 131 or 132 of the Act [1985 Act – ss. 611 & 612 offer the same relief] from the requirement to recognise a share premium account; and

(iii) a reserve arising from a reduction or cancellation of share capital, share premium account or capital redemption reserve.'

This is not an obvious definition of profit to an accountant, but results from discussions with counsel in developing TECH 7/03 and TECH 02/07. An accountant would regard 'profit' as being the result reported in the income statement, and 'total comprehensive income' as being a wider measure of performance. The latter measure equates to 'gains' in the above quotation. Accountants would generally not see any of the three items within (b) in the above quotation as being part of profit, but counsel has advised that they should be so regarded for the purposes of analysing what is treated as a realised profit under the Companies Act 1985.

TECH 01/08 then defines a realised profit at some length, the first part of which is:

'3.9 A profit is realised where it arises from:

(a) a transaction where the consideration received by the company is "qualifying consideration"; or

(b) an event which results in "qualifying consideration" being received by the company in circumstances where no consideration is given by the company; or

(c) the recognition in the financial statements of a change in fair value, in those cases where fair value has been determined in accordance with the fair value measurement guidance in the relevant accounting standards, and to the extent that the change recognised is readily convertible to cash; or

(d) the translation of:
   (i) a monetary asset which comprises qualifying consideration; or
   (ii) a liability, denominated in a foreign currency; or
(e) the reversal of a loss previously regarded as realised; or . . . '

The definition of a realised loss is briefer: 'Losses should be regarded as realised losses except to the extent that the law, accounting standards or this guidance provide otherwise. The statutory position is set out in s. 2 of this guidance'.[6] That is, while not all losses are realised, there is a lack of symmetry in that losses are realised unless there is a specific reason to the contrary, whereas profits are realised only if they meet a complex definition.

A key definition is that of 'qualifying consideration'. This phrase is used extensively in the definition of realised profit.

'3.11 Qualifying consideration comprises:

(a) cash; or
(b) an asset that is readily convertible to cash; or
(c) the release, or the settlement or assumption by another party, of all or part of a liability of the company, unless:
   (i) the liability arose from the purchase of an asset that does not meet the definition of qualifying consideration and has not been disposed of for qualifying consideration; and
   (ii) the purchase and release are part of a group or series of transactions or arrangements that fall within para. 3.5 of this guidance; or
(d) an amount receivable in any of the above forms of consideration where:
   (i) the debtor is capable of settling the receivable within a reasonable period of time; and
   (ii) there is a reasonable certainty that the debtor will be capable of settling when called upon to do so; and
   (iii) there is an expectation that the receivable will be settled.'

Completing the definitions is 'readily convertible to cash', which is used in part (b) of the definition of qualifying consideration.

'3.12 An asset, or change in the fair value of an asset or liability, is considered to be "readily convertible to cash" if:

(a) a value can be determined at which a transaction in the asset or liability could occur, at the date of determination, in its state at that date, without negotiation and/or marketing, to either convert the asset, liability or change in fair value into cash, or to close out the asset, liability or change in fair value; and

6 See para. 3.10.

(b) in determining the value, information such as prices, rates or other factors that market participants would consider in setting a price is observable; and

(c) the company's circumstances must not prevent immediate conversion to cash or close out of the asset, liability or change in fair value; for example, the company must be able to dispose of, or close out the asset, liability or the change in fair value, without any intention or need to liquidate or curtail materially the scale of its operations, or to undertake a transaction on adverse terms.'

Effects of TECH 01/08

Changes in circumstances

Following the principle in para. 3.6 (quoted above), paras. 3.28 to 3.40 of TECH 01/08 elaborate on the fact that treatment as realised (or unrealised) may change over time. First, the principles of realisation may change. An example of this is the change to guidance in TECH 7/03 made by TECH 02/07 regarding which fair value gains are realised; as a result more fair value gains are regarded as realised. Second, and likely to be a more frequent event, a change in law or accounting regulation may affect realised profits. For example, a company changing from preparing its individual company financial statements from UK GAAP to IFRS for the first time will change a number of accounting policies. Depending upon particular company circumstances this might lead to higher or lower accumulated realised profits. Third, there may be a change in commercial circumstances. For example, a sale of goods or services may have led to the establishment of a receivable (or 'debtor') in the balance sheet. At the time, it was thought that the customer would pay, and so this represented 'qualifying consideration'. Subsequently, the customer may get into financial difficulty such that there is then no expectation that the receivable will be settled in cash or any other form of qualifying consideration. At that stage, what was initially regarded as a realised profit would no longer be so regarded. In accounting terms, there would be a provision for bad debts, or a write-off of that particular receivable, resulting in an expense in the income statement.

The fact that circumstances may change in one of these ways does not undermine the validity of treating the profit as realised in the first place, or of having made a distribution based on it in an earlier period.

A particular application of this that has been important in recent years is in relation to pensions. In UK GAAP, FRS 17 'Retirement benefits' was introduced in November 2000, but until 2005 it required only note disclosures, and permitted a continuation of the old accounting rules (SSAP 24) in the balance sheet and profit and loss account in that period. The result was often that the footnoted FRS 17 information showed a much larger deficit than the

SSAP 24 numbers. Hence accumulated realised profits, driven by the SSAP 24 numbers, understated the deficit compared with the amount calculated under FRS 17. Nevertheless, this did not mean that the FRS 17 disclosures supplanted the SSAP 24 numbers, nor did it mean that distributable profits had to be withheld beyond the amount implied by the SSAP 24 numbers.

Paragraph 3.30 of TECH 01/08 explains the situation in the following way:

> 'The effects of the introduction of a new accounting standard or on the adoption of IFRS become relevant to the application of the common law capital maintenance rule only in relation to distributions accounted for in periods in which the change will first be recognised in the accounts. Where items will fall to be treated as liabilities under a new standard in a period after the period in which the dividend is accounted for, directors do not have to pay regard to such future liabilities merely because they are disclosed in the notes to the accounts'.

An additional layer of complexity has been added by the change in timing of the recognition of a liability for a proposed dividend – the change in timing is explained in chapter 9 at page 85. Thus, where directors are considering paying an interim dividend for a financial year, say, 2009, or are considering proposing a final dividend for one year, say, 2008, that will be accounted for in the following year's financial statements, 2009 in the example given, the directors, before paying/proposing the dividends have to consider any known changes in accounting policies that will take effect in the year that the dividend will be accounted, 2009 in the example.

General examples of realised profits

Paragraphs 3.14 to 3.17 of TECH 01/08 give a number of examples of realised profits and losses. Most of these require no amplification. However, it is worth noting that 'a gift (such as a "capital contribution") received in the form of qualifying consideration' is a realised profit. A capital contribution would typically be received from a parent company or other shareholder. In accounting terms, a capital contribution would be recorded in equity and presented in the statement of changes in equity. That is, it would not be reported in the statement of comprehensive income or, if presented, in a separate income statement. Nevertheless, despite being shown as a transaction with shareholders, it is regarded by TECH 01/08 as a realised profit if in the form of qualifying consideration (although as with any transaction, the overall commercial effect has to be considered if it is part of a group or series of transactions). A gift from a third party would also be a realised profit, again if in the form of qualifying consideration, but the accounting treatment would differ: it would be recognised in the statement of comprehensive income.

Some other specific examples are discussed in the sections that follow.

Pension deficits

For companies that are complying with IAS 19 (IFRS) or FRS 17 (UK GAAP), questions arise about the impact of pension deficits on realised profits and as these are often very large numbers the impact can be huge. For a discussion of this, see 'The effect of pensions on realised profits' in chapter 16.

Fair value accounting: gains and losses

Fair value accounting under IFRS and UK GAAP as it now stands is far more widespread than when the original version of TECH 7/03 was issued. Following consultation on the point, TECH 02/07 amended TECH 7/03 to broaden the circumstances when a fair value gain may be regarded as realised; the revised guidance was consolidated into TECH 01/08.

To be regarded as realised, a fair value gain must be 'readily convertible to cash' and have been determined in accordance with relevant accounting standards. The requirement for the gain to be readily convertible to cash (see above for the definition) means that, for example, gains on revaluing property, plant and equipment and unquoted equity instruments will generally not be realised, whereas gains on revaluing, for example, equity instruments traded in an active market, will generally be realised; this will be so irrespective of the type of company that holds the instruments and irrespective of whether the gain has been credited in arriving at profit/loss for the year or has been credited direct to equity as is required for available-for-sale investments (providing that for companies reporting under UK GAAP the credit is to a fair value reserve and not to the revaluation reserve).

Share-based payment

Accounting for share-based payment is dealt with in chapter 18. Various questions arise in connection with the effect of accounting for such arrangements on realised profits. Guidance was given in TECH 64/04, published in 2004 by the Institutes, and has been consolidated into TECH 01/08; this deals with the effect of accounting for share schemes in accordance with UITF Abstracts 38 and 17 (revised), the earlier UK GAAP accounting rules.

TECH 01/08 extends the guidance to deal with expenses arising under IFRS 2 (and FRS 20). The expense charged in arriving at profit/loss will be a realised loss irrespective of whether the scheme is cash-settled or equity-settled. For every charge against profits under an equity-settled share-based payment transaction, there is an equal and opposite credit to equity. Generally, in the case of share options, the credit can be regarded as realised and thus negate the impact of the charge against profits being a realised loss. The credit to reserves will not always be regarded as realised, however, including that arising in a subsidiary's financial statements where the subsidiary reimburses its parent an amount in excess of the IFRS 2 (FRS 20) charge in respect of a share option scheme – see TECH 01/08 for further details.

Preference shares presented as liabilities

Under IAS 32 and FRS 25, an entity presents its capital instruments in accordance with their substance. For example, preference shares redeemable for a fixed amount on a specified date paying a cumulative fixed annual dividend would be classified in the balance sheet as liabilities and the dividend (together with any other finance charge, such as the amortisation of issue costs) would appear in the income statement as an 'interest charge'. TECH 01/08 explains that a preference dividend is a distribution at the time of its making and is not a loss. Thus, accruing for a preference dividend, albeit in arriving at profit/loss for the year, is not a realised loss. It further adds that the accrual for a preference dividend on preference shares presented as a liability does, however, restrict distributable profits for public companies due to the effect on the 'net assets test'.

Dividends out of pre-acquisition profits

Although this is not solely an intra-group issue, it does arise frequently within a group and, as such, is discussed below.

Intra-group transactions

As noted above, TECH 01/08 notes (para. 3.5) that: 'In assessing whether a company has a realised profit, transactions and arrangements should not be looked at in isolation'. This applies in particular in relation to intra-group transactions, because in the past certain transactions have been carried out, involving members of the same group, that have sought to generate realised and distributable profits at the entity level, despite the fact that the transaction is artificial or circular from a group perspective. Section 9 to TECH 01/08 addresses the question of whether, or in what circumstances, intra-group transactions give rise to realised profits. Some of the issues considered in section 9 are discussed below.

In connection with *dividends*, four situations are discussed. The starting point is that, subject to the points made in the following paras, a dividend received or receivable from a subsidiary will be a realised profit if the dividend is in the form of qualifying consideration. Most obviously, therefore, a dividend received in cash will be a realised profit. If a subsidiary declared a dividend to its parent but left it outstanding on inter-company account and had no ability or intention of settling it, that would not give rise to a realised profit to the parent. Paragraph 9.5 of TECH 01/08 also makes the point that it is necessary to consider whether a dividend from a subsidiary has given rise to an impairment in the value of the investment in the subsidiary.

191

Second, the guidance points out that it may be necessary for a subsidiary to pay dividends up to its parent before the parent's year end to ensure that the parent has sufficient distributable profits in its annual financial statements to support the expected level of proposed final dividend without the need to prepare interim accounts under s. 838 of the Act. The guidance therefore discusses what might constitute payment of an interim dividend and examines a number of scenarios.

The third situation outlined relating to dividends is a circular transaction in which a subsidiary pays a dividend to its parent where the parent has provided the funds for the dividend in the first place or the parent uses the proceeds of the dividend to reinvest in the subsidiary. Here, in general, the dividend received would not give rise to a realised profit to the parent, even if received in cash.

The fourth point relates to a dividend being paid by the subsidiary out of pre-acquisition profits. Prior to 1 January 2009, whether the parent was preparing accounts under IFRS or UK GAAP made a big difference to its distributable profits. From 1 January 2009, the accounting treatment, and thus the impact on distributable profits, will be the same under both GAAPs. Whether the dividend from a subsidiary is from pre- or post-acquisition profits, the accounting treatment going forward is to credit the dividend income in arriving at profit/loss for the year and thus the profit is realised if in the form of qualifying consideration. As in the general case, it is important to consider whether an investment is impaired following a dividend, especially one of unusual size.

Further examples of intra-group transactions relate to sales of assets between group companies. First, if a parent sells an asset to a subsidiary, any profit on the sale will not represent a realised profit for the parent if it does not receive an asset which is in the form of qualifying consideration. Second, the overall commercial effect of the sale and any related transactions and arrangements must be considered; for example, the profit would be unrealised if:

- there is an agreement or understanding regarding the repurchase of the asset by the parent; or
- the parent directly or indirectly provided the funds for the purchase, or reinvested the proceeds in the subsidiary by means of a capital contribution; or
- the subsidiary is unlikely to be able to meet its obligations under any borrowings used to fund the purchase without recourse to the parent.

Similar considerations apply where the subsidiary sells an asset to the parent. For example, if a subsidiary sells an asset to its parent and makes a profit on the sale, it could, other things being equal, distribute that profit to the parent. However, the profit would not be realised in the hands of the parent unless the asset which the parent purchased meets the definition of qualifying consideration. The reason is that the transaction is very similar in its overall effect to a distribution of the asset in specie to the parent – which is not a transaction on which the parent would record a realised profit, unless the asset distributed itself took the form of qualifying consideration.

A third example is given in section 9 of TECH 01/08 concerning a sale of an asset from one subsidiary to a fellow subsidiary, followed by a dividend to the parent of the profit made on the sale. Similar principles arise to those discussed above.

The underlying theme in section 9 of TECH 01/08 is to apply a substance over form approach to intra-group transactions, although, of course, looking at the substance in determining distributable profits is not limited to intra-group transactions.

20

Disclosures in published annual reports

Introduction

Published financial information for an IFRS annual report is centred around a company's income statement, statement of comprehensive income, balance sheet and cash flow statement – the main IFRS primary statements. Extensive notes in the financial statements provide more detailed disclosure in support of the numbers in these primary statements. For example, there are notes to give more detail about the categories of property, plant and equipment (land and buildings, vehicles and machinery and so on) and to give details of the movements during the year (the amount at the beginning of the year, the additions, disposals, depreciation and so on). Similar details are given about intangible assets, provisions, share capital and reserves and many other items in the primary statements.

In addition, there are disclosures under a number of headings that do not directly amplify the items in the primary statements, but are free-standing. Some apply to all companies; some to listed companies only; and some to quoted companies (which includes listed companies). Some are within the financial statements while others are outside, albeit within the overall annual report. This chapter contains a brief discussion of these disclosures, under the following headings:

- Corporate governance disclosures;
- Statement of directors' responsibilities;
- Directors' report;
- Operating and financial review;
- Directors' remuneration;
- Related party relationships and transactions;
- Transactions with directors; and
- Segment disclosure.

Corporate governance disclosures

For accounting periods beginning on or after 29 June 2008, the corporate governance disclosures applicable to UK listed companies come from three different sources: the FSA Listing Rules; the FSA Disclosure and Transparency

Rules; and the FRC Combined Code ('the Code'). Rules and recommendations about corporate governance practice (as opposed to disclosures) are to be found in the last two of these three.

Listing Rules

Listing Rule 9.8.6R requires UK listed companies to include in their annual report and accounts a two-part disclosure statement in relation to the Code. The Code comprises both principles and provisions with one part of the Listing Rules' disclosure requirement about the principles and the other part about the provisions.

The first part requires companies to explain how they have applied the main principles set out in Section 1 of the Code. Prior to this (i.e. accounting periods beginning before 29 June 2008), companies had to explain how they had applied the main *and supporting* principles set out in Section 1. However, the resulting narrative reporting was lengthy and tended to include much boiler-plate wording and the change to reporting only in respect of the *main* principles is designed to reduce the amount of boiler-plate reporting. A parallel move may reduce the reporting further; both the FRC, in the preamble to the 2008 Code, and the FSA have stated that where a company has applied the Code's main principles by complying with the associated *provisions* it should be sufficient simply to report that this is the case. Where a company has taken additional actions to apply the principles or otherwise improve its governance, the FRC and FSA say that it would be helpful to shareholders to describe these in the annual report.

The second part of the disclosure is a statement as to whether or not the company has complied throughout the accounting period with the *provisions* (as distinct from the principles referred to above) set out in Section 1 of the Code. If there are instances of non-compliance, the company must specify the Code provisions with which it has not complied, and (where relevant) for what part of the period such non-compliance continued, and give reasons. The FRC, in the preamble to the 2008 Code, stated that where a company has chosen not to comply with one or more provisions of the Code, the company, in its explanation, should aim to illustrate how its actual practices are consistent with the associated principle and contribute to good governance.

A listed company is required to have its auditor review the corporate governance statement disclosures in relation to nine of the forty-eight FRC Combined Code provisions.

Disclosure and Transparency Rules

The FSA has introduced rules on corporate governance into the DTR. They similarly apply for accounting periods commencing on or after 29 June 2008. The rules require a company to have an audit committee (with minimum criteria and responsibilities stipulated) and require various corporate governance

195

disclosures to be included in a corporate governance statement: in the directors' report; separately issued to accompany the annual report and accounts; or made available on the company's website (but with a cross-reference to it in the directors' report). Some of the disclosures are already required by SI 2008/410 to be in the directors' report. With one exception, all of the other corporate governance requirements of the DTR will be satisfied if specific provisions of the Code are complied with. The exception is the requirement to give a description of the main features of the group's internal control and risk management systems in relation to the consolidated financial reporting process.

Combined Code

For accounting periods commencing on or after 29 June 2008, the applicable Code (and thus the one reported on under the Listing Rules) is the 2008 Code; for periods prior to these the Code reported on is the 2006 Code. There are very few differences between the two Codes, with the main changes being to remove the prohibition on an individual chairing more than one FTSE 100 company and to permit the company chairman of a smaller company (that is, outside the FTSE 350) to serve on (but not chair) the audit committee where he or she was considered independent on appointment as chairman (although if he or she sits on the committee this has to be in addition to the two independent non-executive directors already recommended in the 2006 Code).

The Code sets out principles and provisions on corporate governance, both practice that companies should adopt and disclosure of practice, none of which are mandatory under the Code itself. The Code has a 'comply or explain' culture as has been the case since the Code's original forerunner, the Cadbury Code, was issued in 1992. The Listing Rules do not change this; they require disclosure of whether or not the provisions were applied and detail of any departures. Some commentators believe that companies should comply. However, the FRC, in the preamble to the 2008 Code, emphasised the 'comply or explain' culture and sought to promote it. The newly introduced DTR requirements on corporate governance are, however, requirements. Hence in a few areas companies will now be obliged to comply.

Schedule C to the Code usefully summarises the disclosure requirements from all three sources (and runs to five-and-a-half pages). The section setting out the provisions from the Code that, if applied, lead to disclosure in the report and accounts is reproduced below.

> 'The Combined Code
> In addition the Code includes specific requirements for disclosure which are set out below:
> The annual report should record:
>
> * a statement of how the board operates, including a high level statement of which types of decisions are to be taken by the board and which are to be delegated to management (A.1.1);

- the names of the chairman, the deputy chairman (where there is one), the chief executive, the senior independent director and the chairmen and members of the nomination, audit and remuneration committees (A.1.2);
- the number of meetings of the board and those committees and individual attendance by directors (A.1.2);
- the names of the non-executive directors whom the board determines to be independent, with reasons where necessary (A.3.1);
- the other significant commitments of the chairman and any changes to them during the year (A.4.3);
- how performance evaluation of the board, its committees and its directors has been conducted (A.6.1);
- the steps the board has taken to ensure that members of the board, and in particular the non-executive directors, develop an understanding of the views of major shareholders about their company (D.1.2).

The annual report should also include:

- a separate section describing the work of the nomination committee, including the process it has used in relation to board appointments and an explanation if neither external search consultancy nor open advertising has been used in the appointment of a chairman or a non-executive director (A.4.6);
- a description of the work of the remuneration committee as required under the Directors' Remuneration Report Regulations 2002, and including, where an executive director serves as a non-executive director elsewhere, whether or not the director will retain such earnings and, if so, what the remuneration is (B.1.4);
- an explanation from the directors of their responsibility for preparing the accounts and a statement by the auditors about their reporting responsibilities (C.1.1);
- a statement from the directors that the business is a going concern, with supporting assumptions or qualifications as necessary (C.1.2);
- a report that the board has conducted a review of the effectiveness of the group's system of internal controls (C.2.1);
- a separate section describing the work of the audit committee in discharging its responsibilities (C.3.3);
- where there is no internal audit function, the reasons for the absence of such a function (C.3.5);
- where the board does not accept the audit committee's recommendation on the appointment, reappointment or removal of an external auditor, a statement from the audit committee explaining the recommendation and the reasons why the board has taken a different position (C.3.6); and
- an explanation of how, if the auditor provides non-audit services, auditor objectivity and independence is safeguarded (C.3.7).

The following information should be made available (which may be met by placing the information on a website that is maintained by or on behalf of the company):

- the terms of reference of the nomination, remuneration and audit committees, explaining their role and the authority delegated to them by the board (A.4.1, B.2.1 and C.3.3);
- the terms and conditions of appointment of non-executive directors (A.4.4) . . . ; and
- where remuneration consultants are appointed, a statement of whether they have any other connection with the company (B.2.1).

The board should set out to shareholders in the papers accompanying a resolution to elect or re-elect directors:

- sufficient biographical details to enable shareholders to take an informed decision on their election or re-election (A.7.1);
- why they believe an individual should be elected to a non-executive role (A.7.2); and
- on re-election of a non-executive director, confirmation from the chairman that, following formal performance evaluation, the individual's performance continues to be effective and to demonstrate commitment to the role, including commitment of time for board and committee meetings and any other duties (A.7.2).

The board should set out to shareholders in the papers recommending appointment or reappointment of an external auditor:

- if the board does not accept the audit committee's recommendation, a statement from the audit committee explaining the recommendation and from the board setting out reasons why they have taken a different position (C.3.6).'

An appendix to Schedule C to the 2008 Code highlights the overlap between the requirements of the FSA's DTR and the Code's provisions.

Schedule C also points out that the Turnbull Guidance and the Smith Guidance contain further suggestions regarding disclosures that could be included in the internal control statement and the audit committee report respectively. The disclosures set out in the Turnbull report on internal controls are as follows:

'Four – The board's statement on internal control

33 The annual report and accounts should include such meaningful, high-level information as the board considers necessary to assist shareholders' understanding of the main features of the company's risk management processes and system of internal control, and should not give a misleading impression.

34 In its narrative statement of how the company has applied Code Principle C.2, the board should, as a minimum, disclose that there is an ongoing process for identifying, evaluating and managing the significant risks faced by the company, that it has been in place for the year

under review and up to the date of approval of the annual report and accounts, that it is regularly reviewed by the board and accords with the guidance in this document.

35 The disclosures relating to the application of Principle C.2 should include an acknowledgement by the board that it is responsible for the company's system of internal control and for reviewing its effectiveness. It should also explain that such a system is designed to manage rather than eliminate the risk of failure to achieve business objectives, and can only provide reasonable and not absolute assurance against material misstatement or loss.

36 In relation to Code Provision C.2.1, the board should summarise the process it (where applicable, through its committees) has applied in reviewing the effectiveness of the system of internal control and confirm that necessary actions have been or are being taken to remedy any significant failings or weaknesses identified from that review. It should also disclose the process it has applied to deal with material internal control aspects of any significant problems disclosed in the annual report and accounts.

37 Where a board cannot make one or more of the disclosures in paragraphs 34 and 36, it should state this fact and provide an explanation. The Listing Rules require the board to disclose if it has failed to conduct a review of the effectiveness of the company's system of internal control.

38 Where material joint ventures and associates have not been dealt with as part of the group for the purposes of applying this guidance, this should be disclosed.'

As suggested by the above list, the disclosures on corporate governance are lengthy and often run to seven to ten pages (excluding the report on directors' remuneration). Even taking account of any possible reduction in disclosure regarding how the Code's principles have been applied (discussed under 'Listing Rules' above), the disclosures look set to remain lengthy.

Statement of directors' responsibilities

Code provision C.1.1 states that: 'The directors should explain in the annual report their responsibility for preparing the accounts and there should be a statement by the auditors about their reporting responsibilities'. One of the auditing standards governing the work of the auditors requires the audit report to include a reference to the description of the directors' responsibilities or, where one has not been included in the report, a description of those responsibilities. Not all of the directors' responsibilities are listed in the responsibility statement. Both the Combined Code and the auditing standard deal only with the directors' responsibilities in respect of the preparation of the financial statements.

The Companies Act 2006 (ss. 170–81) sets out a statutory statement of directors' duties which apply to all directors, including non-executive directors. The duties are as follows:

- duty to act within the powers conferred by the company's constitution;
- duty to promote the success of the company for the benefit of its members as a whole;
- duty to exercise independent judgement;
- duty to exercise reasonable care, skill and diligence;
- duty to avoid conflicts of interest;
- duty not to accept benefits from third parties; and
- duty to disclose any interest in a proposed transaction or arrangement with the company.

This is not an exhaustive list of directors' duties contained in statute. For example, directors also have a duty to deliver accounts and reports to the Registrar, but this is not contained in the Act's section on general duties of directors. Neither does it codify every duty contained in common law; for example, it does not codify the directors' duty to consider the interests of creditors when the company is on the verge of insolvency.

Although these duties are newly introduced into legislation, they do not relate to the preparation of accounts and so they do not have to be referred to in the statement of directors' responsibilities that is needed to satisfy the Combined Code and the auditing standard. However, regarding the business review required to be included in the directors' report, the Act states that its purpose is to inform members of the company and help them to assess how the directors have performed their duty, under s. 172, to promote the success of the company. See below under directors' report.

The Transparency Directive introduced, for accounting periods beginning on or after 20 January 2007, a requirement for a responsibility statement. The requirement has been incorporated by the Financial Services Authority into its 'Disclosure and Transparency Rules' ('DTR'). The DTR require that the persons responsible within a listed company (that is, the directors) make a responsibility statement setting out that to the best of their knowledge:

(a) the financial statements, prepared in accordance with the applicable set of accounting standards, give a true and fair view of the assets, liabilities, financial position and profit or loss of the listed company and the undertakings included in the consolidation taken as a whole; and

(b) the management report includes a fair review of the development and performance of the business and the position of the company and the undertakings included in the consolidation taken as a whole, together with a description of the principal risks and uncertainties that they face.

The DTR also require that the name and function of any person who makes a responsibility statement is clearly indicated in the responsibility statement.

Both statements (a) and (b) above could be incorporated into the existing directors' responsibility statement. Alternatively, statement (b) could be included in the directors' report.

An example of a statement of directors' responsibilities, for a listed company using IFRS in its single entity accounts as well as in its group accounts, that would satisfy the Combined Code and the auditing standard and that is combined with the statements required by the DTR is set out in Box 20.1.

Directors' report

Section 415 of the 2006 Act requires the directors of all companies to prepare a directors' report.

Much of the content of the directors' report as required by the 2006 Act comes from the requirements in the 1985 Act, two significant parts of which had only been added in 2005: the requirement for a Business Review and the requirement for the directors' statement regarding disclosure of information to the auditors. The content requirements have been further added to by the 2006 Act: in particular, the 2006 Act added to the required content of the Business Review. There is quite a large overlap between the content required in a Business Review and that recommended by the ASB for an OFR (see below).

Requirements for the directors' report include:

- principal activities of the group;
- names of company directors;
- disclosure of any qualifying indemnity provision for the benefit of one or more directors;
- the amount (if any) which the directors recommend should be paid as dividend;*
- a statement (unless the company has taken advantage of an exemption from audit) to confirm, for all directors in office at the time the report is approved, the following:
  - so far as each director is aware, there is no relevant audit information of which the company's auditor is unaware (relevant information is defined as 'information needed by the company's auditor in connection with preparing his report'); and
  - each director has taken all the steps that he or she ought to have taken as a director in order to make him- or herself aware of any relevant audit information and to establish that the company's auditor is aware of that information;
- a business review* containing –
  - a fair review of the group's business, being, a balanced and comprehensive analysis of the development and performance of the group's business during the financial year and the position at the end of the

---

Box 20.1 *Statement of directors' responsibilities in respect of the Annual Report, the Directors' Remuneration Report and the financial statements*

The directors are responsible for preparing the Annual Report, the Directors' Remuneration Report and the financial statements in accordance with applicable law and regulations.

Company law requires the directors to prepare financial statements for each financial year. Under that law the directors have prepared the group and parent company financial statements in accordance with International Financial Reporting Standards (IFRSs) as adopted by the European Union. In preparing these financial statements, the directors have also elected to comply with IFRSs issued by the International Accounting Standards Board (IASB).[1] The financial statements are required by law to give a true and fair view of the state of affairs of the company and the group and of the profit or loss of the group[2] for that period.

In preparing these financial statements, the directors are required to:

- select suitable accounting policies and then apply them consistently;
- make judgements and estimates that are reasonable and prudent;
- state that the financial statements comply with IFRSs as adopted by the European Union and IFRSs issued by IASB.

The directors are also required by the Disclosure and Transparency Rules of the Financial Services Authority and by the Companies Act 2006 to include a fair review of the business and a description of the principal risks and uncertainties facing the group and company.

The directors are responsible for keeping proper accounting records that disclose with reasonable accuracy at any time the financial position of the company and the group and to enable them to ensure that the financial statements and the Directors' Remuneration Report comply with the Companies Act 2006 and, as regards the group financial statements, Article 4 of the IAS Regulation. They are also responsible for safeguarding the assets of the company and the group and hence for taking reasonable steps for the prevention and detection of fraud and other irregularities.

The directors are responsible for the maintenance and integrity of the company's website. Information published on the company's website is accessible in many jurisdictions. Legislation in the United Kingdom governing the preparation and dissemination of financial statements may differ from legislation in other jurisdictions.[3]

Directors' statement pursuant to the Disclosure and Transparency Rules

Each of the directors, whose names and functions are listed in [refer to section of annual report containing details of directors] confirm that, to the best of each person's knowledge and belief:

- the financial statements, prepared in accordance with IFRSs as adopted by the EU, give a true and fair view of the assets, liabilities, financial position and profit [loss] of the group and company; and
- the business review[4] contained in the directors' report[4] includes a fair review of the development and performance of the business and the position of the company and group, together with a description of the principal risks and uncertainties that they face.

By order of the board

Name

Company Secretary

Date

[1] This sentence would not be included if the accounts complied with IFRS as adopted by the EU but not also full IFRS.

[2] This assumes that the parent company takes the s. 230 exemption in the Companies Act 1985 and does not present the parent company income statement.

[3] This paragraph only needs to be included if the financial statements are included on the company's website, and need not be included in the printed version of the financial statements.

[4] Insert here whichever name has been used for the review and wherever it is located within the annual report.

This statement assumes that the directors have given a separate statement about going concern under provision C.1.2 of the Combined Code and LR 9.8.6R(3).

year, consistent with the size and complexity of the business, including, to the extent necessary:

- analysis using financial key performance indicators and, unless medium-sized, other, including environmental and employee, key performance indicators;
- (quoted companies only) main trends and factors likely to affect the future development, performance and position of the group's business;
- (quoted companies only) information, including policies and effectiveness of those policies, about: environmental matters (including the impact of the business on the environment); employees; and social and community issues (or state which information has not been included);
- (quoted companies only) information about persons, so long as it is not seriously prejudicial to such person and contrary to the public interest, with whom the company has contractual or other arrangements which are essential to the business (or state which information has not been included);

○ description of principal risks and uncertainties facing the group;
if any information, required above to be included in the business review, about impending developments or matters in the course of negotiation would, in the opinion of the directors, be seriously prejudicial to the interests of the company, it may be omitted;

- likely future developments;*
- political donations and expenditure;
- charitable donations;
- financial risk management objectives and policies and the group's exposure to price risk, credit risk, liquidity risk and cash flow risk;*
- company's acquisition of its own shares;
- employment of disabled people;
- employee involvement;*
- policy and practice on payment of creditors;*
- (publicly traded companies only) various, including details of the company's capital structure, restrictions in transferring shares, restrictions in voting rights, significant shareholders, significant change of control clauses, and agreements for compensation for loss of office on a takeover bid.

* not required by companies subject to the small companies regime.

In addition, the Listing Rules add some further disclosures, for example, the interests of directors in the company's shares. The DTR now requires various disclosures on corporate governance to be included in the directors' report, although this can be included by means of a cross-reference – see corporate governance above.

The requirements have tended to produce a report containing a somewhat eclectic collection of information, much of it introduced as political imperative or fashion of the day. Especially in the case of listed companies, where the disclosure of the 'business review' tends to be addressed in much more detail in the OFR, with the directors' report containing a cross-reference to the OFR, the directors' report is left as a rather odd document.

The Act states that 'the purpose of the business review is to inform members of the company and help them assess how the directors have performed their duty under s. 172 (duty to promote the success of the company)'. See above for a discussion of the directors' duties (under statement of directors' responsibilities).

The Financial Reporting Review Panel's (see chapter 4) scope was recently extended to include directors' reports, including the business review. The Panel has stated, inter alia, that: 'In its consideration of business reviews, the Panel will consider whether the review is consistent with the accounts and with other material included in the Annual Report and whether it is balanced and comprehensive in the sense that it deals even-handedly with the positive and negative aspects of the development, performance and position of the business'.

The 2006 Act (s. 463) gives 'safe harbour' to directors in respect of statements made within the directors' report that subsequently prove to be untrue or misleading and in respect of information not included that should have been included, provided that the directors did not know at the time of making any such statements that they were untrue or misleading (or were reckless as to whether they were untrue or misleading) or, in the case of an omission, there was not a dishonest concealment of facts. It is expected that this 'safe harbour' would also apply to business review disclosures contained within an OFR provided they are cross-referenced from the directors' report.

Operating and financial review

The OFR has been for some years, and remains today, a voluntary statement published by most listed companies and some other public interest companies. It is primarily a narrative statement outside the audited financial statements, but part of the annual report. It is similar to the US 'Management's discussion and analysis'. The content of OFRs has generally followed the non-mandatory guidance issued by the ASB (originally in 1993 and subsequently updated, the last update being in 2006). Whilst a number of companies head their narrative report with the title 'Operating and Financial Review', not all do so; others, for example, include the relevant content under the heading of 'Chief Executive's review' or in a number of separately headed reports.

Recent government action

Whilst this non-mandatory approach has been reasonably successful, the DTI took the view that narrative reporting across a wider range of issues than just financial performance was increasingly important. Hence they brought forward proposals for legislation in May 2004 for listed companies to prepare a statutory OFR. Final regulations were passed into law in March 2005, being effective for financial years beginning on or after 1 April 2005, requiring quoted companies to prepare and publish an OFR. A new style of document, a 'Reporting Standard', was developed by the ASB on the OFR to complement the legislation, as the legislation was not itself detailed.

Unexpectedly, in November 2005, Gordon Brown, then the Chancellor of the Exchequer, announced that the statutory requirement for an OFR would be withdrawn. Regulations repealing the requirement came into force in January 2006. The reason given was that other new requirements which were simultaneously introducing a business review into the directors' report (see above), in order to implement an EU Directive, had a core in common with the OFR requirements and that government policy is not to impose regulatory requirements on business in excess of those needed to implement Directives.

Reporting Standard 1 was withdrawn by the ASB as it no longer had any statutory underpinning. The document was converted into a best practice statement and issued as 'Reporting Statement 1', retaining the abbreviated title of RS 1. The main difference between the Reporting Standard and the Reporting Statement is the adoption of language appropriate for a voluntary document rather than a mandatory one.

ASB Reporting Statement

As stated above, the 'Reporting Statement' on the OFR is persuasive rather than mandatory. It is aimed at quoted companies, but is also applicable to any other entities preparing an OFR. Quoted companies were the audience of the legislation before its withdrawal and were defined as those admitted to the Official List; or officially listed in the European Economic Area; or admitted to either the New York Stock Exchange or NASDAQ.

RS 1 is principles-based, recommending that directors prepare an OFR addressed to members that:

- reflects the directors' view of the business;
- focuses on matters that are relevant to members;
- has a forward-looking orientation;
- complements as well as supplements the financial statements;
- is comprehensive and understandable;
- is balanced and neutral; and
- is comparable over time.

The OFR should provide a balanced and comprehensive analysis of:

- the development and performance of the business during the year;
- the entity's position at the year end;
- the main trends and factors underlying the development, performance and position of business of the entity during the year; and
- the main trends and factors likely to affect future development, performance and position,

to help members to assess an entity's strategies and the potential for those strategies to succeed.

The statement provides a basic framework for disclosure, but allows directors the flexibility to tailor the OFR to an entity's particular circumstances. The framework covers:

- the nature, objectives and strategies of the business, including a description of the environment in which it operates;
- the development and performance of the business (for current and future periods);
- the resources, principal risks and uncertainties and relationships that may affect the entity's long-term value; and

- the position of the business (including a description of the capital structure, treasury policies and objectives and liquidity of the entity for current and future periods).

In satisfying the above, information should be given about: persons with whom the entity has contractual or other arrangements which are essential to the entity's business; employees; receipts from, and returns to, members in respect of shares held by them; environmental matters, including the impact of the business on the environment; and social and community issues. Additionally, all other matters that the directors consider to be relevant should be disclosed. For environmental matters, employees and social and community issues, the disclosure should include details of the entity's policies and the extent to which they have been implemented.

Directors should, to the extent necessary to meet the framework recommendations, disclose the key performance indicators (KPIs), financial and non-financial, judged to be effective in measuring delivery of their strategies and in managing their businesses. Disclosures that should be made for each KPI included in the OFR are set out in RS 1.

Disclosure need not be given of impending developments or matters in the course of negotiation if, in the opinion of the directors, they would be seriously prejudicial to the entity's interests.

Publication of an OFR on a voluntary basis is in our view a useful and important part of corporate reporting and most listed companies present one. However, as noted above, it is voluntary. If a company does not wish to publish an OFR, it is still subject to the statutory requirement to publish a business review, as discussed in the earlier section on directors' reports. The requirements of a business review are similar to the OFR recommendations, but are less extensive.

Directors' remuneration

By historical standards and compared with practice in most other countries, the current UK requirements for the disclosure of directors' remuneration are extremely detailed, onerous and complex, especially in the case of listed companies. It is a tribute to the complexity of the requirements that a comprehensive treatment of the subject (as in PricewaterhouseCoopers LLP, *Manual of Accounting – Management Reports and Governance 2008* (CCH)) takes over one hundred pages. The details of directors' remuneration, taking the form of a separate report which needs to be approved by members in general meeting in the case of quoted companies, is also one of the most widely read parts of a company's annual report.

The requirements in this area are primarily those in the Companies Act 2006 and its supporting statutory instruments (SI 2008/410 for large and medium-sized companies and SI 2008/409 for small companies). The Listing Rules also include requirements, which for the most part duplicate those in the Act, but also contain some additional disclosures. Accounting standards do not cover this area.

Historically, in the UK, disclosure used to be required of 'directors' emoluments' and it is emoluments to which a number of companies continue to refer. Then, for a period of time, both the legislation and the Listing Rules referred to both directors' 'remuneration' and 'emoluments'.

Until the 2006 Act, generally, 'remuneration' was used to refer to the total package payable to directors, comprising salary, benefits, annual bonuses, long-term bonuses, whether payable in cash, shares or something else, share options, pensions, etc. and 'emoluments' usually meant total remuneration excluding share options, long-term bonuses and pensions. What is within emoluments (defined in this way) will depend upon a director's particular package and could vary from year to year, but in the main, emoluments tends to be the aggregate of salary, benefits and annual bonuses.

Now the regulations made under the 2006 Act and the Listing Rules refer mainly to 'remuneration' and have very few references to emoluments, although they sometimes use the term 'remuneration' to mean what has conventionally in the past been referred to as 'emoluments'. In this section we will use the terms as conventionally used in the past.

The difference between a share option scheme and a long-term incentive plan is sometimes non-existent in legal terms. In practice, the term 'share option' is generally used to refer to an option with an exercise price (other than a nominal exercise price) and long-term incentive plan tends to be used to refer to schemes where there is no (or only a nominal) exercise price.

Directors' remuneration report

Quoted companies must prepare a directors' remuneration report and this has to be approved by the members in general meeting. The content for the directors' remuneration report is largely dictated by regulations, but the Listing Rules do require some additional details to be disclosed. Where information is required to be given for each director, the directors' names must be disclosed so that it is clear what relates to each individual director. Part of the report is required to be audited and reference is made to this in the auditor's report. The required content of the directors' remuneration report includes:

Not subject to audit:

- names of the members of remuneration committee at the time when the committee considered remuneration for the year;
- names and details of persons (which might include a director who is not a member of the committee or might include a company) that materially assisted the committee to determine remuneration for the year;
- statement on the company's policy on directors' remuneration for the following and subsequent financial years, including specified details

such as a summary, for each director (who has served as a director since the balance sheet date), of the performance conditions attaching to share options and long-term incentive schemes (this includes naming comparator companies or index if used), explaining the relative importance of performance-related and non-performance-related elements for each director, and explaining the company's policy on the duration of contracts, notice periods and termination payments;

- (effective for periods commencing on or after 6 April 2009) statement of how pay and employment conditions of employees of the group were taken into account when determining directors' remuneration for the year;
- performance graph showing Total Shareholder Return (TSR) for the company and for a named index for the last five years; and
- details of directors' service contracts: date, unexpired period, notice period and any provision for compensation payable on early termination.

Subject to audit:

- emoluments, analysed into its components (e.g. salary, annual bonus and benefits-in-kind), and compensation for loss of office, for each director;
- the nature of any benefits-in-kind;
- details about share options held by each director (including exercise prices and summary of performance conditions);
- details about long-term incentive schemes for each director (including the share price at the date of award and a summary of performance conditions for interests awarded or vested in the year);
- contributions payable to a defined contribution scheme and various details (including accrued benefits and transfer value of accrued benefits) in respect of defined benefit pension schemes for each director; and
- compensation for past directors.

Notes to the accounts

Whether or not a company is required to present a directors' remuneration report, all companies have to give specified details of directors' remuneration in the notes to the accounts. The information required in the notes is much less than is included in the directors' remuneration report; the actual detail differing between quoted companies, small companies and all other companies. For example, quoted companies have to include the following amounts in the notes to the accounts:

- aggregate emoluments;
- aggregate gains made by directors on the exercise of share options;
- aggregate amounts receivable in respect of long-term incentive schemes; and
- aggregate value of company contributions to defined contribution pension schemes; and

- the number of directors to whom benefits are accruing in respect of (1) defined contribution pension schemes and (2) defined benefit pension schemes.

Some quoted companies include in their notes to the accounts a cross-reference to the directors' remuneration report where the above information can be found. Particular care is, however, needed to ensure that the cross-reference is only to audited information.

Related-party relationships and transactions

Accounting standards require disclosure by companies of related-party relationships and transactions. The international standard (IAS 24) is broadly similar to the UK standard (FRS 8), but see below for key differences.

The underlying reason for the disclosure requirements is that a reader of accounts will assume, unless told otherwise, that the transactions are with third parties and are at arm's length prices. If this is not the case, the reader needs to be put on notice, so that he or she can bear the fact in mind when reading the accounts. For example, a transaction between related parties may be at a non-market price resulting in one party making a loss, or a sub-normal profit, or on the other hand an above-market margin on the transaction. Without knowing that some transactions were between related parties, the non-market profit margins shown in the financial statements would be perplexing.

It is important to note that there is no requirement to substitute an arm's length price for the actual price charged to the related party. It is merely a matter of factual disclosure of the relationship that subsists and the transactions that have taken place.

A key part of the standards is the definition of who is regarded as a related party. Broadly speaking, both IAS 24 and FRS 8 define related party in terms of control and influence. Under IAS 24 one party is related to an entity if:

(a) the party, directly or indirectly:
  - controls, is controlled by, or is under common control with, the entity (this includes parents, subsidiaries and fellow subsidiaries);
  - has an interest in the entity that gives it significant influence over the entity; or
  - has joint control over the entity;
(b) the party is an associate (as defined in IAS 28 'Investments in Associates') of the entity;
(c) the party is a joint venture in which the entity is a venturer (see IAS 31 'Interests in Joint Ventures');
(d) the party is a member of the key management personnel of the entity or its parent;
(e) the party is a close member of the family of any individual referred to in (a) or (d);

(f) the party is an entity that is controlled, jointly controlled or significantly influenced by, or for which significant voting power in such entity resides with, directly or indirectly, any individual referred to in (d) or (e); or

(g) the party is a post-employment benefit plan for the benefit of employees of the entity, or of any entity that is a related party of the entity.

The disclosure requirements of IAS 24 may be summarised as follows:

- disclosure of control – that is, disclosure of the parent and, if different, the ultimate controlling party; where neither produces financial statements available for public use, the name of the next most senior parent that does so has to be disclosed;
- disclosure of transactions and balances, including, separately for each of (a) the parent, (b) entities with joint control or significant influence over the entity, (c) subsidiaries, (d) associates, (e) joint ventures in which the entity is a venturer, (f) key management personnel of the entity or its parent and (g) other related parties:
  - nature of related party relationship;
  - the amounts involved;
  - amounts due at the balance sheet date, their terms and conditions, including whether secured, and details of any guarantees given or received;
  - provisions for doubtful debts;
  - amounts written off in the period; and
- disclosure of key management personnel compensation:
  - in total;
  - for short-term employee benefits;
  - for post-employment benefits;
  - for other long-term benefits;
  - for termination benefits; and
  - for share-based payment.

Where the parent's single entity financial statements, as well as its group financial statements, are prepared using IFRS, the disclosures required by IAS 24 have to be given in both the single entity and group financial statements. In the group financial statements, transactions between group companies that have been eliminated on consolidation do not have to be disclosed. However, where any of these involved the parent, they will be disclosed in its single entity financial statements because intra-group transactions have to be disclosed in the single entity financial statements of the transacting group company.

FRS 8 is a similar standard to IAS 24. Some of the key differences are that:

- disclosure is not required in a parent's single entity financial statements if these are presented with consolidated financial statements;
- transactions with group companies are not required to be disclosed in the single entity financial statements of many subsidiaries;

- disclosure is not required of employee remuneration; and
- disclosure is required of the name of the transacting related party.

Proposals have been published to revise IAS 24 and, separately, to replace FRS 8 with a new standard based on the revised IAS 24. One of the main changes being proposed by the IASB is to require that transactions between an associate of a company and a subsidiary of the same company be disclosed in both the associate's and the subsidiary's financial statements. At the moment, the transactions would be disclosed in one but not the other.

In addition to the accounting standards, the Listing Rules, the Companies Act and SI 2008/410 call for some disclosures. For example, the Listing Rules require disclosure of contracts, exceeding a size threshold, with a group company in which a director of the company is or was materially interested. Some of the disclosures required by the Act are of advances and credits to and guarantees on behalf of directors – see the next section.

Transactions with directors

Transactions with directors is an area that has long been regulated by legislation. The Companies Act 1985 contained various prohibitions and conditional approvals regarding loans, quasi-loans and credit transactions; some were banned whilst others were allowed if specified conditions were met. For example, companies were precluded from making a loan to a director of the company or its holding company unless the loan was for a small amount (not more than £5,000) or lending money was part of the company's ordinary activities (and certain conditions were met).

A number of changes to the regulation of transactions with directors were made by the Companies Act 2006. Of these the most significant is that if a loan, quasi-loan or credit transaction was precluded before, then, generally, under CA 2006 the prohibition is removed if the members approve the transaction. Where the transaction is for a director of the holding company (e.g. a subsidiary wishes to make a loan to a director of its parent company) then the approval of the members of both companies (subsidiary and parent) is required if the loan is to be permitted. As before, there are various de minimis and other exceptions, for example, a loan or quasi-loan of £10,000 or less is permitted without needing to obtain the approval of members.

Disclosure of such transactions has long been required by the Companies Act 1985 regardless of whether or not the transactions were legal. Under s. 413 of the 2006 Act, disclosure is required of advances and credits to and guarantees on behalf of directors.

Segment disclosure

A further area of disclosure required by accounting standards is segment disclosure. Like related-party disclosures, the information required by the relevant standards has no impact on the numbers in the income statement or balance sheet, but it does enable a better understanding of the results and assets, and therefore the financial situation of the whole company or group.

IFRS 8 'Operating segments' is the current standard and is applicable for accounting periods beginning on or after 1 January 2009. IFRS 8 had a difficult passage within the EU; its approval process was protracted with much opposition to its adoption.

Underlying IFRS 8 is the premise that an external reader of the financial statements should see the company 'through the eyes of management'. The standard requires the starting point for determining reportable segments (namely, those segments about which information is reported in the financial statements) to be those revenue-generating activities whose operating results are regularly reviewed by the entity's 'chief operating decision maker to make decisions about resources to be allocated to the segment and assess its performance'. These are called 'operating segments'. Although each operating segment may be separately reported in the financial statements (i.e. each one may be a reportable segment), they may be combined if they are of a similar nature to establish the reportable segments. A company's CEO may well be its 'chief operating decision maker' as defined by IFRS 8, but this is not automatic; it could, for example, be a group of people. IFRS 8 explains that the term 'chief operating decision maker' denotes a function and not a title.

IFRS 8 also takes a management perspective in determining what is disclosed; the measure reported to the chief operating decision-maker is disclosed even if this is prepared on a different basis to the profits, assets, etc. recognised in the income statement and balance sheet. The main disclosures are, for each reportable segment, a measure as reported to the chief operating decision maker of:

- profit or loss;
- total assets; and
- liabilities only if this is regularly reported to the chief operating decision maker.

If the following are included in arriving at segment profit/loss or are otherwise regularly reported to the chief operating decision-maker, they are disclosed by segment:

- third-party revenues;
- inter-segment revenues;
- interest income;
- interest expense;
- depreciation and amortisation;
- material items of income and expense disclosed in accordance with para. 97 of IAS 1 (2007) – see 'exceptional items' on page 83 in chapter 9;

213

- share of results from equity accounting;
- income tax expense; and
- material non-cash items other than depreciation and amortisation.

If the following are included in arriving at segment assets or are otherwise regularly reported to the chief operating decision-maker, they are disclosed by segment:

- investments accounted for by the equity method; and
- certain additions to non-current assets (principally PPE and intangible assets).

If the measure of profit reported to the chief operating decision-maker is before interest and tax, this would be what is reported by segment. Neither interest nor tax would then be reported by segment by that entity, whereas if another entity reported after-tax profit to its chief operating decision-maker, then as well as reporting this level by segment each of interest and tax would have to be reported by segment.

Factors used to identify the segments and types of product and service in each reportable segment are to be disclosed as well as reconciliations from the total of all reportable segments to the relevant amount included in the income statement and balance sheet. In addition, certain entity-wide disclosures are required: an analysis of revenues for each product and service; a geographical analysis of revenues and of certain non-current assets (principally PPE and intangible assets); and information about the extent of reliance on major customers.

These disclosures thus give a greater insight into how the profit and net assets are made up and managed, enabling users to understand the components of profit and to understand which parts of the overall business are showing growth. Not all entities, however, are required to give these disclosures; IFRS 8 applies to entities whose securities are publicly traded or that file, or are in the process of filing, financial statements with a securities commission or other regulatory organisation for the purpose of issuing any class of instruments in a public market.

For UK GAAP reporters, certain disclosures (limited to analysis of turnover) are required by legislation[1] and thus have to be given by all companies, although small and medium-sized companies may omit the disclosure from the version of the accounts filed with the registrar. SSAP 25 adds further requirements, but only for public companies, banking or insurance companies or groups, and other companies whose size exceeds ten times the Act's criteria for defining a medium-sized company (note, however, that many of these companies now prepare their financial statements under IFRS rather than UK GAAP). SSAP 25

---

1 See para. 68 of Schedule 1 to SI 2008/410 and para. 60 of Schedule 1 to SI 2008/409.

requires less disclosure than the international standard; for companies within its scope it requires an analysis, by class of business and by geographical segment, of:

- turnover;
- profit or loss before tax (before or after interest); and
- net assets.

Appendices

Appendix 1
50 questions for non-executive directors to ask

We set out here a selection of accounting questions that non-executive directors might find appropriate to ask at meetings of the board or audit committee. The questions are necessarily generic and it is for non-executive directors to consider whether, or how, they apply in the case of a particular company.

Introduction (chapter 1)
1. Which GAAP do we use (UK GAAP, IFRS, etc.) in the group financial statements?

Accounting in the UK and international harmonisation (chapter 2)
2. Which GAAP do we use in the financial statements of the subsidiaries?
3. If the group uses IFRS, have we considered whether the accounts of the subsidiaries should also be on IFRS?
4. Which new IFRSs are we adopting this year and have they been adopted by the EU?
5. (Where the company is also listed in the US) Do we adopt full IFRSs as well as IFRSs as adopted by the EU?

The legal framework for accounting (chapter 3)
6. Have we updated all of our references to the Companies Act 2006?

The accountancy profession and the regulatory framework for accounting and auditing (chapter 4)
7. Have we had any letters from the Financial Reporting Review Panel or any similar regulators?
8. What are the Financial Reporting Review Panel's priority sectors for this year?
9. Have the auditors given qualified or modified opinions on the financial statements of any companies within the group?

Substance over form (chapter 5)
10. Are we sure that the financial statements reflect the substance of the transactions that we have entered into?
11. Are there any special purpose entities in, or related to, the group? Have we consolidated them?

Communicating accounting information (chapter 6)

12. Do we disclose, or should we disclose, 'alternative performance measures', i.e. adjusted, or non-GAAP numbers? If so, are we careful to make sure that they do not dominate the GAAP numbers?

Current trends in accounting (chapter 7)

13. How much do we use fair value for the valuation of assets and liabilities? Does it help the understanding of our financial position or does it hinder? How do we explain it?

14. Do our results present a smooth trend? If so, is that realistic? If they do not, are we using narrative reporting to explain the meaning of the volatile trend?

Individual entity accounts and consolidated accounts (chapter 8)

15. Have we identified all of the subsidiaries and SPEs for consolidation?

16. Are there any other entities for which we have moral responsibility? How are these being treated?

Presentation of financial statements (chapter 9)

17. Should we adopt the income statement plus separate statement of other comprehensive income, or a combined statement?

18. Whichever is chosen, does it enable us to make our economic performance clear?

19. Do we present separately from our trading transactions, in some way, our gains and losses arising from fair valuing certain items?

20. Have we explained our accounting policies clearly? Do they relate to transactions that we actually carry out? If we use IFRSs do our policies adopt IFRS terminology or do they still retain UK GAAP wording in places?

Earnings per share (chapter 10)

21. Do we disclose, or should we disclose, any adjusted EPS numbers?

22. If so, are we careful to make sure that they do not dominate the GAAP numbers?

Mergers and acquisitions (chapter 11)

23. Are our acquisitions accounted for under IFRS 3 or IFRS 3 (revised)?

24. Are there any gains and losses reported in the income statement as a result of acquisitions? Have we explained these properly?

25. Have we reviewed our goodwill and intangibles for impairment? If so, which discount rate did we use and what were the other critical assumptions?

Interaction of accounting with tax (chapter 12)

26. What does the deferred tax liability (or asset) on the balance sheet mean?

Assets (chapter 13)

27. Do we have any non-current assets that are not being depreciated or amortised? Is that justifiable? Have we tested them for impairment?

Liabilities (chapter 14)

28. Have we provided for all liabilities such as warranties and other claims against us?
29. Have we given proper disclosure of contingent liabilities?

Leases (chapter 15)

30. Have we properly identified all leases (even if they are not called leases)?
31. Have we correctly categorised our leases as operating leases or finance leases? Are our judgements at the margin supportable?
32. Have we considered leases of land separately from leases of buildings?

Pensions (chapter 16)

33. What method of accounting are we adopting for defined benefit schemes (immediate recognition of gains and losses or the 'corridor' method)?
34. Have we given proper disclosure of our pensions obligations?

Financial instruments (chapter 17)

35. Have we properly analysed our capital instruments as between equity and debt?
36. Do our accounting policies make it clear which financial assets and liabilities are carried at amortised cost and which are carried at fair value?
37. Have we given a clear presentation and explanation of any gains and losses arising from measuring financial instruments at fair value?
38. Are our hedges effective commercially? Do they qualify for hedge accounting?
39. Have we provided all the disclosures required by IFRS 7?

Share-based payment (chapter 18)

40. Have we properly identified all the arrangements (with employees and others) that fall within share-based payment?
41. Have we provided all the disclosures required by IFRS 2?

Realised and distributable profits (chapter 19)

42. Are we sure that this transaction does indeed generate a realised profit (especially for circular or structured transactions)?
43. Are we satisfied that we have sufficient distributable profits to support the dividend that we are proposing?
44. Do we need a subsidiary to pay up a dividend to us so that we will have sufficient distributable profits?
45. Do we need to prepare and file interim accounts to support the distribution?

Disclosures in published reports (chapter 20)

46. Have we fully embraced IFRS 8's approach to segment reporting, that is, allowing an external reader to see the group through the eyes of management?
47. Have we given all the required disclosures (statutory business review, directors' report, directors' remuneration report, etc.)?
48. Do we seek to disclose only the minimum or do we go beyond that, taking a more enlightened attitude that fuller explanation (e.g. in the Operating

and Financial Review) of strategy, markets, KPIs, etc. will lead to a better understanding of the group and hence be to our advantage?

49. Which Corporate Governance Combined Code are we reporting on this year? Have we fully complied or do we need to disclose one or more departures? What are our institutional shareholders' views on our corporate governance?

50. Have we given the responsibility statements under the FSA's Disclosure and Transparency Rules?

Appendix 2
List of international accounting standards (IFRSs and IASs) and IFRIC interpretations as at 30 June 2008

International Accounting Standards

IFRS 1	First-time adoption of International Accounting Standards
IFRS 2	Share-based payment
IFRS 3	Business combinations (2004 and 2008 versions)
IFRS 4	Insurance contracts
IFRS 5	Non-current assets held for sale and discontinued operations
IFRS 6	Exploration for and evaluation of mineral resources
IFRS 7	Financial instruments: disclosures
IFRS 8	Operating segments
	Improvements to IFRSs
IAS 1	Presentation of financial statements (2005 and 2007 versions)
IAS 2	Inventories
IAS 7	Statement of cash flows
IAS 8	Accounting policies, changes in accounting estimates and errors
IAS 10	Events after the reporting period
IAS 11	Construction contracts
IAS 12	Income taxes
IAS 14	Segment reporting
IAS 16	Property, plant and equipment
IAS 17	Leases
IAS 18	Revenue
IAS 19	Employee benefits
IAS 20	Accounting for government grants and disclosure of government assistance
IAS 21	The effects of changes in foreign exchange rates
IAS 23	Borrowing costs (1995 and 2007 versions)
IAS 24	Related party disclosures
IAS 26	Accounting and reporting by retirement benefit plans
IAS 27	Consolidated and separate financial statements (2005 and 2008 versions)
IAS 28	Investments in associates
IAS 29	Financial reporting in hyperinflationary economies
IAS 30	Disclosures in the financial statements of banks and similar financial institutions

IAS 31	Interests in joint ventures
IAS 32	Financial instruments: presentation
IAS 33	Earnings per share
IAS 34	Interim financial reporting
IAS 36	Impairment of assets
IAS 37	Provisions, contingent liabilities and contingent assets
IAS 38	Intangible assets
IAS 39	Financial instruments: recognition and measurement
IAS 40	Investment property
IAS 41	Agriculture

IASB statements

Preface to international financial reporting standards including IFRIC and SIC interpretations
Framework for the preparation and presentation of financial statements

Interpretations – SICs and IFRICs

IFRIC 1	Changes in existing decommissioning, restoration and similar liabilities
IFRIC 2	Members' shares in co-operative entities and similar instruments
IFRIC 4	Determining whether an arrangement contains a lease
IFRIC 5	Rights to interests arising from decommissioning, restoration and environmental rehabilitation funds
IFRIC 6	Liabilities arising from participating in a specific market – waste electrical and electronic equipment
IFRIC 7	Applying the restatement approach under IAS 29 'Financial reporting in hyperinflationary economies'
IFRIC 8	Scope of IFRS 2
IFRIC 9	Re-assessment of embedded derivatives
IFRIC 10	Interim financial reporting and impairment
IFRIC 11	IFRS 2 – group and treasury share transactions
IFRIC 12	Service concession arrangements
IFRIC 13	Customer loyalty programmes
IFRIC 14	IAS 19 – the limit on a defined benefit asset, minimum funding requirements and their interaction
SIC 7	Introduction of the euro
SIC 10	Government assistance – no specific relation to operating activities
SIC 12	Consolidation – special purpose entities
SIC 13	Jointly controlled entities – non-monetary contributions by venturers
SIC 15	Operating leases – incentives
SIC 21	Income taxes – Recovery of revalued non-depreciable assets
SIC 25	Income taxes – Changes in the tax status of an entity or its shareholders

Appendix 3
List of UK accounting standards (FRSs and SSAPs), Statements and UITF Abstracts as at 30 June 2008

Financial Reporting Standards

FRSSE	Financial reporting standard for smaller entities
FRS 1	Cash flow statements
FRS 2	Accounting for subsidiary undertakings
FRS 3	Reporting financial performance
FRS 4	Capital instruments
FRS 5	Reporting the substance of transactions
FRS 6	Acquisitions and mergers
FRS 7	Fair values in acquisition accounting
FRS 8	Related party disclosures
FRS 9	Associates and joint ventures
FRS 10	Goodwill and intangible assets
FRS 11	Impairment of fixed assets and goodwill
FRS 12	Provisions, contingent liabilities and contingent assets
FRS 13	Derivatives and other financial instruments: disclosures
FRS 15	Tangible fixed assets
FRS 16	Current tax
FRS 17	Retirement benefits
FRS 18	Accounting policies
FRS 19	Deferred tax
FRS 20 (IFRS 2)	Share-based payment
FRS 21 (IAS 10)	Events after the balance sheet date
FRS 22 (IAS 33)	Earnings per share
FRS 23 (IAS 21)	The effects of changes in foreign exchange rates
FRS 24 (IAS 29)	Financial reporting in hyperinflationary economies
FRS 25 (IAS 32)	Financial instruments: presentation
FRS 26 (IAS 39)	Financial instruments: measurement
FRS 27	Life assurance
FRS 28	Corresponding amounts
FRS 29 (IFRS 7)	Financial instruments: disclosure

Statements of Standard Accounting Practice

SSAP 4	Accounting for government grants
SSAP 5	Accounting for value added tax
SSAP 9	Stocks and long-term contracts

SSAP 13	Accounting for research and development
SSAP 19	Accounting for investment properties
SSAP 20	Foreign currency translation
SSAP 21	Accounting for leases and hire purchase contracts
SSAP 25	Segmental reporting

ASB statements

Statement of aims
Foreword to accounting standards
Statement of principles for financial reporting
Foreword to UITF Abstracts
Guidance notes on SSAP 21 'Accounting for leases and hire purchase contracts'
Half-yearly reports
Preliminary announcements
Operating and financial review (RS 1)
Retirement benefits – disclosures
A review of narrative reporting by UK listed companies in 2006

UITF Abstracts

UITF Abstract 4	Presentation of long-term debtors in current assets
UITF Abstract 5	Transfers from current assets to fixed assets
UITF Abstract 9	Accounting for operations in hyper-inflationary economies
UITF Abstract 11	Capital instruments: issuer call options
UITF Abstract 15	Disclosure of substantial acquisitions
UITF Abstract 19	Tax on gains and losses on foreign currency borrowings that hedge an investment in a foreign enterprise
UITF Abstract 21	Accounting issues arising from the proposed introduction of the euro
UITF Abstract 22	The acquisition of a Lloyd's business
UITF Abstract 23	Application of the transitional rules in FRS 15
UITF Abstract 24	Accounting for start-up costs
UITF Abstract 25	National insurance contributions on share option gains
UITF Abstract 26	Barter transactions for advertising
UITF Abstract 27	Revision to estimates of the useful economic life of goodwill and intangible assets
UITF Abstract 28	Operating lease incentives
UITF Abstract 29	Website development costs
UITF Abstract 31	Exchanges of businesses or other non-monetary assets for an interest in a subsidiary, joint venture or associate
UITF Abstract 32	Employee benefit trusts and other intermediate payment arrangements
UITF Abstract 34	Pre-contract costs
UITF Abstract 35	Death-in-service and incapacity benefits
UITF Abstract 36	Contracts for sales of capacity

227

UITF Abstract 38	Accounting for ESOP trusts
UITF Abstract 39	(IFRIC Interpretation 2) – Members' shares in co-operative entities and similar instruments
UITF Abstract 40	Revenue recognition and service contracts
UITF Abstract 41	(IFRIC Interpretation 8) – Scope of FRS 20 (IFRS 2)
UITF Abstract 42	(IFRIC Interpretation 9) – Reassessment of embedded derivatives
UITF Abstract 43	The interpretation of equivalence for the purposes of s. 228A of the Companies Act 1985
UITF Abstract 44	(IFRIC Interpretation 11) – FRS 20 (IFRS 2) – Group and treasury share transactions
UITF Abstract 45	(IFRIC Interpretation 6) – Liabilities arising from participating in a specific market – waste electrical and electronic equipment

Appendix 4
Table of origins for CA 2006 references

Chapter	Topic	CA 2006	CA 1985
1	What is GAAP	ss. 393–474	ss. 226–62A
3	The Companies Act 2006	Part 15 Sch. 1 to SI 2008/410 Sch. 6 to SI 2008/410	Part VII Sch. 4 to CA 85 Sch. 4A to CA 85
	Accounting provisions of the Act applying to IFRS and UK GAAP companies	ss. 394–7 & 407	ss. 226, 226A, 226B & 227C
	The requirement for group accounts	ss. 398–406 & 408	ss. 227–30
	Annual accounts and the true and fair view	s. 396 s. 404 s. 393	s. 226A s. 227A N/A
	Approval, distribution and filing of accounts	s. 414 ss. 434, 475–84, 495–7 and 503–6 ss. 419 & 422 s. 423 s. 430 s. 437 s. 441 ss. 454–7	s. 233 ss. 235–6 and 249A–B ss. 234A & 234C s. 238 N/A s. 241 s. 242 ss. 245–5C
	Exemptions and special provisions	Sch. 2 & Part 2 of Sch. 6 of SI 2008/410 Sch. 3 & Part 3 of Sch. 6 of SI 2008/410	Sch. 9 to CA 85 Sch. 9A to CA 85
	Accounting provisions of SI 2008/410 applying to UK GAAP companies only	Sch. 1 to SI 2008/410	Sch. 4 to CA 85
4	Audit reporting	ss. 495–7 ss. 503–6	s. 235 s. 236

(cont.)

Chapter	Topic	CA 2006	CA 1985
	Audit reporting: limitation of liability	ss. 532–8 para. 8 of SI 2008/489	s. 310 N/A
5	Form v. substance (financial statements to give a true and fair view)	s. 393	ss. 226–7B
	FRS 5 'Reporting the substance of transactions' (definition of subsidiary undertaking)	s. 1162	s. 258
	Examples of FRS 5 in practice in the UK (definition of subsidiary undertaking)	s. 1162	s. 258
6	Background	ss. 393–474	ss. 226–62A
	Summary financial statements	ss. 426–9 and SI 2008/374	s. 251 and SI 1995/2092 (as amended by SI 2002/1780 and SI 2005/2281)
8	When to consolidate – General approach	ss. 398–402	ss. 227, 228, 228A & 229 and, for small and medium-sized companies, 248 & 248A
	Exemption re. holding company income statement	s. 408	s. 230
	What to consolidate – Exclusions from consolidation	ss. 405(2) & (3)	ss. 229(2) & (3)
9	Statement of comprehensive income – income statement formats	Sch. 1 to SI 2008/410 and Sch. 1 to SI 2008/409	Sch. 4 to CA 85 & Sch. 8 to CA 85
	Balance sheet	ss. 414 & 433	s. 233
11	Share premium, merger relief and group reconstruction relief	ss. 610–16	ss. 130–3
12	HM Revenue & Customs and the move to IFRS	s. 407	s. 227C
13	Depreciation – amortisation of goodwill	ss. 393 & 396 together with para. 22 of Sch. 1 to SI 2008/410	ss. 226A & 227A together with para. 21 of Sch. 4
17	Equity shares in the Companies Act	s. 548	s. 744

Chapter	Topic	CA 2006	CA 1985
	Issue of shares	s. 610	s. 130
	Treasury shares	ss. 724–32	ss. 162–2G
	Accounting under UK GAAP	SI 2008/410 – Sch. 1 paras. 47–9 and SI 2008/409 – Sch. 1 paras. 46 & 47	Sch. 4, paras. 38–40
19	General rules on distributions	Part 23 s. 829 s. 830 s. 831	Part VIII s. 263 s. 263 s. 264
	Relevant accounts	s. 836 ss. 837–9	s. 270 ss. 272–4
	TECH 01/08	s. 853 s. 838	s. 262(3) s. 272
20	Statement of directors' responsibilities	ss. 170–81, excl. s. 172(1) s. 172(1)	N/A s. 309(1)
	Directors' reports	ss. 415–9 Sch. 7 to SI 2008/410 s. 236 s. 463	ss. 234, 234ZZA, 234ZZB, 234ZA & 234A Sch. 7 to CA 85 N/A N/A
	Directors' remuneration	ss. 420–2 Sch. 8 to SI 2008/410 s. 412 Sch. 5 to SI 2008/410	ss. 234B & 234C Sch. 7A to CA 85 s. 232 Part I of Sch. 6 to CA 85
	Transactions with directors	ss. 197–214 & 223 s. 413	ss. 330–44 Part II of Sch. 6 to CA 85
	Segment disclosure	para. 68 of SI 2008/410 and para. 60 of SI 2008/409	para. 55 of Sch. 4 to CA 85

Index

Law Practitioner Series